PREJUDICE
AND PRIDE

PREJUDICE AND PRIDE

Discrimination against gay people in modern Britain

Edited by Bruce Galloway

Routledge & Kegan Paul
London, Boston, Melbourne and Henley

First published in 1983
by Routledge & Kegan Paul plc
39 Store Street, London WC1E 7DD, England
9 Park Street, Boston, Mass. 02108, USA
464 St Kilda Road, Melbourne
Victoria, 3004, Australia and
Broadway House, Newtown Road,
Henley-on-Thames, Oxon RG9 1EN, England

Photoset in Times by
Cambrian Typesetters,
Aldershot, Hants
and printed in Great Britain by
Billing & Sons Ltd
Worcester

Library of Congress Cataloging in Publication Data

Main entry under title:
Prejudice and pride.
Bibliography: p.
Includes index.
1. Gay liberation movement − Great Britain − Addresses,
essays, lectures. 2. Homosexuality − Great Britain −
Addresses, essays, lectures. 3. Homosexuality − Law and
legislation − Great Britain − Addresses, essays, lectures.
4. Sex discrimination − Great Britain − Addresses, essays,
lectures. I. Galloway, Bruce.
HQ76.8.G7P73   1983   306.7'66'0941   83−11185

ISBN 0−7100−9916−9 (pbk.)

CONTENTS

INTRODUCTION

This book is one of the few written by gay people about themselves. It offers no theory on the causes of homosexuality, and no analysis of the homosexual as a social or medical problem. We are not the problem. Women and men of all ages in all societies have felt attracted to others of the same sex, yet their experience has been censored from literature, excised from text books, condemned by the religions and labelled sick by the medical profession. To give physical expression to those feelings once warranted death in Europe, and still does in some countries. In Britain today our social and sexual activities remain extensively criminalised. We are ostracised by our families, ignored at school, assaulted on the streets, harassed by the police and patronised by the media.

What demands analysis is the systematic suppression of all forms of behaviour other than the rigidly heterosexual. Social prejudice and legal discrimination affect many other groups: transvestites, transsexuals, prostitutes, the celibate, paedophiles, unmarried mothers, independent, assertive women and gentle, non-masculine men. But their needs and experiences are not necessarily the same as ours, and are not discussed here. We can, however, make common cause against prejudice, violence, ignorance, biased law-making and the denial of basic civil rights. We are all entitled to impartial justice.

With one exception the essays in this book have been written by members of the Campaign for Homosexual Equality, and arise from research done by CHE over many years. They are not simply a grim catalogue of systematic discrimination. The gay movement in Britain retains its pride and its determination, and this book records many victories gained since 1967, and presents a programme of action for the years ahead. As chairperson of CHE I congratulate the authors of *Prejudice and Pride* on producing this book.

I ask you, the reader, to do more than read what they have written. At first this may seem to be simply a chronicle of prejudice; and if it does, no harm will have been done. Few people − even gay people − realise the extent of the oppression we suffer from society and its laws. Sometimes the oppression arises from irrational prejudice, sometimes from ignorance, often from the self-oppression of those who cannot come to terms with the homosexual aspects of their own personalities. Inevitably the authors have had to ignore those who do not display prejudice against gays. There are many magistrates and judges who do not believe that the law should interfere in the private lives of people who are not harming or threatening others; this book is not about them. Nor is it about the many persons in our police forces who, despite the attitudes of their colleagues, are perfectly reasonable in their behaviour towards gay people.

Similarly there are many employers who do not, and would not, discriminate against employees because they are gay. Indeed in 'blue-collar' jobs the gay worker may have more to fear from the prejudice and hostility of workmates than from the employer. The known cases of discrimination in employment come almost entirely from the 'white-collar' sector. Here, as elsewhere, there are encouraging signs. The Confederation of British Industry has made clear to me its total opposition to discrimination, though it can do no more than advise its members. A number of local authorities, including Nottinghamshire, South Glamorgan and the GLC, have recently made it their policy that they will not discriminate against any person on grounds of race, sex, religion . . . or sexual orientation. Some may also refuse to deal with a firm which does so discriminate. Clearly this marks an important development. We would like to see such statements adopted by all local authorities, as well as by commercial employers.

Since the nineteenth-century campaigns against slavery the United Kingdom has regarded itself as a leading defender of human rights and individual liberties. That claim is no longer valid. Homosexuals are, in terms of British law, second-class citizens. In this respect Britain is far behind many European countries where gay people have something like equality before the law with others. In many of those countries for instance the age of consent is the same for homosexual and heterosexual activity; several have no law criminalising homosexual conduct by members of their armed forces; and some even take positive steps to discourage discrimination against gay citizens. The Parliamentary Assembly of the Council of Europe recently called on member governments (including the UK) 'to assure equality of treatment . . . for homosexuals with regard to employment, pay and job security, particularly in the public sector'; yet the law still discriminates against us, and by doing so encourages other forms of discrimination. We are proud of what has been achieved in recent years to change this. Much must still be done to create a free and equal society which welcomes and celebrates the rich diversity of human personality, a society of which the gay person is as much a part as the non-gay.

Michael G. Jarrett
CHE Chair

1 AT HOME
Anna Durell

Everyone who reads this book will have been raised on a questionable mythology. Our deepest feelings about ourselves, our emotions, ambitions, needs and beliefs are coloured by assumptions we pick up as we learn to speak and read. English language and culture, like that of other major linguistic groups, is riddled with assumptions about gender characteristics, sexual identity and the nature of sexuality. These assumptions are not proven: indeed many of them are by nature unprovable. They do work systematically to the disadvantage of women and non-heterosexuals.

Very few people have conducted anything like a mass survey of sexual experience and preference. This is because it is assumed that there is a 'norm', only deviations from which need to be measured. This concept of normality pictures the human male as dominating, sexually aggressive, physically strong and mentally dispassionate, while the human female is submissive, sexually passive, physically weak and mentally sensitive and intuitive (if not actually unstable). It is 'natural' that these two stereotypes should be attracted (like magnetic poles), to their 'opposite', whose qualities they 'complement'. It is assumed that this electro-chemical lovemaking arises from the need to procreate. It is 'natural', since only the female can give birth to children or suckle them, that she should be solely dependent on the male. It is also 'natural', since certain other primates pair-bond, that each male should marry one female and the two live happily in a nuclear family unit.

These latter-day Anglo-Saxon attitudes have been extensively analysed and successfully debunked by the women's movement, and severely rocked by the evidence of anthropologists and sociologists. It is not necessary to rehearse the criticisms here. However, these notions keep a firm hold on the popular imagination in this and other countries. They are embodied in the very medium in which debate and argument about them is conducted — language. They are also essentially not descriptive, but prescriptive. The cultural 'norm' is not so much what everybody does, but what everybody *ought* to do. If it turns out that almost no one does conform to 'normality', the response is not to redefine the normal but to wail that the moral fabric of society is crumbling.

What a society does define as the 'norm' also necessarily defines the nature of the 'abnormal'. This is more than a mere truism. Both Muslim and Judaeo-Christian cultures, for example, place a very high value on the role of the 'Patriarch', and consequently on sex-role differentiation. As a result, female independence, male passivity, cross-dressing and same-sex attraction have all been lumped together as *sexual* deviations, although there is no necessary connection between clothing, economic activity, and sexual orientation. However, by praising or punishing a child for activities which initially seemed to her or him to be quite unconnected, adults in fact structure that child's notion of what is sexual.

In twentieth-century America, and to some extent in Britain, a picture has been built up of isolated, two-adult, two-point-four-child units, in which only the 'father' is economically active, while 'mother' has sole responsibility for child-rearing. As Ehrenreich and English point out in *For Her Own Good*,[1] 'mother' has certainly been inundated with thousands of millions of words of authoritative advice on how to rear 'normal' children. The American books of the 1950s and early 1960s, notably Dr Spock, seem oddly obsessed with the 'problem' of boy babies (by linguistic convention, baby is always 'he') being raised by women. How is 'he' to emulate and acquire the proper masculine virtues of independence, reasoning ability and aggression? If 'Mom' cuddles him too much, might not the smell of her perfume and the feel of her dresses inspire Oedipal longings? The phrase 'mother's boy' became synonymous with 'homosexual'. When the Gay Liberation

Front emerged in the 1970s, much of its political fury was directed against 'the family' in its unholy alliance with paediatricians and child psychologists, as the prime instrument of sexual repression. The 'gay' whom GLF was determined to rehabilitate was precisely 'mother's boy': an outrageous, screaming queen in radical drag and make-up. There was of course, and is, no necessary connection between same-sex attraction, affection for one's mother, transvestism or emotionality: the package was a political fabrication to start with, and GLF had quite self-consciously decided to hit society where it hurt most.

It is also important to remember that 'the family' described above was itself an invention for political purposes. It is not, and never was, characteristic of families in the USA or Britain. Most married women work for a significant proportion of their wedded lives. We also live in a multi-cultural society. Ethnic minorities and many urban working-class groups have quite different patterns of child-rearing. Greek, Hispano-American, Muslim, Hindu, Jewish, and the religious groups such as Catholics, Baptists and Plymouth Brethren, also have their own particular categories of, and attitudes to, sexual non-conformity. Young people within those groups may quite clearly perceive themselves as 'deviant' within their immediate environment, and may feel also in some way at odds with the 'mainstream' culture, but not feel that they have anything in common with 'homosexuals' or what appears to be a predominantly middle-class, 'WASP' gay movement. This alienation is particularly acute for women, since the media images of the homosexual, information about 'gays' and the visible gay movement are all almost exclusively male.

> I always wanted to be a boy, from before I went to school. I was
> jealous of boys until I was 11 or 12. They had freedom and
> could go out and climb trees and do things I wasn't allowed to. I
> used to day-dream about girls. I had an experience with a
> schoolfriend when I was 13. But I tried my hardest to be
> bisexual.[2]

In cultures where women are viewed as socially passive, economically dependent, and sexually only 'receptive' rather than appetitive, a young woman who wishes to be physically or economically active and to choose or refuse her own sexual partners is *per se* 'deviant'. For many women, this issue totally overrides any simple choice about being celibate or lesbian. Women's sexuality is so generally suppressed that girls often feel no attraction they could classify as sexual.

> . . .after our fourth year at school, Charlotte got herself a boyfriend. . . . I remember being really upset, and yet I didn't know why. . . . We had this amazing row one afternoon about some soppy little thing, I can't remember what, but at the height of it she called me a frigging lesie, and I remember being shocked, because I'd heard the word 'lesbian' and 'lesie' before but I didn't really know what they meant. It never occurred to me that my scene with Charlotte was anything but a normal friendship. After this I sort of forgot about her and our gang and kept myself to myself.[3]

It is quite usual for young women, however they subsequently choose to live, to experience a split between their emotional, and sometimes sensual, attachment to other women, and the often strained, self-conscious role-playing involved in relating to boys and men, who are viewed as both physically and intellectually superior and immature and unreliable. Girls may perceive themselves as 'male' in their desire for freedom or autonomy, or as 'frigid' in the absence of the expected desire for boyfriends or a husband. Whether they connect these feelings with the idea that they might be lesbian depends very much on what they happen to have read or been told.

> I am John I am 15 and gay I know I am Gay because I have had sex with Gay Men. I know I was Gay at 13 my mother and farther say I am too young to know my sex life but I am writing to you because I wanted to know more on this sort of life. Please help me Please.[4]

Boys, more commonly brought up to see themselves as sexual, are much more likely to identify their non-conformity with experiencing sexual desire for other males, which happens to coincide with the popular understanding of 'homosexuality'. But they may instead see themselves as 'not-male', because they lack aggression or sexual appetitiveness, and have strong emotional and sensual needs. This may be reinforced by a perception, real or imagined, of themselves as physically or genitally underdeveloped. They may rationalise this through effeminacy, or 'camp', or they may stumble into another cultural slot: that of the *travesti* or transsexual. Again, how the individual structures his identity does depend greatly on the attitudes of his immediate circle. What we clinically label transvestite or transsexual, the youth or man who dresses and sometimes lives as a woman, is regarded by other cultural groups in a whole range of different ways, from amused tolerance to religious awe — a kind of holy fool. This life-style also may or may not involve sexual relationships with other males. The experience of counselling organisations in this country suggests that there is exactly the same range of sexual orientation among those who cross-dress, or who wish to change gender, as there is in the population at large.

Our concept of 'homosexuality' is defined against, and by, our concept of 'heterosexuality'. This does great injustice to the diversity of individual experience. In order to be counted as 'gay' people have either so to define themselves or to live a recognisably 'gay' life-style. But just as our notion of sex, and the sexual 'act' is defined in male terms, so 'gayness' and 'the gay life-style' are characterised in ways which reflect male experience. Large numbers of people, particularly women, do not come out as gay simply because they do not see that those words, as commonly understood, properly apply to them. However, young people in this country are subjected, at an increasingly early age, to enormous pressure to define themselves sexually. In the last twenty years the music, fashion and cosmetics industries have taken an almost obsessive interest in the teenage and pre-teenage market, using images of (hetero)sexual fulfilment as the hook in exactly the same way as in advertising aimed at adults. As a result growing numbers of teenagers see themselves as 'deviant', non-conformers or freaks. If they are lucky they will come across some authoritative information about sexual non-conformity which will allow them to relate their experience to that of other quite rational and likeable people. If they do not, they will become desperate.

In 1969 Rose Robertson founded *Parent's Enquiry*, an advisory service for young people intended to help them and their parents to come to terms with homosexuality. By the beginning of 1982 the service was receiving about 115 new contacts a week, including those referred by social workers and other agencies. Sadly, over 55 per cent of young people contacting her have already made some more or less serious attempt at suicide. Similar stories of isolation and despair emerge from the case histories collected by the Joint Council for Gay Teenagers, from whose book *Breaking The Silence* some of the quotations in this chapter are taken. The Joint Council was established in 1979 by representatives from gay switchboards and other gay groups who were concerned about the rapidly increasing number of calls from teenagers and the inability of adult groups to provide an effective support network.

The major difficulty in this area is the state of the law. The age of consent for male homosexual activity is 21. Homosexuality, while technically legal in certain highly restrictive circumstances, is not lawful (see Chapter 5). Any organisation fostering contact between gay people might be liable to prosecution for 'conspiracy to corrupt public morals'. It is important to remember here that this might still be true even if the organisation dealt solely with lesbians: for a conspiracy charge to succeed, it is not necessary that any specific criminal offence be proven, or even relevant. The Joint Council collected extensive statistical evidence from switchboards and counselling agencies on the numbers of people under the age of consent who were contacting them, and organised a lobbying exercise at the House of Commons. However, despite the fact that a minority group, women members of the Policy Advisory Committee, were convinced that the age of consent for male homosexuals should be reduced to 16, it seems unlikely that this will happen for some years.

'Do you ever feel all the older guys are after you?'
'I used to think that, but I don't now.'
'(Laughs) You wish they were?'
'(Laughs) I wish they were, yeah!'
'Do you ever worry about the law? It being illegal?'
'No, it excites me, actually.'

Interview with David (17)[5]

I'm 14 now. My parents don't know I'm gay. . . . I go to the Gay Centre and the gay clubs. I like discos. . . . I see myself as gay now, and I don't want to be straight. Once the cops stopped a few of us in Birmingham, and asked if we were queer. That made me nervous, but on the whole I think being gay is great.

Interview with Paul[6]

There is little evidence that the high age of consent has much effect on the behaviour or attitudes of young people once they have managed to establish their own sense of sexual identity. Many boys have been sexually active through casual contacts in public lavatories or in relationships with friends or relatives since the age of 10 or 11 in any case. What the legal situation does do is restrict publicity for, and the activities of, organisations attempting to provide care and support for young lesbians and gay men, as we shall see later.

Secrets and silence: the marriage trap

The majority of people who experience doubts about their sexual orientation during adolescence do not come out. Undoubtedly one of the biggest reasons for this is the widespread acceptance of the 'passing phase' theory. Enormous numbers of people spend years of quiet misery waiting for the 'phase' to pass. Many of them tragically accept the well-meant but lethal advice of family doctors or friends that 'marriage will cure it'. It is impossible to judge the number of gay people who are married, because this is one of the groups that is least likely to come across any information about gay switchboards, most frightened of admitting the truth, and best provided with an excuse for not identifying with the popular image of the lesbian or homosexual male. The married have, after all, successfully established a heterosexual relationship. Many of them have children.

During periods when London Lesbian Line has maintained publicity in newspapers or magazines read by non-gays, or has done extensive 'sticker' campaigns, the call rate has averaged 130 a week. Of those, nearly one-third would be married women. In 1981, Deirdre Sanders printed a 'letter from a married lesbian' (which she described as a conflation of several hundred similar letters which she had received) on the problem page of the *Sun*. Her reply, which was sympathetic and supportive, included the number of London Lesbian Line. The Line received 250 calls in the following three weeks from women who identified themselves as married lesbians. Most had experienced strong emotional attachments to women prior to marriage, but had not felt any specifically sexual attraction to be present. They 'were fond of and respected' their husbands, had wanted children and loved them, but were generally troubled by the feeling that something was lacking from their sexual relationship in marriage, and they were quite often deeply 'in love with' a woman friend, a social worker or health visitor. Most were incredibly relieved to have been able to discuss this with another lesbian at all, and totally daunted by the idea of leaving their marriage and attempting to establish a lesbian relationship.

Apart from the obvious desire to avoid hurt, and the fear of losing their children, the major deterrent was economic. Once married and a mother, a woman tends to become trapped: without saleable skills or independent resources, leaving home is a near-impossibility. It was a severe deterrent even in the few cases where the marital sexual relationship had totally broken down, and the woman had been subjected to repeated rape and other physical violence. The fear of being separated from one's children is also a very real and justified one. It is extremely rare for a homosexual partner to retain custody of children after a divorce in which their homosexuality has been publicised. It is quite common for the courts to allow denial of access, and in a classic case (Re D. – 1977, 1 All ER 145) a male child was adopted by the mother and her new husband against the wishes of the homosexual father, who had taken the case to the House of Lords. Custody seems likely to be granted in contested cases only where the heterosexual partner is clearly unsuitable by reason of a history of violence or inability to offer any kind of home, and then with extreme reluctance.

In July 1982 a lesbian was awarded custody of her daughter against the wishes of her husband, after the Court of Appeal had heard evidence that she 'lived discreetly' with her lover, that the husband was quite unable to offer any home to the child, and that it was the opinion of the social services that the only alternative to awarding the mother custody was to place the child in care. The woman gave evidence that she had been subjected to extreme physical and sexual abuse by her husband during the marriage, incuding his forcing her to have sex with other men in his presence and then 'going for her like a wild animal'. Refraining from commenting on these heterosexual mores, Lord Justice Watkins gave it as his opinion that

> if a parent becomes homosexual after a marital breakdown the
> courts should not allow children to be brought up in a

homosexual household . . . and should only consider awarding custody . . . to the homosexual parent if there is clearly no acceptable alternative and they are satisfied that it is in the best interests of the child.[7]

Although they are certainly subject to the same degree of prejudice, it seems likely that married men, with their greater economic and social freedom, and generally greater physical and psychological power within the marriage relationship, find it easier to lead a double life. It is dangerous to generalise from a very small and possibly atypical sample, but of the men contacting a London advice line during the first quarter of 1981 who admitted to being married, the majority were not prepared to consider telling their wives, nearly three-quarters had recently had gay sexual experience, and the most commonly given reason for contacting a gay agency was simply to find 'a bit on the side'. Most had found their sexual experience through 'cottaging' (using public lavatories as a way of contacting willing sexual partners). The risk these men run, as is borne out by literally thousands of reports in local newspapers, is that of 'coming out' in the most painful and damaging way to their families: after a widely reported prosecution for gross indecency, soliciting or indecent assault. The married man who does not come out is of course also desperately vulnerable to blackmail, and to police pressure to plead guilty in exchange for a promise of 'no publicity'.

Johnny-no-home

True to form, when the media uncovered the story of the hostel for homeless boys run by the so-called 'Bishop of Medway', the scandal which most attracted their attention was the homosexual element. The real scandal, that homelessness is a chronic and growing problem, particularly in major cities and particularly among the single, received little attention. Lesbians and gay men, seeking housing as gays, are by definition single. They may be living in long-term, stable couples, they may have children, but they do not qualify for any of the special housing association or mortgage facilities offered to 'young marrieds' or married couples with children. They also encounter special difficulties in obtaining or keeping housing because of the prejudice against their sexual orientation.

> A letter telling 24-year-old Lynne C. to go was handed to her just one day after she moved in. . . . It said 'Hi, Lynne, Toby told me that you are lesbian and it is just happens that I cannot stand them. . . . Besides, if I knew that you were one of them, I would have told you this before you move in. At this point you will have to move out next Sunday.'[8]

> Two lovers have fled their home after death threats from neighbours. . . . A twenty-seven-year old psychiatric nurse and his lover . . . were ambushed by a crowd of local men and women. The crowd said they were looking for a man who had assaulted a 13-year-old boy . . . Brian, they claimed, fitted the man's description. . . . 'There were four or five vans outside our place. As we reversed and were getting out . . . two white mini vans pulled up. They all had CB radios. . . .' The two lovers were surrounded by an angry crowd of forty. 'They made it plain they would murder us.' (The Deptford police confirmed that they were looking into a case of child abduction, but assured reporters that there were no sexual undertones in the case.)[9]

The problem is particularly acute for young lesbians and gay men, more so if they are black. They are likely to be unemployed or in low-paid or insecure jobs, and may have recently moved to a large town in search of employment and gay contacts. In London, where the system of 'holiday lets' is widely used to circumvent the Rent Acts, it is not unusual for lessors to ask the equivalent of one-quarter of the average industrial wage (over twice the standard DHSS 'rent allowance') of each person for a bedroom shared with one or even two others. It is also standard practice for all agencies to charge a fee of one month's rent in advance, with another month's rent payable as deposit to the lessor. West End hostels offer only temporary emergency accommodation and in any case regularly have to turn people away. The homeless young therefore drift, cadging a bed for the night where they can, or sleeping rough. With over 80,000 empty homes in London, many in public ownership, squatting is a more attractive and in many ways politically more satisfying alternative.

We are all 'gay punks' three white males and one black woman.
During the year prior to moving to this house we lived in five
different squats. The first, in Holloway, we shared with two
others. In its four months' life we were joined by five other
punks. The squat ended abruptly when it was attacked by a
gang of local heavies. The house and many of our belongings
were ruined and we were left homeless. For two months we
lived in Kings Cross with another group. During this period
there would be up to forty people living in two derelict, two-
roomed flats . . . many were gay, many had had or were having
problems with the police, probation officers, social workers,
parents, etc, a large number came from out of London. . . .
Again these squats ended abruptly, this time as a result of a
dawn raid by a group of British Movement skinheads. We then
opened another squat in Archway . . . this squat was finally
burnt out by British Movement skinheads. . . . We squatted
three flats in an estate in Waterloo . . . other flats were
squatted by other punks who were homeless, again a lot of
these were gay. We left . . . after three months of constant
police harassment, raids by various groups of heavies and two
successful arson attacks.[10]

In October 1979 a group of gay people involved in housing
through Shelter and the squatting movement, formed 'Gays in
Housing', an organisation to campaign for improved access to
housing for lesbians and gay men. With advice from this group, a
number of gay short-life housing co-operatives were formed,
taking from local authorities, under licence, housing that was in
too poor condition to be rehabilitated or used for the standard
waiting list. The punk household described above became part of
one of these co-ops, and for nine months acted as an unofficial
emergency refuge for the homeless young. During those nine
months, seventy-four people stayed in the house for more than
one night, with well over twenty being turned away for lack of
space. The average number staying in the house at any one time
was twenty. Of those who stayed, fifty-five were under 21. Of the
total, 55 per cent identified as gay or bisexual, 56 per cent were
homeless on arrival, and 24 per cent came from out of London.[11]
In 1981 Gays in Housing, together with the Joint Council for
Gay Teenagers, London Gay Switchboard, and several non-gay

housing advice or emergency services (Piccadilly Advice Centre, Soho Project, Alone in London, Basement Youth Project, Centrepoint and Homeless Action) set up a committee to approach the GLC and London Boroughs for funds to establish a properly organised refuge for young gays. All the agencies agreed that on the basis of their experience such a facility was urgently needed. London Gay Switchboard, for example, had received 200 calls from gay people in 1980 who were actually homeless at the time of contact.

The official bodies approached were highly sympathetic to this project, but the steering committee were advised to take legal opinion. The opinion they were given, and there is no reason to suppose that it was ill-founded, was that any group advertising or providing a hostel for young gay persons might be charged with procuring, running a disorderly house, and/or conspiracy to corrupt public morals. These possibilities arise out of the decision in the *IT* case (see page 87) and the nature of the 1967 Sexual Offences Act (see page 109). The restrictions within which the hostel would have to operate in order to provide reasonable defences against such charges (including, for example, admitting no one under 18!) rendered the whole project unworkable, and it was abandoned. Homeless young gays continue to be housed, if at all, by an unofficial and 'underground' network of 'safe houses' and squats. No official publicity can be given to these as the mere presence of gay males over 21 in the same house as those under age inevitably attracts police attention, while openly gay houses tend to attract the attention of the British Movement and the National Front in any case. Two houses within the Pink Triangle co-operative were attacked three times in one year, on one occasion by over twenty skinheads at 3 a.m. The same house was forcibly entered by the police on a different occasion, who removed all the records and address lists for the co-op.

Gays in Housing continues to campaign for housing rights for gay people, and a number of co-operatives have now succeeded in registering with the Registrar of Friendly Societies. Initially, difficulties were expected with adapting the 'model rules' to restrict membership, but Seagull, a women-only co-op, registered with a restrictive membership clause, and clauses restricting membership to 'those who define themselves as lesbians or gay men' are now acceptable. There has also been some success in approaching local authorities to get equal treatment in the allocation of council housing. A number of authorities (e.g. London Boroughs of Islington, Hackney, Haringey, Brent and Greenwich, and the councils for Avon, Oxford, Nottinghamshire and West Midlands) have undertaken to review their allocations and points systems to ensure that individuals and long-standing couples who are gay are treated in the same way as their heterosexual counterparts.

Private lives?

> . . . my sister started going out with her first serious boyfriend and then she started asking me when I intended to start going out with a boy. I wanted to say that I'd thought about it but I was afraid she'd think I was stupid or something so I invented a boy called Joey. I don't think she believed me because she was always asking about him and why he never came to the house.[12]

People who identify as heterosexual have little idea how far identifying as gay affects our everyday lives. Every family gathering, every social occasion, every school outing, shop, office or factory tea-break, involves dodging or confronting questions about relationships or sexual conquests. Many job interviews involve references to marital status or marriage prospects, all DHSS interviews include questions about the relationship to others in the same house. We do ourselves an injustice if we lie: we often experience injustice if we don't.

If our families are strongly religious — strict Baptists, Adventists, Christian Scientists, etc. — we are expected to sit impassively through sermons in which those who 'sin the sin of Sodom' are condemned to burn alive in the eternal flames of hell. If our family traditions include arranged marriage, we are forced into open rebellion or a life of shared misery. But coming out can cut black lesbians and gay men off from the only support network which protects them against the crude sexual exploitation, discrimination and random violence of the white majority.

In public we are expected to maintain puritanical standards of behaviour which have never applied to heterosexuals. Apart from provoking violence, many acts which others take for granted are actually criminal in a same-sex context: holding hands, kissing, chatting someone up, even minimal sexual contact in any place the public can enter may all result in arrest and prosecution. Should we actually commit a crime or require treatment for an 'illness' such as depression, we still run some risk of being 'sectioned' under the Mental Health Acts.[13]

> I remember . . . when I was working in a mental hospital, a young sixteen-year-old boy who had been committed to us by order of the Courts, was admitted to a locked ward, along with patients whom the hospital had found to be most disturbed. . . . When I asked about his diagnosis, I was told that he was 'another fucking queer'. Apparently, he had been caught 'indulging in a homosexual relationship'. . . . Once in the hospital, he was subjected to the usual ridicule of the staff . . . one of his daily tasks was to clean the ward lavatories . . . woken at 6am, Sundays and Christmas included, and his first task was to clean the toilets.[14]

In 1981, a caller to London Lesbian Line said that she had been admitted to hospital with concussion and a fractured arm when her father had thrown her downstairs after she told him she was lesbian. When she attempted to discharge herself from hospital on the second day, the doctor told her that he was thinking of having her transferred to a psychiatric ward, as the reason she had received her injuries indicated that she was suffering from a mental illness. She was then threatened with an order under Section 26 of the Mental Health Act.

Some improvements in the law (1982 amendments), and considerable changes in the attitudes of the medical profession, now make 'sectioning' on grounds of homosexuality alone unlikely, but enormous powers of interpretation still rest in the hands of those acting for statutory bodies. For example, some local authority social services departments still interpret their 'protective' powers over children 'at risk' or 'in moral danger' to mean an obligation to place young persons who are involved in homosexual relationships or who are associating with gay people into the care of the local authority.

> I told the hospital what had happened to me. The (male) nurse put something up my arse . . . he said, 'you'll enjoy this, this is what you queers like, isn't it?' It hurt like hell. They were really rough. I'd been torn inside and needed eighteen stitches. (Male

rape victim, describing his subsequent treatment in hospital to the author.)[15]

Any accident, assault or illness leading to hospitalisation can expose the gay patient to further humiliation. It can also involve extreme suffering and financial hardship for the patient's lover. Because gay people cannot marry, they cannot be each other's next-of-kin. We may be refused visiting rights, cannot give or withhold consent to operations (although some enlightened London hospitals now do treat gay lovers as the equivalent of spouses for these purposes, presumably at the doctor's own risk should legal relatives choose to make an issue of it), cannot claim dependent's benefits, taxation relief or allowances for care and nursing, do not receive pensions as 'relics', and cannot, in the absence of a recognised will, administer the estate or benefit from it. We have no rights over the body or to make funeral arrangements, and are not entitled to trade union or Friendly Society death benefits or grants.

For the same reason, lesbians and gay men cannot confer citizenship on their lovers. The sexist and racist nature of the Immigration Acts strike lesbian and gay male non-citizens with double force: they have no way of securing residence in or entry to this country. International travel is in any case fraught with difficulty for us. Although US Immigration has now undertaken not to seek evidence of homosexuality there are instances of visitors being refused entry to Britain when letters are found on them indicating that they are homosexual. In one case, a visitor arriving in February 1982 was stopped and searched, and his lover, a policeman in the Diplomatic Protection Squad, visited by the local force, who removed gay magazines and correspondence from his flat. The policeman was instantly taken before his commander and forced to sign a letter of resignation.[16]

Every aspect of our lives, however central or trivial, is a potential minefield. The classification of homosexuality as a peculiarly *sexual* 'deviation' leads to an equation with psychotically aggressive sexuality, and an identification with 'child molesters'. (Usually, in fact, sexual assaults on children are carried out by undeniably heterosexual, and often married, men.) As a result, the media have an obsessive interest in lesbians or gay men (and transvestites or transsexuals) who have, rear or work with children. Many single women of course do want children, and large numbers of lesbians have conceived through AID, arranged by doctors in private practice, clinics, or by groups of friends where gay men act as donors. In 1978 two journalists, one posing as a lesbian, contacted women's advisory services on the pretence of seeking AID. They subsequently ran a 'shock-horror' exposé of the practice, incidentally placing the careers and security of a large number of families at risk, forcing the doctor to whom most had been referred to stop the provision of AID, and eliciting fierce disapproval from the BMA of any doctor who assisted lesbians in conceiving children. More recently, a journalist managed to trace and interview a woman who had conceived by the 'test-tube baby' method. Sterilised at 28, and now living with a woman lover, P. was desperate for a child but unable to conceive *in utero*. With an agreeable donor posing as her husband, she sought help from Mr Patrick Steptoe. The journalist arrived at her home to conduct the interview shortly after she had lost the child through miscarriage. As the result of publicity in a Sunday newspaper, P. also lost her job.[17]

At the other end of the scale, a letter in *Gay News*[18] is a good example of the daily, trivial frustrations gay people suffer. A male couple were visited by officials from the Television Licence Enquiry Office, after one partner had purchased a second television. The TV licence was in the other partner's name. Such a licence is valid 'for the person named and any member of his/her family and domestic staff while they are living with him/her at the address shown'. It was not, in the opinion of the visiting official, valid for non-legal relationships. Such discrimination however is not merely directed against the non-married *per se*. Many companies, clubs, the Automobile Association, etc. accept the validity of 'common-law' marriages, but will not extend shopping discounts, reduced membership fees, fringe benefits of other kinds, to same-sex partners. The usual reason given is the difficulty of proving that a gay relationship is anything more than a temporary and *ad hoc* alliance. Since few bodies seem to expect the same difficulty with couples of opposite sex, one can only assume that their judgment is coloured by the presumption that gay relationships are inherently unstable, promiscuous and transient.

In recent years lesbians and gay men have managed, through the women's and gay movements, to provide themselves with many facilities and support networks denied them by conventional society. But this, and the removal of legislative barriers to progress, is only part of the answer. We live in a society in which powerful social and economic forces work to the prejudice of all those who do not conform to the favoured stereotype – which is, in effect, that of the middle-class, dominant, heterosexual, white male. The majority of the population do not fall into this category. The creation of a just society involves dismantling the myths and attitudes which oppress not merely homosexuals, but women, blacks, the young, the elderly, the single, and the physically and mentally less able. A society based on a lie is doomed to be perpetually disappointing.

Notes

1   Barbara Ehrenreich and Deirdre English, *For Her Own Good*, London, Pluto Press, 1979.
2   Joint Council for Gay Teenagers, *Breaking the Silence*, 1981, p. 10.
3   Ibid., p. 54.
4   Unpublished letter to a gay counselling agency.
5   *Glib*, magazine published in Birmingham, 1979, p. 16.
6   Ibid., p. 12.
7   Court of Appeal decision, reported in *Capital Gay* no 53, 23 July 1982.
8   *Capital Gay*, 2 October 1981.
9   *Capital Gay* no. 69, 12 November 1982.
10 P. Smith, unpublished report to Gays in Housing for the 'Crashpad' project.
11 Ibid.
12 *Breaking the Silence*, p. 17.
13 See *The Law and Sexuality*, published by Manchester Law Centre and Grass Roots Books, Manchester, 1978, pp. 61–71.
14 *Come Together* no. 2, 1970, republished in an edition by Aubrey Walter, Gay Men's Press, 1980, p. 53.
15 See also *Breaking the Silence*, p. 36.
16 *Gay News* no. 235, March 1982.
17 *Gay News* no. 237, April 1982.
18 *Gay News* no. 253, November 1982.

2 AT SCHOOL
Malcolm Dobson

Introduction

In this chapter I hope to demonstrate how discrimination against lesbians and gay men operates in education. To do this, it will be necessary to examine briefly the nature and purpose of 'education', and the structure and philosophy of the system which provides it to the majority of people in this country. I will be concentrating on the state education system, since it is here that the major trends are most visible, and it is also where the most wide-reaching changes can be achieved through the efforts of those involved in the process, via pressure on LEAs and central government. The term 'independent sector' is a classification which encompasses widely differing schools and educational philosophies, and because of this diversity it is impossible to examine them adequately here. However, the importance of the private sector in forming institutional attitudes to homosexuality should not be underestimated; for example, the majority of top civil servants (60 per cent), principal judges (80 per cent) and Anglican bishops (85 per cent) were educated at public schools.

Educational philosophy and purpose

As Anna Durell has pointed out in Chapter 1, we are all raised on some sort of mythology, which controls the way we live. Many, if not all, of these myths are necessary for the maintenance of the

structure of society, and the education system is the major institution responsible for their propagation and reinforcement. The society we live in is based on a capitalist structure, which depends for its survival on reproduction of a supply of labour. This needs two conditions – the reproduction of the necessary skills, and the reproduction of ruling-class ideologies and their acceptance by the working class. It is education's role to bring these two conditions about.

The history of education in England and Wales reflects that process. Louis Althusser suggested that in a pre-industrial society the church was the dominant 'Ideological State Apparatus',[1] a role taken over by the education system in a capitalist society. It is not insignificant that the state education system was established during the rise of the industrial capitalist society in the nineteenth century, taking over, to a large extent, the role of the church school. In the present century one of the major provisions of the 1944 Education Act was the establishment of the secondary level of education in the form of grammar schools for academic pupils, technical schools for courses leading to technical qualifications, and secondary modern schools, for which the minister advocated *ad hoc* courses leading to no qualifications. The full structure was rarely implemented, and there was some overlapping between schools; however, the intention and significance in emphasising the social structure is clear.

Part of that social structure is the nuclear family, and the ruling classes have recognised its importance in the reproduction of the labour force. Government social policies, throughout the nineteenth and twentieth centuries, have had a strong emphasis on protecting the family, specifically the working-class family. Education has played no less a role in this. The physical separation of the sexes (with single-sex schools, and separate entrances for girls and boys in mixed schools) owed much to a desire to preserve morality, but there was a correspondingly strict separation in the curriculum. Subjects such as needlework, child care and domestic science were designed specifically to educate girls for their future roles as wives and mothers.

The school's role in maintaining and supporting the family has a potential for creating strong tensions within the system. From the time of the Education Act of 1870, which established that a child should not receive religious teaching at variance to its parent's wishes, to the current debate over the right of parents to withdraw their children from sex-education classes, schools have been in a position of conflict, within themselves and within society as a whole. The school is considered to be *in loco parentis*, which creates tensions between what the school wants to do, what parents expect of it, and the prevailing educational philosophy of both local and central government (which can often be in conflict). Further conflict stems from the fact that the school is supposed to educate the young in the 'correct' social behaviour, which means accepting society and its institutions; the 'correctness' of the role of the police, for example, and the supremacy of the 'nuclear family'. For many, if not most, of the young people at school such a view of society does not match up to the reality that they experience.

It is against this background that I will examine how lesbians and gay men experience the education system. Anti-gay discrimination − heterosexism and homophobia − affects more, indeed considerably more, people than just teachers, who are its most obvious victims. It also affects gay students and the curriculum, both manifest and hidden. (The manifest curriculum is what is consciously taught in lessons; the hidden curriculum is what is conveyed in what actually happens in school: the attitudes put over in the way staff relate to students; the images presented in teaching materials and examples used in the classroom, and so on.) In addition, the school community will include children whose parents are lesbian or gay; those children will receive at school negative images of their parents, either through explicit or implicit condemnation, or because the existence of homosexuality is ignored. These areas of discrimination, of course, directly concern what happens within the school; there is, however, more to school and education than that. It should be remembered that the school exists in and is part of the wider community; this will inevitably include lesbians and gay men, who should be taken into account in the work the school is doing.

'Corruptors of youth'

Discrimination against gay staff is probably the most 'visible', in that the media (especially the local press) publicise dismissals (especially when connected with court cases over cottaging, for example) of teachers and other people working with children. The 'sensitivity' of employing lesbians and gay men in jobs involving contact with the young arises from the belief that the young people will be seduced or corrupted, either physically or ideologically. The fear of physical assault arises from the belief that lesbians and gay men are predatory by nature, and the identification of homosexuality with paedophilia. Both ideas are without foundation: in fact Home Office statistics show that the vast majority of 'assaults' on young people below the age of consent by adults are by heterosexual men on girls. The other fear, that of ideological corruption, seduction to the homosexual way of life, is more basic, and lies, for example, behind Mary Whitehouse's objections to homosexual 'proselytizing' in schools (in other words, to the facts rather than the myths about homosexuality being taught).

The fear is that if homosexuality is presented as 'normal', and a valid alternative life-style, young people will find it so attractive that they will immediately embrace it. This, of course, connects with the idea that the only life-style schools can be seen to endorse is that of the nuclear family. It can be argued that in the dismissal of the gay teacher, John Warburton (see Chapter 3), the problem wasn't his homosexuality *per se*, but that it became public knowledge inside the school, and, even worse, that he defended himself positively and without shame or apology. If his employing authority (the Inner London Education Authority) had supported him it would have been supporting his 'deviant' life-style, contradicting its support for 'normality'; therefore the authority had to dismiss him to demonstrate its disapproval of his life-style. Similarly, I was told by the borough librarian of my employing authority that I had 'brought the [library] service' into disrepute and was threatened with dismissal after a head teacher had complained that I had worn a badge saying 'Gay Pride 78' when visiting a school as part of my work as a children's librarian.

What had happened in these two cases is that the concept of 'invisibility' had been breached. This idea (which has not, I think, been formally stated or acknowledged, but can be seen behind the comment that 'teachers should never in any circumstances lift the veil from their own private lives'[2] arises from the conflict referred to earlier, the question of how much schools should influence children, and the authority that the school has as an official body and as an organ of the state. This question of 'authority' and 'influence' gives rise to the convention that teachers (and anyone else working with children) do not reveal or discuss their private lives with the children in their charge. However, a little thought will show that this convention does not and cannot work, especially if staff live within the school's catchment area. The personal life, at least in general terms, of a heterosexual member of staff is usually common knowledge. Most married women, and some married men, wear a wedding ring; when women are pregnant they can hardly conceal it; spouses sometimes accompany staff on school trips. This is all so 'normal' as to be unremarkable. It is only when an 'abnormal' life-style is involved that the convention of 'invisibility' is invoked. This, indeed, affects not only gay and lesbian staff. Unmarried staff living with heterosexual lovers present an 'unacceptable' life-style (although, of course, few are sacked if news of their domestic arrangements leaks out), and in a recent case a head teacher newly appointed to a post in a Catholic school was sacked when it was discovered that he was divorced.

'It's just a phase'

Young lesbians and gay men are in an even worse position, since it is their own existence that is being denied. At best (and it is a very poor best), they are allowed to go through a homosexual 'phase' which they grow out of, into 'normal' sexuality.

> The pubescent teenager naturally goes through a phase which is designated as 'homosexual' by the psychiatrists — but seen by the layman simply as the 'hero worship' which characterizes adolescence and which is a precursor to normal mature heterosexuality.[3]

> At fifteen I spoke to a teacher who I liked. He told me I'd grow out of it . . .[4]

> People have been telling me for years that it was just a phase. It first came out at school when I was 14. I told a friend that I fancied her friend and she told everyone and I mean everyone. I had long talks with teachers about it . . . All of them said it would go away in the end . . .[5]

Official recognition and support of young lesbians and gay men is virtually non-existent. One of the questions in a survey of local education authorities carried out by CHE in 1981 (unpublished) asked chief education officers, 'Do you have specific provision for the counselling of gay students?' Out of forty-two replies, only four referred to this question. Two said 'No', one mentioned college gaysocs and one referred to student counselling services in further and higher education. The only education authority to have made any commitment to young lesbians and gay men is the Inner London Education Authority (ILEA), by its grants to the London Gay Teenage Group. At the end of 1979/beginning of 1980 the group was registered with ILEA, after an exhaustive two-year period of negotiation through twelve area youth committees, area youth worker groups, individual committee members, and so on. In January 1982 the following small advertisement appeared in a number of periodicals, including ILEA's own *Contact*.[6]

LONDON GAY TEENAGE GROUP

Islington. Part-time youth worker. Applications are invited for the post of youth worker to work with the above group of young people aged 16–21 years. The successful applicant will be expected to work for seven hours per week. These hours are split between one mid-week evening (three hours) and Sunday afternoon (four hours). Applicants should have experience in working with groups of young people, and have skills and experience in counselling and organisation. Salary according to qualifications £3.54—£4.76 per hour. Applications and further details from: Islington Area Youth Office, White Lion St, N1 9PW. Tel: 278 1802. Closing date: 5 February 1982.

YOUNG LESBIAN GROUP

Islington, N7. Part-time youth worker. Applications are invited for the post of youth worker to work with the above group of young women aged 16–21 years. The group meets on Monday evenings each week from 7pm—10.30pm. Applicants should have experience in working with groups of young people and have skills and experience in counselling and organisation. Salary according to qualifications £3.54—£4.76 per hour. Applications and further details from: Islington Area Youth Office, White Lion St, N1 9PW. Tel: 278 1802. Closing date: 5 February 1982.[6]

It immediately provoked criticism. On 1 February in the House of Commons, Mr Greenaway, Conservative member for Ealing North, 'asked the Secretary of State for Education and Science if he will use his powers under the Education Act of 1944 to direct any local authority which maintains Youth Clubs run for homosexuals below the age of consent to cease to do so; and if he will make a statement.'[7] Mr William Shelton, in a written answer for the Secretary of State, said, 'My Right Hon. Friend is investigating reports that the ILEA is supporting work with groups of young homosexuals. He will reach a view on what action should be taken in the light of the facts established.'[8] The proposals to employ youth workers also drew this response from a school parent/ governor, published in the ILEA magazine *Contact*:

'BETTER USE OF MONEY' Sir - I have read in one of the national newspapers that the ILEA have placed two advertisements for two youth workers to lead teenage homosexual and lesbian groups. It is ludicrous in these days of redundancies and education cuts — surely the money offered for these two posts could be better used to buy other things more beneficial to our children.[9]

Opposition to individuals who come out, or who are forced out in their school can come from staff or students. The accounts given in *Breaking the Silence* make this clear, and these represent only a small proportion of what actually happens. The opposition from staff usually runs in the 'it's just a phase' mode, through displeasure that the pupil's activities are disrupting the surface-smoothness of the running of the school ('I had to have a fairly stiff talk with the head. . . . He made it clear that his main worry concerned the school's reputation'[10], to outrage that a pupil should commit such an offence. This outrage can lead to the parents of the pupil being informed, usually without the knowledge or consent of the pupil in question: in one recent case the head teacher of a London school informed the parents of one of the pupils that their son was gay. The pupil was out at school, quite happy and adjusted about his sexuality, and wanted to tell his parents, but in his own time. Fortunately, his parents supported him and complained strongly to the head.

Opposition within the peer group is simpler, yet more difficult to analyse. There is, of course, great pressure from the peer group to conform, in all sorts of ways. Any deviation of any sort — liking the wrong sort of music, wearing the wrong clothes, etc. leads to exclusion. This also applies to personal relationships. The types of roles that boys and girls are expected to conform to are strongly heterosexist: girls are supposed to make way for the boys, and must not be seen to be challenging their status, either academically or socially. They have to be popular with boys, so that they aren't accused of being 'frigid' or 'lezzies', but not so popular that they can be accused of being a 'slag' — a difficult line to tread. Boys, in their turn, have to conform to the macho role; they have to have had, or at least say they have had, sex with as many girls as possible. To be reluctant to conform to this role can lead to them being labelled 'queer' or 'poof', the worst insults in the book.

Everyone keeps on at you about whether or not you have a boyfriend . . . I can't tell them my real feelings.[11]

I found I was acting a role and that was a strain.[12]

I've not taken girls out though I have talked about them to show that I'm interested. I remember an incident in the third year when some lad asked me if I was queer. I denied it of course.[13]

No one knew about me, at first, but I soon got a reputation at school, not because I looked or acted queer but because I never joked or boasted about this girl or that girl.[14]

These roles are constantly reinforced, by peers, and by the media popular with the young. Anybody who comes out as lesbian or gay within such an atmosphere risks being rejected by her or his peers as well as by the school authority structure, and, what is worse, physical violence. The organisers of the Gay Self-Defence sessions in London report increasing numbers of 14- and 15-year-olds attending, after experiencing violence at their schools. This active rejection, coupled with the passive rejection in the lack of any positive image, indeed any image, of homosexuals and homosexuality within the school environment, can have severe effects on the young lesbian or gay man. Indeed, far from it being 'callous' to enable young lesbians and gay men to accept their sexuality in a positive way, as Mary Whitehouse so frequently says, it is callous not to.

The pressure to conform, which is so pervasive through their lives, can lead to problems at school which the school pastoral system and its back-up system are unable to cope with, and are probably unwilling to face. Pupils who feel rejected by school, or who feel that education is irrelevant to them, revolt against the institution and its ideals by being disruptive in class or withdrawing voluntarily from the institution; in other words, by truanting:

> Well, anyhow, when I kept playing truant they finally kicked me out of school for being too much trouble, I guess.[15]

Of course, this happens for many other reasons, and it is probably too simplistic to say that they arise only from one cause, but it is probably only too accurate to say that the homosexuality of a pupil is never recognised as a factor. This is because the people involved in the pastoral system are probably unaware of it, and also because most young people would be reluctant to divulge their homosexuality to someone who is likely to be totally unsympathetic, especially when, as I have pointed out above, the 'pastoral' system, which is (presumably) supposed to act in a supportive, advisory role, is so often identical to the disciplinary structure which, as its name suggests, is there to punish wrongdoers. Members of the Gay Youth Movement who attended the Gays in Education Conference in November 1982 were quite clear that the last people they would have approached for advice or assistance were the people who, officially, they should have. Again, to return to the CHE survey carried out in 1981, no education authority said that it had any provision for gay pupils, and this presumably means that there is no consideration of them in pastoral provision. One small example of this is in the reaction to an Education Welfare Officer for the ILEA. When he came out to his superior, the reaction was not that he may have some useful input on counselling young lesbians and gay men, but the conventional one of, first keep quiet about it, and then pressure to make him resign his post.

'Fairies and butch young maids'

Some of the pressures young lesbians and gay men experience arise out of their experience of their formal education. Many look for positive support in the curriculum and teaching materials, but in vain:

When these feelings intensified, I'd go to the [school] library in the hope that somewhere in all those books I'd find someone like myself. I would read about boys who were lonely, unpopular, sensitive, misunderstood; about boys who hated sports and were ridiculed by their mates. But nowhere in all those books did I find anyone like me![16]

The sex education talks never mentioned homosexuality and I assumed it was so uncommon that it wasn't worth mentioning.[17]

Those areas, such as social studies or sex or health education where one might expect to find some references to homosexuality, are on the whole unhelpful. The official position on health (which usually includes sex) education can be summed up by the words of the chairman (sic) of the Gwynedd Health Authority at a conference organised by the Health Education Council in Llandudno in 1982:

Health education in schools had an important part to play in supplementing and reinforcing the values and habits of family life . . . 'catch 'em young and point them the right way' was an attractive proposition, but it was important that pointing them the right way should not be seen as indoctrination.[18]

Quite – reinforcing the values of family life would, presumably, not be seen as indoctrination, whereas providing positive support for young lesbians and gay men would. Similar evidence can be found in the threat from the government to withdraw the government grant from the FPA if *Make it Happy* (Jane Cousins, Virago, 1978. Winner of *The Times Educational Supplement*'s Information Book Award) was not removed from its recommended list. The view of the Department of Education and Science (and its predecessor the Ministry of Education) can be judged from the instructions it gives in its pamphlets on health education (which includes sex education). In 1957 the Ministry of Education issued a pamphlet (fourth impression in 1964) which forbore to mention the subject of homosexuality at all, except in the vaguest possible terms of 'crushes' which the young boy or girl would grow out of. However, it is interesting to note what was said about sex education in general, especially bearing John Warburton's case in mind:

Older children, particularly around puberty, often ask more searching and profound questions [than younger children]; these too should be answered by giving information within the limits of a boy's or girl's maturity and comprehension, just as with questions on any other subject.[19]

In 1977 the Department of Education and Science said,

Homosexuality, both male and female, is probably best dealt with in passing if and when it arises, as it may do with older boys and girls from their studies of literature, visits to the theatre and cinema, and from television programmes.[20]

What price the ILEA's demand that John Warburton should sign a document saying that he would not discuss 'homosexuality with pupils, except in the course of a completely structured programme of sex education of which the Headmaster/Head-mistress has full knowledge'?[21] It is interesting to read what the DES says about the effects of social change on sex education:

the past decade has seen the growing effects of six factors whose full significance has yet to be evaluated. Perhaps the most important are the growing acceptance of the contraceptive pill and the judgement which allowed the publication of 'Lady Chatterley's Lover'. The others are changes in the divorce laws making divorce easier; the abortion laws; . . . a multi-racial society . . .; and lastly an appreciation that sexuality is a problem [sic] for the handicapped.[22]

Where, one might ask, is the reference to the partial decriminal-isation of male homosexual acts that occurred during that same decade? Again, in connection with John Warburton, and relating to attempts by gay rights campaigners to make it acceptable for gay staff in schools to be open about their sexuality, it says that:

it is vitally important that the privacy and reticence of boys and girls are respected by teachers, and that teachers should never in any circumstances lift the veil from their own private lives.[23]

This brings us back to the concept of 'invisibility' which was discussed earlier, and which, as we saw, does not work. There can be no doubt that sex education is still firmly directed towards the mechanics of procreation and as such cannot encompass homo-sexuality.

Social studies, designed to introduce pupils to the society they live in, are almost as bad. Any mention of homosexuality is usually under the heading of 'deviancy', which, although it might be a sociological concept and term, conjures up images of wilful disobedience, wickedness and maladjustment that are unlikely to support a young lesbian or gay man in her or his emerging sexuality. What of other subjects? The Ministry of Education said that:

> questions involving human sex and reproduction are particularly liable to arise independently, during lessons on other subjects such as religious instruction, English literature, history, geography and science, and teachers of these subjects should be ready for them; sometimes related social and ethical issues will come up for discussion in this way.[24]

To use the ministry's words in a way which (presumably) was not intended, this can be even truer of homosexuality. But where is it discussed? Not in history, unless you count the occasional disparaging reference to James I of England, VI of Scotland, or Edward II. Not in art, where there *might* be some mention of the effect of Michelangelo's homosexuality on his art; not in English literature, where E. M. Forster's *A Passage to India* is a set book on many syllabuses.

Attempts to rectify the absence of any mention of homosexuality, or to refer to it in a positive way, are frequently attacked. One of the reasons for the attack by the government on *Make it Happy* was that book's positive references to homosexuality. The tape/slide kit, *Homosexuality: a fact of life*, produced by Tyneside CHE in 1978, has been attacked for its 'bias' and 'propaganda', that is, because it was produced by a gay organisation, and has been banned by the City of Newcastle-upon-Tyne Education Committee, amongst others. Similarly, even quasi-official organisations are attacked; the Schools Council's resources list *Relationships and sexuality*, prepared as part of its Health Education 13–18 Project, was the subject of questions in Parliament, no doubt partly because of the fact that it included *Homosexuality: a fact of life*.

However, although what is taught in the manifest curriculum is important, the hidden curriculum is probably more important in creating and reinforcing ideas and beliefs. For a pupil who is coming to terms with her or his emerging homosexuality (or trying to), or even for those pupils going through a 'phase' (and they probably need as much positive support and reassurance as those pupils who are certain of their homosexuality, and not just the vague promise that 'you'll get over it eventually'), there is not much support to be gained. Teaching materials in areas where sexuality or personal relationships are relevant (and this is more often than might be supposed) are overwhelmingly heterosexist. Staff attitudes are usually hostile − the cliché of the macho games teacher using 'cissie' or 'pansy' as terms of abuse is no less true for being a cliché. Attempts to introduce equal opportunities into such subjects as home economics or crafts lead to jibes that 'boys are to be turned into fairies and girls into butch young maids'.[25]

Come the revolution

It would seem from the above that an improvement can only come about with a fairly radical change in the way 'education' operates in society, which itself will only occur with a fairly radical alteration in the nature of our society. But, while we are waiting (or, preferably, working) for the revolution, what can be done?

The areas of discrimination outlined in this chapter, although discussed separately for simplicity's sake, are inextricably linked, and action in one area has profound implications for the others. Probably the most important step is for education authorities, the DES, individual schools and people to stop thinking of homosexuality as something 'out there', which has no connection with what happens in schools, and to accept that it has a fundamental connection with what happens in school. One of the strongest motivating forces in the establishment of equal opportunities/anti-sexist and multi-ethnic/anti-racist policies in schools is the recognition that there are female and black pupils in schools who need positive recognition of their existence and needs and positive role models amongst the staff and in the overt and hidden curriculum to identify with. The basic foundation to any improvement in the situation is a recognition that there are young lesbians and gay men in schools with similar needs.

Any attempt to cater for these should have several intertwined strands. The basic need is for visibility; unlike women and members of ethnic minorities who are immediately visible, lesbians and gay men are not identifiable as such until they declare themselves. Before this can happen lesbians and gay men, both pupils and staff, should feel that they can come out at school. If they are going to do so, there have to be a number of pre-conditions. Staff need to feel secure in their jobs; therefore they need to have the support of the senior management (head teachers, etc.) in their school, and also the knowledge that their education authority will not dismiss them. This latter requires not only anti-discrimination employment clauses, but also specific support for staff who come out to pupils. Lesbian and gay pupils will also need to be assured of the support of staff in school, and also of the education authority's support.

Such official support is no good if staff and pupils who are out (and those who choose not to come out) are met with abuse in their daily lives. The school atmosphere and staff and pupil attitudes would have to be supportive; such an atmosphere depends on the development of positive attitudes to homosexuality amongst the whole school community. This can be done through the formal curriculum, and through the hidden curriculum – the way in which heterosexual members of staff relate to lesbian and gay colleagues and pupils, the correction of anti-gay abuse directed at heterosexual as well as lesbian and gay staff and pupils can have a telling effect. The school community, as I have pointed out above, also extends beyond the school boundaries; with a more positive atmosphere within the school, lesbian and gay parents and their children will feel able to be more open about their home situation. The place of the school in the wider community can be recognised by the appointment of community governors who are lesbian or gay, as the London Borough of Brent did in the summer of 1982 (even though their plans to advertise in *Gay News* did bring the wrath of Rhodes Boyson, MP for Brent North, down on their heads).

Any moves that are directed at fighting homophobia and heterosexism would have to be discussed thoroughly in a school. Most people working in schools are aware of the need for multi-ethnic, if not anti-racist, teaching; many are accepting the need for equal opportunities. So far, few people have any idea of the extent or nature of discrimination against lesbians and gay men in our society. It will be up to those of us working in education to initiate and lead the necessary discussions. However, to do so is tantamount to coming out; for many, it would mean coming out into a situation the very opposite of the one they want to bring about. Would it be a case of 'out of the closet, into the fire'?

Notes

1 'Ideological state apparatus' is the term coined by Louis Althusser to describe those institutions which include the mass media, the church, the law, and education, which promote the ruling ideologies of society. An introduction to Althusser's analysis of education's role in society can be found in *Sociology: Themes and Perspectives* by Michael Haramblos (University Tutorial Press, 1980). Those interested in the relationship between the family and education should read *The State, the Family and Education*, by Miriam E. David (London, Routledge & Kegan Paul, 1980).
2 Department of Education and Science, *Health Education in Schools*, London, HMSO, 1977, p. 117.
3 Mary Whitehouse, *Whatever happened to sex*, Hove, East Sussex, Wayland, 1977, p. 68.
4 Michael Burbidge and Jonathan Walters, *Breaking the silence*, Joint Council for Gay Teenagers, 1981, p. 21.
5 Ibid., p. 49.
6 ILEA, *Contact*, January 1982.
7 House of Commons, *Hansard*, 1 February 1982, Column 33.
8 Ibid.
9 ILEA, *Contact*, 5 February 1982.
10 Burbidge and Walters, op. cit., p. 38.
11 Ibid., p. 17.
12 Ibid., p. 26.
13 Ibid., p. 26.
14 Ibid., p. 51.
15 Ibid., p. 30.
16 Ibid., p. 33.
17 Ibid., p. 52.
18 *Health Education News*, no. 36, May/August 1982.
19 Ministry of Education, *Health Education*, London, HMSO, 1957, p. 55.
20 DES, op. cit., p. 118.
21 Letter to John Warburton, in 'Open and Positive', Gay Teacher's Group (London), n.d.
22 DES, op. cit., p. 111.
23 Ibid., p. 117.
24 Ibid., p. 55.
25 *Gay News*, no. 157, 14 December – 10 January 1979, p. 13.

3 AT WORK
Mike Daly

The scandal of current unemployment ought to quickly dislodge any impression that with the so called employment protection legislation of the last decade the job security of workers has become established. Industrial tribunals do offer dismissed workers the opportunity to challenge their dismissal but not all are qualified to claim. Generally speaking the recently dismissed employee must have had at least a year's full-time employment with the employer against whom the complaint is brought. But of the qualified relatively few, perhaps a quarter, succeed in establishing that their dismissal was unfair and it is only in a tiny proportion of 'successful' cases that tribunals make an order for reinstatement. The majority have to be content with compensation – minimal financial recognition of the injustice they have suffered.

Unfair dismissal?

Given such bleak prospects for any sacked employee, how does the homosexual fare in challenging a dismissal for reasons simply of sexual orientation? An analysis of three decisions will suffice to illustrate the major themes that emerge from those industrial tribunal cases which have considered the unfairness of a dismissal for reasons connected with the employee's homosexuality.[1]

A first category of the 'reasoning' proposed for dismissal might

be characterized as 'customer/client/fellow worker objection' to the homosexual employee. In taking advantage of the supposed prejudice of others and in not even having to prove that their perceptions are well grounded, employers do not have to display their own prejudice. Indeed, since the enactment of the 1980 Employment Act, the employer bears no burden of proving that s/he acted reasonably in dismissing the employee.

Louise Boychuk worked as an accounts clerk in the office of an insurance broker for a little over a year when she was dismissed for wearing a badge which bore the legend 'Lesbians Ignite'.[2] She had worn various badges for many months without objection from her employer prior to the inflammatory button which led to her dismissal. It is perhaps understandable, given the norm, that people assume that their colleagues are heterosexual. It is equally understandable − but rarely understood − that lesbians and gay men may object to that assumption and some wish to declare that they are homosexual by, for example, wearing a badge. Some employers, however, choose to see such badges as 'flaunting one's sexuality' whilst overlooking or even engaging in precisely that behaviour − wolf-whistles, bottom pinching, and other harassment − by which too many (male) heterosexuals declare their sexuality. And how might employers characterize the wedding ring? As a display of heterosexuality?

Ms Boychuk was told to either remove the offending badge or be dismissed. She refused and the employer's reason for dismissing her was that he found the badge offensive and thought his customers, especially Arabs (!) would take a poor view of the firm if they saw such a badge on the lapel of an employee in the reception area.

Neither the reasonableness of the fear nor the reasonableness of the imagined prejudice were examined by the tribunal. On the contrary, the tribunal Chairman agreed with the employer that his Arab and non-Arab customers 'would not like it' and upheld the sacking. On appeal the employment appeal tribunal upheld the decision saying that it was within the area of an employer's discretion to lay down reasonable standards of dress and behaviour for employees. The EAT did not qualify that discretion, however, by saying that where an employer restricts or prohibits certain styles of dress so as not to cause offence to customers, for instance, there must be some reasonable basis for the restriction and it should not be based on mere whim. They did not consider the reasonableness or otherwise of the belief that badges with a lesbian message would cause alarm and offence to Arab purchasers of insurance and, ultimately, damage the business.

A second argument used to justify the homosexual's dismissal focuses on the employee's *'misconduct'* and subsequent criminal conviction. Even universal support for the dismissed worker is of little avail, as is shown in the case of Gordon Wiseman.[3] A large number of students, course users, health administrators, fellow staff members and many others sent unsolicited letters of support for Wiseman to the college authorities with objections to the dismissal. There was no evidence that anyone sent in unfavourable remarks to the college but in spite of this impressive level of support Mr Wiseman was dismissed and an industrial tribunal upheld the dismissal.

Gordon Wiseman was a lecturer in drama therapy at the Salford College of Technology. His courses were known and respected nationally and his personal reputation as a leader in his field was considerable. The law report reads as follows:

On November 2nd, 1979, Mr. Wiseman was lonely and depressed in the afternoon. He decided to meet a consenting adult and take him to the privacy of his home — it must be inferred, for sexual purposes. He went to a public lavatory in Dean Lane which is a known meeting place for homosexuals. He sat down in a cubicle. Someone (a stranger) entered the next cubicle and began to make advances. As Mr. Wiseman was going to respond, the police, who had been keeping watch, burst in and arrested them both. Subsequently, on the 6th December, Mr. Wiseman pleaded guilty to an act of gross indecency with [a named man]

A newspaper report of Gordon Wiseman's court appearance and conviction was shown to his college authorities. He was suspended, subjected to a disciplinary procedure and eventually dismissed. As is usual in gross indecency convictions, the only 'criminal' aspect of behaviour was to engage in sexual activity in a place defined by law as 'in public', albeit behind locked doors and entirely out of public sight. As the dissenting member of the industrial tribunal argued, in all of these grey areas of moral judgement and sexual predisposition, objectivity is difficult to achieve, but it is helpful to gain a perspective by asking the question: 'Would a male or female heterosexual lecturer have been dismissed if discovered soliciting or indulging in promiscuous behaviour?' We have no evidence certainly, but we must find it difficult to imagine that this would be the case.[4]

The majority had no such difficulty or perspective and accepted that the college principal had acted reasonably in the belief that Wiseman had 'given way to temptation' and shown 'lack of control'. Not only might young people be at risk but, conversely, Wiseman may have been vulnerable to approaches from his students. The repute of the college was at stake, it was argued, yet the tribunal also accepted that 'there was no evidence to suggest that his "inclinations" had affected his teaching duties in the past or his attitude towards his students.' They also considered his good professional record, national reputation and the very wide measure of support he had received from students, staff and others. Although the evidence before the tribunal was entirely speculative and contrary to actual experience the majority found the dismissal fair. Argued the dissenting voice of the tribunal, 'In treating a homosexual male more harshly because of his homosexuality, the governors had shown themselves to be less than "unprejudiced" and "open-minded" as the Employment Appeal Tribunal requires them to be.'

The appeal tribunal did not adopt the dissenting view but upheld the dismissal as fair. For them the 'real question raised before us is: is it a self evident proposition that someone who has done what Mr. Wiseman told the disciplinary bodies and the industrial tribunal he had done, and takes his view about his own conduct (incautious and foolish), cannot be a risk to teenage boys in his charge?'[5] The appellate tribunal thought the proposition not self-evidently right and that it was, therefore, for the industrial tribunal to evaluate the reasonableness of the employer's action in treating the appellant's conduct as a reason for dismissal. 'Whether or not we would have agreed with the answer they gave, we find no error of law, which alone would give us power to interfere.'[6] It is worth adding a word from the law report: 'The applicant [Wiseman], as a rule, dealt with mature students but there were a considerable number of students ranging from the ages of 16 to 19 involved.'[7] Teenage boys whom the tribunal feared might be at risk!

Such talk of risk and vulnerability figures as a third category of 'reasoning' in this area of unfair dismissal which views the homosexual (whether 'convicted' or not), as *corrupter and sexual predator*. Legal authority can now be claimed as weighty reinforcement of these popular prejudices with the recent judgments in the Saunders case.[8]

John Saunders had been responsible for site maintenance at a camp for teenage children in Perthshire. For over two years he had worked without there being any significant complaint until his employers learnt from a 'trustworthy' source (undoubtedly the police), that he was a homosexual. He readily confirmed the fact that, as his employers put it, 'he indulged in homosexuality'. The Scottish National Camps Association Secretary proposed that 'at a camp accommodating large numbers of school children and teenagers it is totally unsuitable to employ any person with such tendencies.'

Mr Saunders claimed that his dismissal was unfair. He argued that he was well able to keep his private life separate from his work and that, in any event, he had no sexual interest in children or young persons. An industrial tribunal concluded that the dismissal was for 'another substantial reason of a kind such as to justify the dismissal' and that it was, in the circumstances, fair.

Before the employment appeal tribunal it was argued that such a conclusion was wrong, primarily because a psychiatrist had given evidence that, after examination, he did not consider Saunders's homosexuality to constitute a risk to children. The psychiatrist had also given evidence that in his opinion heterosexuals were as likely to interfere with children as homosexuals. However, the tribunal found that a considerable proportion of employers would take the view that the employment of a homosexual should be restricted, particularly when required to work in proximity with children. 'Whether that view is scientifically sound,' concludes the EAT, 'may be open to question but there was clear evidence from the psychiatrist that it exists as a fact.'[9]

There is surely a central flaw in the 'reasoning'. The court appears to consider the views of a 'considerable proportion of employers' to be synonymous with the standards of a 'reasonable employer'. The mere fact that a considerable proportion of employers would take the view that homosexuals create a special risk to the young (a view that is readily and very widely challenged) does not become the view of the reasonable employer simply because it 'exists as a fact'.

Is prejudice the more reasonable because it is the more popular? The case and its principle have been cited with approval — 'Where the belief is one which is genuinely held, and particularly is one which most employers would be expected to adopt, it may be a substantial reason even where modern sophisticated opinion can be adduced to show that it has no scientific foundation.'[10]

Is homosexuality, *per se*, established as a substantial reason for fair dismissal? In an attempt to sidestep such questionable conclusions (and yet not dislodge them) the Court of Session (the Scottish Court of Appeal) insisted that 'there were other relevant considerations in the mind of the employer at the relevant time' and Saunders 'had not been dismissed simply on the ground that he was a homosexual'.[11] And these other relevant considerations?

The court put it to junior counsel (whose task under the Scottish system is to establish a prima facie case — the QC was not, in the event, called upon to speak) that the employers also considered the parents of the children using the campsite, who would be concerned were the camp to retain a homosexual as employee. Junior counsel conceded the point and yet surely the court is drawing a false distinction? These 'other relevant considerations' amount to the same thing — homosexuality, or rather the employers' view of it, was at the root of their concern for parents and their dismissal. The appeal court concluded in an exceedingly brief judgment, 'on the facts found and accepted by the industrial tribunal applying the proper test we cannot say that the tribunals below were not entitled to reach their decisions for the reasons which they state.'[12]

Mr Justice Bristow (who chaired the employment appeal tribunal in the Gordon Wiseman case) was challenged by counsel when he referred to homosexuality as a 'misfortune'. 'In the present case,' replied the judge, 'it is obviously a misfortune, since you get taken to a magistrates' court and subjected to a fine *and* you lose your job.'[13] Such considerations of 'double punishment' have been dismissed as 'mere distraction' in the case of another college lecturer also dismissed after a conviction for gross indecency.[14] But as is well established in the CHE catalogue of some forty dismissal cases, it isn't only the 'convicted' who suffer for their 'misfortune'.

Most at risk

The employment security of homosexuals is at risk simply because of the 'colour' of their sexuality rather than because of any considerations of competence. The law is not at all likely to offer redress nor to dislodge the popular prejudices which provoke the dismissals. From the many such dismissal cases a picture emerges of the employee most particularly 'at risk'.

The gender of the dismissed employee will generally be male.[15] He will have been 'discovered' to be homosexual rather than be a 'visible' gay person. (In only a quarter of the catalogued cases had the employee 'come out'. Leaving aside the suggestion of its desirability and virtue there might even be less risk in visibility.) The 'discovery' might well have been a consequence of court proceedings and criminal conviction for gross indecency or some other such 'crime'. (This was true in one-third of the cases catalogued in the CHE report.) The employment from which he was dismissed is likely to have been in some way connected with children or young people, probably in a white-collar capacity. Thus the 'identikit' of the person most 'at risk' is of a homosexual man employed as a teacher or social worker brought forcibly 'out of the closet' by a criminal conviction. Tribunals and employment protection legislation would seem to offer no protection.

The insecurity of such white-collar employment is compounded by the terms of the Rehabilitation of Offenders Act 1974. The act establishes certain categories of criminal conviction which are to be considered 'spent' after a period of years provided, broadly speaking, that the sentence was no more than a term of two and a half years imprisonment. With a conviction 'spent' a person is entitled to deny that s/he was ever convicted. If an employer asks a job applicant or an existing employee if s/he has any previous convictions the response can be a denial — such denial sanctioned by law. The act, however, excludes certain categories of employment from its reference and such areas of work include those where the homosexual employee is most at risk — social work and teaching. Indeed, if such workers are convicted of a sexual offence, the police pursue the practice of notifying the employer or appropriate professional body of the conviction.

Nor do the repercussions of a conviction for a sexual offence (however minimal its proportions) stop there. Teachers might, upon subsequent convictions, be barred from teaching for life. The Department of Education and Science is known to operate a 'black list' (List 99) of such sexual 'criminals', among others, information which it circulates to local authority and other employers.

Thus the worker whom the evidence establishes to be most at risk − the male teacher/social worker convicted of a sexual offence − is the person to whom the law offers the least protection. Such vulnerability can produce untold and prolonged suffering not just for the employee but also for his family, as is shown by the case of Peter Johnson.[16]

In the early 1970s Johnson was convicted of gross indecency and fined £25 − a measure of the crime's gravity. His wife's nervous breakdown and the pressures on himself forced him to change jobs and move to another part of the country where he worked happily and successfully. Ten years later he successfully applied for a job in a social services department. His interviewers did not ask about previous convictions nor, understandably, did Johnson volunteer details of his ten-year-old conviction. As a result of gossip it became known to his employers that he had previously been found guilty of gross indecency. He did not deny the fact and since his type of work was specifically excluded from the scope of the Rehabilitation of Offenders Act, he could not rely on its protection. Despite the support of his colleagues and immediate supervisors he was given no choice but to resign or be sacked.

Because Mr Johnson did not have the required length of service (fifty-two weeks) he was unable to argue that his resignation amounted, in the circumstances, to a dismissal − a 'constructive dismissal'. His MP was contacted and would have helped him fight the case but the prospect of having to relive the bitter experience of his fight ten years previously was too much for him and his wife.

> He resigned quietly in order to protect his family from the inevitable glare of publicity that was his only possible route to reinstatement. The cause of it all was a brief sexual encounter ten years before with another consenting man in a dark and private place, unseen by all but a couple of hidden policemen.[17]

It would be far from straightforward to pinpoint employer discrimination against homosexuals. Such is rarely blatant, is often disguised in other reasons for discipline and dismissal or is proposed to be an unwilling but necessary business concern for the prejudices of fellow workers, customers and clients.

There have in recent years been two attempts to gauge the current state of employer attitudes to the employment of homosexuals and the prospects for anti-discrimination policies in employment. Both enquiries, undertaken by the National Council for Civil Liberties, have been concerned with the public sector and local authority attitudes − in education and social services, areas of work in which the homosexual is most 'at risk'. The survey findings offer little cause for optimism, the more disturbing in that both areas of employment profess a concern for personal relationships and a preoccupation with human behaviour, development and dignity.

Homosexuality and the teaching profession

In 1973 the Inner London Education Authority wrote to the Campaign for Homosexual Equality,

> The Authority has no policy which excludes homosexuals from employment as teachers. Any such teacher in our service has therefore no need to fear for his position provided of course that there is no question of misconduct or risk to children.

This response was to serve as an initiative for the NCCL survey, published in August 1975 under the title *Homosexuality and the Teaching Profession*.[18] Of the 104 local education authorities canvassed in England and Wales, forty-seven replied. Ironically, the Inner London Education Authority was excluded from the survey since its response to CHE had in large measure encouraged the enquiries of other authorities. Ironically, because at the very time that the questionnaire was being canvassed the ILEA were at the centre of a controversy over the sacking of one of their probationary teachers for reasons related to his homosexuality.

In December 1974 John Warburton was banned from teaching in ILEA schools. His job at the Marylebone Church of England Girls' Secondary School was terminated after he had held a short dialogue with his students on the subject of homosexuality, subsequent to his being seen on a demonstration and then being greeted by his class with chants of 'poof' and 'queer'. He was banned from teaching in any ILEA school unless he was prepared to give a written undertaking 'not in future to discuss homosexuality with pupils, except in the course of a completely structured programme of sex education of which the Headmaster/Headmistress has full knowledge, and with which he/she is in full agreement.' Mr Warburton felt unable to comply with this request despite the advice from the NUT that it would be in line with their policy for him to sign the undertaking. (A full account of the Warburton case can be found in *Open and Positive*, published by the Gay Teachers' Group in 1978.)

Was this case a freak, an isolated example of discrimination? How would Mr Warburton have fared had he been employed by another of the education authorities in England or Wales? Not at all well. In the words of the NCCL survey,

> Nowhere has this (discrimination in employment against homosexuals) been more evident than in the field of education which must rank alongside the higher grades of the civil service as the area where the greatest discrimination exists.[19]

Only one authority (Solihull) said that they would not object *per se* to teachers being open with pupils about the fact of their homosexuality. The NCCL characterized two-thirds of the replies as unbigoted although a good half of these had hedged their answers around with qualifications of the type, 'unless, of course, a teacher allowed this [homosexuality], or any other aspect of his/her private life, to interfere with the proper professional exercise of his/her duties' (Leeds). Reflects the NCCL, 'such qualifications could be regarded as fair and proper, provided that they applied equally to heterosexuals. In many cases, however, the implication is that a homosexual's private life is a threat to the pupils, in a way which a heterosexual's is not.' Bury, for example, 'would need to be satisfied that children would in no way be at risk before appointing a known homosexual.' Although one might be reassured by the response from Durham that 'homosexual tendencies, of themselves, present no more automatic threat to children than heterosexual ones,' the respondent goes on to wonder 'whether these tendencies [might manifest] themselves in a way which was likely to interfere with the maintenance of a reasonable standard of discipline.'

Was an interference with reasonable standards of discipline the cause of ILEA's sacking of the probationer John Warburton? More persuasive, perhaps, were arguments similar to those marshalled by the Sheffield Authority. 'It is possible to say that in appointing teachers this Authority does not enquire into the sexual habits of candidates, any more than it does into any other aspect of teachers' private lives. If, however, these habits become public knowledge they assume a different quality, whether the person concerned is homosexual or heterosexual, and then, inevitably, such knowledge would be a factor in the appointment process, but the weight of the factor would depend upon the quality of the display of the sexuality.'

What then is the nature of the display if a teacher were to live with a companion of the opposite sex or, indeed, were to marry? So prevalent is the heterosexual norm that such conduct might not even be viewed as a display of sexuality. Would a homosexual menage be so neutrally considered or might 'sexual habits' be thought displayed for public knowledge?

'Public knowledge' in the shape of pupils' taunts and insults — 'poof' and 'queer' — provoked Warburton to his classroom discussion. Said the ILEA in a standard letter of reply they addressed to every correspondent who had written expressing unease at the dismissal, 'The policy of this Authority is that a teacher's private life is of no concern to the Authority so long as it does not intrude into his professional life in school. Unfortunately with Mr. Warburton, it did to an extent which could not be overlooked, nor be allowed to recur.' Could not be overlooked — by whom, it might be asked — John Warburton?

Tameside are at least willing to recognise that 'it is statistically certain that there are homosexual teachers in the employ of the Authority but we have no plans to make any special issue of their employment.' Not all of the replying authorities displayed such recognition. Prejudice is evident in a reply from Croydon. 'Members of a local Education Authority are elected and must have regard to the views of those who elected them. I am fairly certain that electors would hold to account their representatives if in a given case they acted so as to confer a cachet upon a way of life which the great majority of those electors would not desire for their own children.'

All of the authorities fail to recognise any positive benefit for the pupil in having a known homosexual as teacher. Might not the school environment prove a most appropriate place in which prejudiced images can be examined, challenged and dislodged? The appointment, employment and promotion of teachers must be based upon their aptitude, personal qualities and qualifications. Sex, race, creed and colour are beginning to be recognized as irrelevant factors in employment. If sexual orientation is to achieve the same irrelevance then employing authorities must be encouraged and perhaps obliged to adopt and enforce a non-discriminating policy.

Homosexuality and the social services

Social work is another area of employment which shares with education a concern for human development and behaviour, in all of its variety. Since both the social worker and the teacher are expected to serve as models, to some extent, of acceptable behaviour, both are susceptible to public prejudice and ignorance or rather, perhaps, an employer's fears of what is believed to be public prejudice. What follows is one of the responses to the NCCL survey of local authority social service committees,[20] a letter from West Yorkshire:

> Dear Sir or Madam or Whatever. . . . Your audacity is beyond belief. I have to accept the fact that due to an Act of Parliament that sexual acts between consenting males is within the law, but to suggest that homosexuals should be allowed to work with vulnerable children is uppalling [sic — the original spelling], I wonder would H. Sammuels [sic] employ a kleptomaniac. . . . I can assure you that if it is brought to my knowledge that person [sic] with these tendencies are employed in the Social Services Department of the authority that I represent I shall do everything in my power to have them removed.

And the unbelievable audacity? The submission of a question-naire which attempted to establish the range of prevalent attitudes which inform the world wherein homosexuals might seek assistance as clients or equality as employees.

The attitudes to the homosexual client are particularly revealing. Said the respondent from North Yorkshire, 'I have no evidence to suggest that problems associated with homosexuality are, at present, a source of major referral to our social workers.' And asked whether the department employed specialists to advise on the social problems of homosexual clients the director responded, 'No, not specifically. It would not appear that this is a problem often referred to social workers in North Yorkshire.' One would be wrong to imagine that the homosexual client is 'invisible' only in North Yorkshire. Not one of the local authorities employed such specialists.

While one would not urge that homosexuality will, in itself, be the 'problem' with which the social worker is asked to deal, it must surely be recognized that the homosexual does face particular social problems, not least establishing a self-respect in a world which may well threaten, at worst, hatred and contempt, and at best, offer an incomprehension that fails to recognize the pressures which might provoke conduct of a type likely to come within the purview of a social worker's caseload. Testimony to the need for specialists is found in the response of the Wakefield director of social services who states that homosexuals are not employed to advise on problems faced by homosexuals 'but we do not especially employ physically handicapped people to advise physically handicapped clients, criminals to advise criminal clients, or alcoholics to advise alcoholic clients.' The identification of homosexuality with disability, criminality and illness can't but contribute to the sense of alienation experienced by many homosexuals.

And what of the homosexual as social worker and employee of a social services department? The very recent case of Susan Shell is most instructive.

Having failed to gain promotion in her job at a 'youth treatment centre' because, said the administator, she was a lesbian and therefore a danger to the children, 30-year-old Susan sought employment, in the spring of 1982, as a night care attendant in a hostel for disturbed teenage girls in Dagenham. Her application, one of 200 submitted, was successful and her duties were to include supervising the girls' suppers and distributing school fares. The matter of her homosexuality was never raised at interview although she mentioned such in conversation with the officer in charge some two days after starting her job. Within a week Susan was informed that she must resign and go quietly or take a week's notice. Attempts to persuade Barking Council to reinstate her at a council's employment hearing were met with three main arguments. Susan would be a bad influence on difficult and disturbed girls. She might be vulnerable to allegations made by the girls and, thirdly, if Susan were to assault one of the girls [sic!] the council would be open to severe criticism of malpractice.

Such views of the homosexual as corrupter of youth, vulnerable, inadequate and sexual predator, echo the responses to the NCCL survey as exemplified, albeit crudely expressed, in the question posed (and mentioned earlier) by the West Yorkshire respondent: 'but to suggest that homosexuals should be allowed to work with vulnerable children is uppalling. I wonder would H. Sammuels employ a kleptomaniac?' This question highlights two commonly held misconceptions: that the homosexual is more likely than the heterosexual to be attracted to children, and that all paedophiles take advantage of children. Such confusion and ignorance of homosexuality are only to be expected since popular attitudes are, after all, fed on a newspaper diet of the 'gay vicar assaults choirboy' variety.

Such proposals of sexual misconduct, homosexual influence and risk emerge in the arguments of other authorities against the employment of homosexuals in certain posts.

Positions in which staff provide care for vulnerable people. (*Leicestershire*)

I think a person's homosexuality might be considered a relevant factor in relation to residential staff in children's homes. The Council must consider the attitude of parents. (*Buckinghamshire*)

I can see particular problems where a field social worker and more particularly a residential child care worker is trying to provide an identification model for a child or young person. (*Suffolk*)

Homosexuality might, for example, be considered a relevant factor in relation to a post to be filled in a children's home where the applicant would be in close contact with children at the age of puberty, pre-adolescence and adolescence. The Authority takes the view that in our society heterosexuality is still the norm and would wish children in its care to be looked after by staff of that orientation. (*Fife*)

Children are vulnerable and easily influenced, and for a well-liked figure to reveal homosexuality might be sufficient to change the orientation of a child from heterosexuality to homosexuality. (*Wakefield*)

Is homosexuality such an attractive model and sexual orientation so easily dislodged? Such popular prejudices thrive in spite of the fact that there is no reason to believe that a person will choose a different sexuality because of the example of another person. Indeed, as was argued in 1981 before the European Court of Human Rights,

Homosexuality, like skin colour, is fixed at an early age. All experts agree that this happens before the onset of puberty. One cannot be seduced into homosexuality, nor is it a matter of choice.[21]

Might not the presence of a well-liked, self-respecting, openly homosexual adult have the salutary effect of leading young people to reject the stereotypical images offered in popular prejudice and ignorance?

However, Derbyshire urge, I do not think we are naive enough to suppose that the particular nature of much of our work, relying as it does on close relationships between individuals, does not present special risks both to workers and clients. Our responsibilities to our clients and to the general public require us to take account of these potential risks when appointing and counselling staff.

The argument is that, no matter how responsible, the homosexual employee is particularly vulnerable to the charge of sexual misconduct.

The recognition, urged by social workers in their Code of Ethics,[22] of human dignity 'irrespective of origin, status, sex, sexual orientation, age, belief or contribution to society' can hardly be advanced if a proportion of the profession's membership feel compelled, for whatever reason (job security, promotion opportunities, popular prejudice, the charge of unprofessional conduct, etc.), to pretence, secrecy and deceit.

And yet could there not be wisdom, if to gain a job or remain employed, in the homosexual's staying hidden? Said the St Helens respondent,

> every appointment made in this department is done in the best interests of the client and all relevant factors are considered by staff who are responsible for making appointments.

And how relevant a factor would homosexuality be considered to be? The question is prompted by replies such as that from Hampshire:

> I would not, in normal circumstances, be prepared to condone the employment of homosexual men and women in posts in this department which carry a responsibility for the care of people and especially the care of children.

Such unwillingness is not an isolated example when thirteen of the authorities state directly or imply that there are posts in which they would not employ homosexuals.

Invisibility certainly protects the homosexual from the grosser forms of prejudice suffered by racial minorities but by no means guarantees employment security. Equality of opportunity and employment security will only begin to be assured when employers are persuaded to adopt a policy of non-discrimination. Such policy will, it seems, only be urged by a pressure group of 'visible' homosexuals, but with increasingly widespread support. Thus we have the paradox that only in 'coming out' and making an issue of their homosexuality can working people establish the irrelevance of such homosexuality as an issue in employment.

But 'making an issue of homosexuality' has its risks of disadvantage and dismissal. There is much evidence to suggest that homosexuals are discriminated against both in employment and in the provision of services. If this is true of such an untypically 'liberal' environment as social services, what are the prospects for establishing equality in other areas of work?

Gay rights and the trade unions

In the face of such lack of protection and job insecurity the trade unions could have an important and, indeed, central role.

Ironically the case that best illustrates the potential significance of a trade union's support for the homosexual member is the one and only case in which an industrial tribunal recognized as unfair the dismissal of an employee for reasons of his homosexuality *and* ordered his reinstatement. The employer's refusal to abide by the tribunal decision provoked the union membership to industrial action although, it must be said, action to challenge the employer's disregard of the legal decision rather than to champion gay rights at work.

Ian Davies was a principal social worker employed by the London Borough of Tower Hamlets. In 1975, having pleaded guilty, he was convicted of an act of gross indecency with another man, a consensual encounter which would not, were the participants a man and a woman, be characterized as criminal activity. The reaction of the disciplinary panel of the Tower Hamlets council to the conviction and £25 fine was that Ian should be instantly dismissed. This second penalty, a good deal harsher than the court's fine, was changed after an intervention by the director of social services and it was decided that Ian was to be employed elsewhere in the department at a greatly reduced salary.

The case eventually went to an industrial tribunal which took into account such 'significant' facts as that the offence was committed outside the Tower Hamlets area and that the other man involved was not a client of the Tower Hamlets social services department. The tribunal decided that the incident did not affect Ian's work in any way and that therefore he should be reinstated in his original job. The council then announced that it did not want to employ a homosexual as a social worker and that they would refuse to accept the tribunal ruling.

Ian's colleagues at the area office where he had been working then came out on strike in his support and the strike spread to the rest of the social services department. NALGO's national executive made the strike official but insisted that this was solely because a tribunal decision had been ignored and not because of the 'gay issue'. When it appeared that the strike was likely to spread to the whole of the borough's white-collar staff the council conceded defeat and Ian was reinstated in his job. The council at first insisted that he should not have a personal caseload but after further pressure from the local union branch this condition was withdrawn.

This was one of only a handful of decisions to overturn the dismissal on an employee for reasons of her/his homosexuality, and the only decision to order re-employment. Was the Davies case, then, unique in law? Might it also be considered unique in the response it achieved from a trade union? How likely is it that a trade union would support the member who claims to be suffering discrimination on the grounds of sexual orientation? Is such an issue recognized as a trade union's concern?

In an attempt to answer such questions the Campaign for Homosexual Equality embarked upon a survey of trade union attitudes.[23] A survey exercise which provoked a less than 50 per cent response rate could hardly be proposed as providing a representative sample. Of the sixty-three unions whose views were canvassed only thirty-four acknowledged receipt of the questionnaire. Of this number four preferred to make 'no comment' while eleven of the unions thought a letter the more appropriate vehicle for their views. None the less the following general observations might be offered as conclusions of the survey.

1. Few trade unions have yet come to see the issue of discrimination against homosexuals at work as being an issue of importance for a trade union.
2. Most progress in establishing the 'industrial' significance of the issue has been made in a limited number of white-collar unions.
3. Trade unions, when presented with a reasoned campaign — usually by groups of homosexuals active within their ranks — are generally willing to adopt a formal policy on gay rights.

Although the enquiries emanated from a group who profess a specific concern — homosexual equality — the survey also attempted to examine the discrimination policies of trade unions with regard to other groups. Questions were asked about discrimination on the grounds of race, colour, creed, sex and sexual orientation. Although only nineteen of the unions completed the questionnaire these answers are instructive, if only in confirming the suspicion that the trade union movement has hardly begun to grasp the nettle of discrimination on whatever grounds.

While every union reply to the questionnaire expressed a willingness to take up and support the case of a member who alleged discrimination, less than half of these unions monitor discrimination or incorporate the matter of discrimination in their education programme for officials, officers and members. None the less fourteen of the replies do suggest that attempts, albeit many of them unsuccessful, have been made to influence union policies to discrimination in its many varieties, with motions to conference, etc. But only two of the unions, EIS and SCPS,[24] employ an officer specifically charged with a concern for discrimination cases.[25] Neither of these union's rulebooks makes mention of discrimination and, in fact, such explicit reference (a testimony to outmoded rules) is made in only four cases – ACTT, ASTMS, CPSA and NALGO – all of them white-collar unions. Evidence, perhaps, of a membership aware of and unwilling to countenance sexual and racial discrimination.

If unions have yet to cope, by the establishment of appropriate 'machinery', in the face of sexual and racial discrimination, now outlawed in well-established legislation, then, *a fortiori*, their appreciation of and response to discrimination against homosexuals is woefully non-existent – although the Bakers' Union have, it would seem, in submitting a completed questionnaire, moved on from the bigotry of their late General Secretary, Sam Maddox. His response, in 1978, to an enquiry about homosexual equality was terse. 'What do you want equality with – dogs or pigs? These too lead loving, caring and useful lives.'

Whilst all of the nineteen responding unions, except ACTT and SOGAT, would challenge a management attempt to dismiss the homosexual (and any other worker) as a 'disruptive influence', and a dozen would support the homosexual (and any other worker) who alleged discrimination, only two unions, SCPS and NALGO, include the topic of sexual orientation in their education programmes. Explicit reference to sexual orientation in the union rules is made solely in the cases of NALGO and CPSA, the latter including among its objects, 'To oppose any force in society which seeks to foster divisions based on race, creed, religion, sex or sexual orientation.'

Although five unions register that attempts have been made to influence their policy towards homosexuals, the overall impression gained from the survey is of the trade unions seeing themselves as organizations whose 'conditions and policy . . . do not involve us in the question that you raise' (Sir John Boyd, General Secretary, AUEW). Nor did the Society of Post Office Executives 'regard such questionnaires as having high priority'. For the Civil Service Union 'the issues raised in it [the questionnaire] have never presented themselves for attention within the Union . . . neither my conference nor my National Executive Council have been called upon to form any judgement' (L. H. Moody, General Secretary).

However, not all of the eleven 'letter only' responses are so unwilling to recognize the issues. Laurie Sapper of the Association of University Teachers suggests that it would be 'unthinkable to discriminate in terms of membership on race, colour, creed, sex or sexual orientation. It is also a fundamental point that no university who employs our members should exercise any discrimination on any or all of the above grounds.'

Mr Spanswick, General Secretary of the Confederation of Health Service Employees, insists that 'we represent those who are homosexuals whether lesbian or gay men in the same manner from the point of view of having the service of the union as any other members. In fact we do not have heterosexuals or homosexuals in membership − we have members.' This commits the union to nothing in discrimination cases in that it totally ignores the existence of discrimination against an employee on the grounds of sexuality.

One wonders whether the unions who did not respond to the questionnaire, nor acknowledge its receipt, would be willing to even recognize that homosexuals are numbered among their membership. A lack of response was most evident among the major blue-collar unions − NUPE, Transport and General Workers, three sections of the AUEW; Miners, Electricians, Seamen and Railwaymen, and both ASLEF and NUR.

Those white-collar unions with a membership in education and the public services and also those unions involved in management and the entertainment industry demonstrated some awareness of the issues, if only in taking the time to reply: of the teaching unions, four replied; health and local governments, three; civil service, three; clerical and management, three; entertainment and media, three − evidence perhaps of a membership willing to tolerate the homosexual who is, consequently, more willing to be visible within the union, and where the issue of gay rights is more likely to become a topic of union debate and policy.

It is perhaps reassuring for the homosexual teacher to find four of the teaching unions − NUT, EIS, AUT and NATFHE − responding to the issue of homosexuality since, as has been suggested, such a person is one of the employees most 'at risk' of dismissal or disadvantage. However, a member of the National Association of Schoolmasters/Union of Women Teachers might wonder about their union's lack of response to the survey, especially in view of their general secretary's expressed views that 'people who manifest themselves as homosexuals do teaching a disservice in that they cause parents to withdraw confidence from teachers generally'. Terry Casey continues, 'any normally sexed teacher who flaunted his views or was a known womaniser would also constitute a similar threat.'[26] The equation of homosexuality with promiscuity, the view of a simple assertion of sexuality as 'flaunting', together with the implication that homosexuals are abnormal is hardly indicative of much understanding of those homosexuals among his union's membership. Nor does the implicit sexism of his remarks show much sympathy for female members of the union.

Evidence of some moderating of view, or at least a little circumspection, is to be found in the remarks of the union's assistant secretary, Nigel de Grunchy, writing to the Gay Teachers Group early in 1980. 'The NAS/UWT believes that teachers' private lives are their own affairs. They should however keep their private lives private. Any teacher who publicly proclaims his or her homosexuality would in our view be inviting serious difficulties.'[27]

Hardly a testament of support for the homosexual teacher in advising that sexual orientation should be kept hidden if job security and promotion prospects are not to be threatened. And to what extent, it might be asked, is the heterosexual teacher well advised to such similar 'discretion' and secrecy in their day-to-day dealings at school?

The Gay Teachers Group in their discussion of 'homosexual teachers in our education system and the place of education on homosexuality in areas of the curriculum' draw interesting parallels with racial discrimination and highlight the National Union of Teachers clear statement of principle:

Conference urges Union members . . . to discourage as strongly
as possible the myths and stereotypes on which prejudice and
hatred feed, drawing upon the widespread evidence throughout
the curriculum of the contributions made by individuals,
peoples and civilizations all over the world. . . . (NUT
Conference resolution, 1978)

Although this declared policy might lack the appropriate machinery, the parallel of a challenge to the stereotypes of sexual
orientation is easily drawn but not, it would seem, sufficiently
obvious for the NUT to register willingness to take up a member's
complaint of discrimination on the grounds of homosexuality.

We [the Gay Teachers Group] are far from happy with the
policies of the education unions with regard to homosexual
members and homosexuality in the education system. . . .
[T]he ignorance about homosexuality that is widespread in
society generally is unfortunately also to be found in the official
policies, or lack of them, of our unions. . . . [J]ust as debate on
women's rights is now conducted reasonably properly at NUT
Conference (having been disgracefully and frivolously treated
initially) so too will gay rights in the 1980s.[28]

A campaign for the 1980s?

It is more than a quarter of a century since the Wolfenden
Committee recommended changes in the law as it affected
homosexual conduct. The Sexual Offences Act 1967 decrimi-
nalized the 'private' dealings of male homosexuals over 21 so long
as the participants were not members of the armed forces nor
merchant mariners 'at sea'.[29] But male homosexual conduct
remains, in principle, unlawful.

Whatever the criminal sanctions, they pale into significance
in the face of the other penalties sustained by both women and
men simply because of their sexual orientation − the loss of
their employment. The law in sanctioning an employee's
dismissal for reasons which are blatantly unjust and rooted in
irrational prejudice sustains the myths and stereotypes of the
popular view which legal reforms have done little to dislodge.

Many have argued that an extension of the employment

protection legislation could help to remedy the situation by rendering unfair any dismissal from employment for reasons of sexual orientation. Such remedy could also be effected by the addition of a clause to the Sex Discrimination Act 1975 proposing that 'A person discriminates against another if, on the grounds of sexual orientation, s/he treats that other less favourably than s/he would someone s/he believed not to have that sexual orientation.'

Trade unions could have a central role in provoking such legal reforms and in the vital monitoring of anti-discrimination policies when such have been introduced. But trade unions must first of all themselves be provoked to a twofold recognition – that there are homosexuals within their ranks, and, that the gay rights issue has industrial significance.

The impetus for such recognition and reform will only come from visible homosexuals within the ranks of a trade union since they are the people ideally placed to work together as a pressure group for the adoption of anti-discrimination motions and policies – a campaign that demands patience, determination and an understanding of the complexities of union machinery. But trade unions *can* be persuaded by reasoned and sustained argument. Testimony to the crucial role of the trade union gay group is the fact that several trade unions have adopted policies on gay rights at work.[30] At its 1976 conference, for example, NALGO adopted the following resolution: 'That this conference instructs all NALGO negotiators to attempt to add "sexual orientation" to the non-discrimination clause in all collective agreements.' The adoption and monitoring of such policies is, campaigners suggest, *the* route to union recognition of the issue of discrimination against homosexuals as an issue appropriate for a trade union's concern and thus, ultimately, to the outlawing of discrimination on the grounds of sexual orientation.

Nor can the issue be seen as solely, or primarily, one for the trade unions. What are at stake are civil liberties that concern all citizens. The political parties have an obligation to legislate to secure those liberties by amending discriminatory Acts of Parliament and persuading the public to accept the need for those amendments.[31]

Notes

1   Evidence that these cases are not isolated nor untypical
    examples will be found in the report *What About The Gay Workers?*
    (London, CHE, 1981) in which the Campaign for Homosexual
    Equality have marshalled a catalogue of three dozen or more recent
    and similar cases reported in the law reports and in the national and
    provincial press. In not all of these cases, by any means, has the
    dismissed employee pursued a claim before an industrial tribunal
    nor, on the evidence of appeal court judgments, would such be
    advisable.
2   Boychuk v. H. J. Symons Holdings Ltd [1977] IRLR 395.
3   Wiseman v. Salford CC [1981] IRLR 202.
4   Chris Beer, *Gay Workers, Trade Unions and the Law* London,
    NCCL, 1980.
5   IRLR (1981), p. 204.
6   Ibid.
7   Ibid.
8   Saunders v. Scottish National Camps Association Ltd [1980] IRLR
    174, [1981] IRLR 277.
9   IRLR (1980), p. 175.
10 Harper v. National Coal Board [1980] IRLR 260.
11 IRLR (1980), p. 175.
12 Ibid., p. 277.
13 *Gay News*, no. 218.
14 Gardiner v. Newport CBC [1974] IRLR 262.
15 Over 90 per cent of the cases involve men (see *What About The Gay
    Workers?*, op. cit.). Several reasons are offered for such imbalance:
    the temporary/part-time nature of much female working and thus the
    failure to qualify to claim unfair dismissal under employment
    protection legislation; the low levels of female membership of trade
    unions and the consequent lack of any guidance or support in the face
    of discrimination; the criminal law does not respond to lesbian
    behaviour with any category of 'sexual offence', which contributes to
    the 'invisibility' of gay women since discrimination often follows upon
    conviction for an 'offence'. 'However, one disturbing feature of
    recent years clearly shown in the cases is the growing tendency to
    extend long-standing fallacies about "predatory" or "corrupting" gay
    male behaviour to cover lesbians as well' (*What About The Gay
    Workers?*, p. 13).

16 Peter Johnson is a pseudonym used in the NCCL publication *Gay Workers: Trade Unions and the Law*, London, 1980.
17 *Gay Workers: Trade Unions and the Law*, op. cit., p. 39.
18 London, NCCL, 1975.
19 With its practice of 'positive vetting' (security clearance) the civil service and the Foreign Office in particular attempts to avoid the recruitment of homosexuals. Prejudice is entrenched: homosexuality is thought to disqualify on security and social grounds and the homosexual is regarded as vulnerable to blackmail — an assumption that is wholly circular and self-fulfilling. Such intolerance enshrines the prospect of blackmail. The more you insist on people not being homosexual the more you ensure that such people are targets for the blackmailer. If society did not work on the assumption that homosexuals are a security risk then there would be no pressure to conceal the fact and thus no liability to blackmail.
20 *Homosexuality and the Social Services*, London, NCCL, 1977.
21 *New Statesman*, 1 May 1981.
22 *Homosexuality and the Social Services*, op. cit., p. 38.
23 *What About The Gay Workers?*, op. cit.
24 The following abbreviations are used to refer to trade unions:

ACTT	Association of Cinematographic, Television and Allied Technicians
ASLEF	Associated Society of Locomotive Engineers and Firemen
ASTMS	Association of Scientific, Technical and Managerial Staff
AUEW	Amalgamated Union of Engineering Workers
AUT	Association of University Teachers
CPSA	Civil and Public Servants Association
EIS	Educational Institute of Scotland
NALGO	National and Local Government Officers Association
NAS/UWT	National Association of Schoolmasters/Union of Women Teachers
NATFHE	National Association of Teachers in Further and Higher Education
NUPE	National Union of Public Employees
NUR	National Union of Railwaymen
NUT	National Union of Teachers
SCPS	Society of Civil and Public Servants
SOGAT	Society of Graphical and Allied Trades

25 Of course the appointment of such an officer might divert complaints away from the normal union procedure for dealing with workplace problems and isolate discrimination as an extraordinary issue which the shop steward neither has to face nor deal with. Conversely such

an appointment might offer an alternative to a racist, sexist or anti-gay shop steward or local branch.

26   *Queers Need Not Apply*, London, CHE, 1979.
27   *Gay Rights and The Teaching Unions*, London, Gay Teachers Group, 1980.
28   Ibid., p. 10.
29   The phrase 'at sea' means on board a UK merchant ship but not, it would seem, on board a deep sea oil-rig!
30   Such trade unions include First Division Association, Institute of Professional Civil Servants, National Union of Journalists, CPSA, EIS, NALGO, NATFHE, NUPE and SCPS. Of course the adoption of such policies is no guarantee of vigilance against discrimination.
31   Tony Benn, in *Gay Workers: Trade Unions and the Law*, op. cit., p. 6.

4 ON THE STREETS
Julian Meldrum

When a man or woman is labelled 'queer', a 'lezzie' or a 'pouffe' —
there are many alternatives — the unthinkable becomes feasible.
The application of the language, itself an act of aggression,
exaggerates a real-or-imagined difference, dehumanising the
person against whom it is used, diminishing the humanity of the
person who applies it to the point where violence may seem to be a
reasonable course of action.

> A man 'went berserk' when he found his daughter in bed with a
> married woman. He shouted that his daughter was 'a slut and a
> lesbian', jumped onto the bed and kicked her with his boots,
> cutting her lip. The 17-year-old girl had apparently got into the
> bed so her father wouldn't know she had been with her
> boyfriend. The father was fined £100 for the assault, and a
> further £100 for assaulting the police officer who arrested him.
> (*Western Daily Press*, 14 March 1980; *Attacks on Gay People*
> (hereafter referred to as *Attacks*), case 2A, p. 2, The Hall-
> Carpenter Archives (hereafter referred to as TH-CA), 80–657).

Anti-gay violence may be as bad as the worst examples of racist
violence and is as firmly rooted in British social history. Although
surveys have shown that the great majority of gay men and women
have never experienced violence as a result of being gay,[1] it is
equally true that most openly gay people will know at least one
person who has. The existence of anti-gay violence is therefore
harder to deny or ignore than are many of the other aspects of the
oppression of gay people in modern Britain.

A man with multiple sclerosis who is unable to walk unaided was kicked to the ground, punched and slashed in the face with a steel comb. His attackers — two young men aged 20 and 21 — assumed that he was gay, when they saw him walking arm-in-arm through Earl's Court with a male companion, in the early hours of the morning. One of the attackers dented the steel toe-cap of his boot in the attack. He was jailed for 4 months; his companion got the same with an additional month suspended from a previous sentence for football hooliganism. (London Newspaper Group, e.g. *Kensington News and Post*, 2 February 1979 and *South Kensington News and Chelsea Post*, 16 February 1979; *Attacks* case 2C, p. 2, TH-CA, 79–135).

Were the victims gay? Does it matter? Of course, it matters deeply to the victim, whether or not he or she is gay. The feelings of guilt experienced by many innocent victims of crime may be exaggerated unbearably when that victim is gay. But should it matter to society at large?

A boy's first understanding of the connection between violence and sexuality came at the age of 11 or 12, when he found himself under attack from a heavier and stronger opponent, out of sight of the pavilion on a school games afternoon. Giving up the fight as lost, he planted a kiss on the other boy's lips. The effect was electrifying. The heavier boy leapt up and back, suddenly separated with a repeated cry: 'You're a 'mo! Meldrum's a homo!' The hearer felt strangely diminished and isolated and vulnerable.

Gay people, then, are not arbitrarily picked out for dehumanisation. The attacks occur because *we break the rules*, because the existence of gayness does challenge widely held assumptions about masculinity and femininity, about the way men and women ought to relate to each other.

Normal behaviour

It is not only gay people, and those taken for gay, who suffer violence in the system described. Some of the most pathetic victims are the very women and men who strive hardest to conform to what is expected of them. This can be seen in the

"Fearlessly I
advanced
into the
Twilight
World of the
Homosexual
!"

violence that sometimes erupts when a 'heterosexual' is confronted by an element of sexual attraction in a friendship with someone of the same sex. The compulsion to deny such an element is illustrated by the address of the Archbishop of Canterbury, Robert Runcie, to the General Synod of the Church of England in 1981:

> Kisses, tears and embraces are not in themselves evidence of homosexuality. Hrothgar embracing Beowulf — Johnson embracing Boswell — a pretty flagrantly heterosexual couple. And all those hairy old toughs of centurions in Tacitus, clinging to one another and begging for last kisses when the Legion was breaking up. All pansies? If you can believe that you can believe anything.[2]

While the archbishop deplores the tyranny of the categories of 'homosexual' and 'heterosexual', his own remarks do nothing to break down such categories, which currently seem to exist as a defence against homosexuality. The verbal violence of the archbishop's 'All pansies?' shows an irrational defensiveness against the idea that 'hairy old toughs' could be as 'homosexual' as any of the women whose relationships among themselves are apparently of no interest to the church or to social historians like the archbishop. In fact, it is only when the sexual and homosexual element in all relationships is recognised and affirmed that it is possible to attack the categories into which human sexuality is now organised.

Twenty years ago

One of the major crime stories of 1962 (TH-CA, 62–1) was the case of the 'wardrobe killer'. This story, still fresh in the minds of older gay men some twenty years later, was at the time practically the only context in which a gay man or woman could have learned from the mass media of the existence of gay pubs and clubs. Here are some extracts from Jack Miller's report, 'Murders in a half world' (*News of the World*, 25 February 1962):

> These are the twilight murders. . . . Two men, if you can call Norman Rickard and Alan Vigar men, lived in the twilight world of the homosexual and they died in the garrotter's noose.

And unless Scotland Yard can find him with more speed than
seems humanly possible, the garrotter may strike again. He is
one of four types: a 'Ronson lighter' which, for some reason, is
what the puff calls the pimp who finds clients for him; a
blackmailer, to which these unfortunates are always prey; a
homosexual whose lust suddenly turned to murderous frenzy,
or . . . . Or, I suspect, a man who hates homos with the same
soul torturing bitterness that Jack the Ripper hated prostitutes.

The next night, he dressed himself in tight, blue faded jeans, a
cowboy plaid shirt, cowboy buckled boots and an epauletted
leather jacket. And he went on the town, probably to West End
clubs where his kind gather, or Bayswater pubs they use in
streets where phone boxes are scrawled with invitations like:
'For a nice night with Charles ring PADdington — .' And he
met a man.

A film has been found in Rickard's camera and there are men's
faces on it. His diary, and Vigar's too, have been found and
there are men's names in them. Simenon has written about
'Maigret and the reluctant witness.' In this case, I fancy, there
are going to be many reluctant witnesses, for friends of both
men have already left their haunts. Their strange world is in
chaos. For there's an awful lot of murk in the twilight.

J. W. M. Thompson's report, 'They walk in the shadow of
fear . . .: Two London murders again bring an undercover world
into discussion' (London *Evening Standard*, 22 February 1962) was
even clearer in its message:

But no one can pretend that homosexuality does not cast its
shadow on our society. This week the shadow has grown
momentarily darker. There have been two London murders
displaying signs of a homosexual element. And, by coincidence,
a new Private Member's bill is proposed [by Leo Abse, MP] to
change the law on homosexuality.

The spectacular homosexual cases, whether they involve
violence or the disgrace of a public figure [such as junior Tory
minister Ian Harvey], always evoke horror and sympathy.

Two aspects of the problem need attention. One is blackmail. The other is: Can science help to release the homosexual from his secret life-sentence?

Of course, a desire to end the blackmail racket implies no kind of approval for the homosexuality the blackmailer preys upon.

The article goes on to detail alleged 'cures' by the staff of the Portman Clinic of homosexual men sent to them by the courts, concluding:

The proposed Bill would make medical reports obligatory. It is argued that this procedure would also strengthen the protection of the public. For those medical reports could, sometimes at least, 'screen out' the homosexual who is in danger of becoming a violent psychopath. *And a potential killer might be spotted in time.*

The CHE survey

This chapter draws heavily on a survey of cases reported during a period of three years, published by CHE as *Attacks on Gay People*.[3] There was clear evidence of more than 250 incidents, of which about 15 per cent led to the death or disablement of the victim. However, the reported cases are only a small and select sample of those that actually take place. Many serious crimes go unreported because the victims fear, and not without reason, that they will themselves be on trial, sometimes literally, for their gayness. In other cases the anti-gay nature of an attack may be suppressed by the victims, their relatives, the police and the press. In any case, as we have seen, the press is in the business of myth creation and tends to use court-case reports as lessons in morality.[4]

The Portsmouth defence

It is quite common for men accused of attacking other men to claim they were 'defending themselves' from 'homosexual advances' by their victims: the so-called 'Portsmouth defence'. The reasons for such violence have already been hinted at: the most important point to understand in reading reports is that a 'homosexual advance' can mean practically anything, from a gentle smile or prolonged eye-contact through to a violent sexual assault or unbearably prolonged sexual harassment. Then again, it may be either a delusion or an outright fabrication by a violent offender. One of the most disturbing aspects of these cases is an assumption that if a victim of assault is shown to be gay, this proves that a homosexual advance was made. This assumption is based on a myth of the homosexual as a sexual predator, which owes more to the prep-school nightmares of judges and MPs than to the reality of gay life-styles.

Generally speaking, the victim in murder cases is as much on trial as the victim in a rape case. Serious assault cases where a gay victim survives are important because they demonstrate the extent to which anti-gay assaults are supported by the anti-gay bias of the courts and legislation. The maximum penalty for 'indecent assault' — which need not be violent at all — is two years when the victim is an adult woman, ten years when he is an adult man. If a man makes a pass at another — 'persistent importuning' is the usual term, but 'attempting to procure an act of gross indecency' is also employed — he commits a criminal offence: women simply have to put up with it. Sometimes the police will employ such arguments to dissuade a gay victim from pressing charges, although obviously such cases don't make the news. Occasionally the victim of a violent assault finds himself in court, while his attacker goes free.

> A young gay man was acquitted by a jury on a charge of 'indecent assault' against a man who admitted that 'I hit him hard in the face . . . He fell back into the hedge and I hit him again. I lost my temper.' The victim of this attack said he had no idea why the man should have hit him, adding that 'I would not have touched him wth a barge-pole.' (*West Briton and Royal Cornwall Gazette*, 7 December 1978; *Attacks*, case 6i, p. 11, TH-CA, 78–211)

Invariably the court is faced with a choice between two conflicting accounts, usually without independent evidence. In such a situation, there is a serious danger that personal prejudice may determine the outcome of a case.

> An off-duty policeman was assaulted as he apprehended a thief. The 22-year-old offender said he hit out because he thought the

policeman 'was a poof'. The young man had previously been drinking: he was fined £75 on each of two assault charges and £50 for theft. (*Kentish Observer*, 23 December 1977; *Attacks*, case 6B, p. 10, TH-CA, 77–164)

Within gay relationships

There are comparatively few examples of violence reported within mutual gay relationships. There may well be under-reporting of such incidents, due to the reluctance of gays to get involved with the police in any way at all, and due also to the reluctance of the police to get involved in domestic disputes, even when serious injury occurs.

A married man was jailed for four years for wounding another married man with whom he had an affair over a period of several months. The relationship came under severe pressure when the wife of one of the two discovered them making love at their home; he wished to terminate the sexual side of their relationship as a consequence. The other man arranged to meet him, and suggested they go away to live together. His friend, however, preferred to end the relationship. In a state of extreme distress the rejected lover threw petrol in the face of the other man, then stabbed him in the chest. He later took an overdose in an attempt to kill himself. The QC defending the assailant had no doubt where the blame lay: 'The tragedy is that the two men ever met. There was some unfortunate attraction between them that led to this dreadful episode.' (Bristol *Evening Post*, 28 July 1980; *Attacks*, case 7K, p. 16, TH-CA, 80–639)

There is probably a lower incidence of chronic long-term violence, in that unsatisfactory gay relationships dissolve more readily than bad marriages, although there is of course a degree of cultural continuity. When the gay relationship is closely modelled on marriage, with a rigid and sexist division of roles and power, the pattern of violence may show the classic 'battered wife' syndrome.[5]

A young gay transvestite man was acquitted of wounding his lover when a jury accepted that he hit out in defence of his

brother and himself, against a man who had on several
occasions become violent when drunk. The [24-year-old] lover
had been out drinking with the [19-year-old's] brother and an
argument broke out when they returned to the flat, where the
younger man had been left to do the housework, when he
declared his intention to leave. In the course of the fight, the 24-
year-old lover allegedly hit out with a broom-handle, then tried
to choke the brother with his hands. He was in turn struck
several times with the blade of an axe, temporarily losing his
sight. (*Manchester Evening News*, 2 May 1980, *Stockport
Advertiser*, 8 May 1980 and *Stockport Express*, 15 May 1980;
Attacks, case 7H, p. 16, TH-CA, 79–348)

While it would seem clear from the reported cases that the major
threat, if any, to lesbian women comes from men (and in particular
the husbands of married women), it cannot be forgotten that
Britain's longest-serving prisoner is Mary Scorse, sentenced to
death in 1952 for killing her lover.

It would appear that Mary Scorse's continued detention is due
to an equation made by the Home Office, between her
lesbianism and a tendency towards violence. Joyce Reynolds,
her lover, was killed when she wanted their relationship to end:
the 20-year-old Mary had become heavily dependent on her.
Mary has been released on licence three times in the last thirty
years, for a total of 42 months. Each time she has been recalled
with no official reason given. She was last released in 1974 and
recalled 27 months later, in August 1976, apparently on the
basis of inaccurate and misleading information supplied by the
Cornish probation service to the Home Office, to the effect that
Mary made sexual advances to her landlady and the landlady's
18-year-old daughter, threatened them with a knife and took an
overdose of sleeping-pills. (The claim about sexual advances
and threats has since been contradicted by the landlady, and
there is good reason to believe the overdose was accidental.)
(*New Society*, 6 July 1978, *Time Out*, 20 July 1979, *Gay News*, 17
April 1980 and the National Council for Civil Liberties;
Attacks, p. 15, TH-CA, 52–1)

There is a folk-wisdom to the effect that gay couples are
peculiarly prone to jealous rows over third parties. The evidence

to support this is not so easy to find: the more serious problem seems to be that if inadequate support is given to gay relationships while they exist, there is even less support available as they break up. This is largely a problem of general education for relationships, which deserves more consideration than it gets.

In pubs and clubs

Violence in gay pubs and clubs must be seen in relation to the general level of violence in licensed premises. From a survey directed by Peter Marsh and Anne Campbell[6] it is apparent that much of the violence reported by licensees involves attacks on pub staff: it is also apparent that about three-quarters of their 2,000 respondents claimed not to have experienced violent incidents at their pubs. While Marsh and Campbell did talk to at least two publicans whose clientele was predominantly gay, their report does not discuss violence in gay pubs as such. They did, however, find a number of licensees who claimed to exclude certain classes of people – such as punk-rockers, football-fans, blacks and gays – depending on the general nature of their clientele. Such exclusions generally result from 'previous unhappy experiences' by the licensees. In the case of gays, there is reason to believe that such experiences involve attacks on identifiably gay customers by other customers. Licensees react variously to such incidents. Sometimes they side openly with the anti-gay customers or give tacit support to them, but in other cases staff and customers in a (non-gay) pub or club have rallied to the defence of gay people. These cases do none the less show a strong reason why there *is* a separate gay scene, namely physical security. Violence on that gay scene differs significantly from that associated with other pubs and clubs, and appears to be less frequent. Whereas fights at heterosexual discos, for example, generally start with quarrels between male customers who may have gone there to pick a fight, open hostilities between customers in gay discos are extremely rare. Where violence does arise it usually involves attacks by outsiders.

A picket of an Aberdeen public house was attacked by two men. A woman received a black eye, one man on the picket had a split lip and another lost three teeth. The men who committed the assaults were arrested and fined £25 each. The picket had been organised in protest at the refusal of the publican to serve gay people, and was strongly supported by non-gay customers (neither of the injured men was in fact gay). (Aberdeen *Press and Journal*, 9 December 1977 and 22 December 1977, *Gay News*, 12 January 1978, *Peace News*, 13 January 1978 and *Outcome*, no. 6, 1978; *Attacks*, case 9D, p. 20, TH-CA, 77–166)

One-night stands

Some of the most gruesome incidents, including a number which made national headlines, arise from something between a calculated robbery and a simple misunderstanding between two or more men who agreed to go home together and (possibly) share a bed. It is clear that the official reaction to such violence is determined by the attitude of the police and courts to the sexual activity. Broadly speaking, there are two competing views. The first, which is firmly ensconced in British law, is that while homosexual activity is partly exempt from criminal sanctions, it is not fully lawful. It is seen as a form of 'corruption' and people who 'corrupt' themselves should not expect the state to intervene when they become victims of violence. The alternative view is that gay men whose life-style depends on a high degree of mutual trust should be protected, by exemplary sanctions if these can be shown to be effective, when such trust is betrayed.

A man was beaten, tied up and robbed of property worth £1000 by a young man he met near Piccadilly Circus one evening, who accompanied him home: 'He was a forthcoming sort of person and made it clear he wanted to come home with me for sexual reasons.' The 20-year-old assailant was jailed for four years for that and another offence which followed the same pattern but netted £3000 in cash and jewellery. The judge commented: 'These are very serious offences and victims such as this are very vulnerable. The courts have a duty to protect them as far as possible.' (*Gay News*, 15 May 1980, and *Camden and St. Pancras Chronicle*, 29 August 1980; *Attacks*, case 10T, p. 28, TH-CA, 80–123)

The conflict between these views is most intense when the sexual activity is in fact illegal. In 75 per cent of the cases in the CHE survey where the age of the attacker was published, he was between 16 and 21 years old. The age of consent for male homosexual acts is 21 years, and young men between 16 and 21 are themselves liable to prosecution when it is infringed (this is what is known as a 'protective' law).

> A 30-year-old man was approached by a 19-year-old on Earl's Court Station, only to find that after they reached the man's flat and had sex the younger man produced a shotgun and held his partner, terrified, for three-quarters of an hour. The victim escaped through a window and called the police — who arrested both men and charged them with gross indecency (to which both later pleaded guilty). The teenager was also charged with firearms offences and put on probation for three years; his victim was given a 12-month prison sentence suspended for two years. The judge 'justified' the latter sentence saying: 'I am not going to waste public money by sending you to prison. At least make sure you do not pick up any young men in the streets of London. . . . The reason I am not sending you to prison is because it would look rotten having dealt with the other man so leniently. The fact that you were faced with this gun may teach you a lesson in the future.' (London Newspaper Group, e.g. *South Kensington News and Chelsea Post*, 23 May 1980; *Attacks*, case 10U, p. 28, TH-CA, 79–100)

The lesson, presumably, is that such incidents should not be reported to the police.

Brief encounters

'Cottaging' is a term used by men to describe their sexual encounters in public lavatories. The classic form involves a ritual escalation of intimacy in total silence, entirely within the cottage, although contacts may be developed outside it. The pattern varies depending on the clientele and the location — rural or urban, in department stores or by railway stations. In general, it seems that most of the men are married, many do not define themselves as being gay, and no more than a small minority would be openly gay.[7] The main advantage of cottaging is that it offers a quick and easy sexual release which does not require emotional commitment to one person and therefore need not disrupt any primary relationship. For some, especially those who do regard themselves as being gay and are more or less integrated into the gay scene, there is an element of gambling in the attraction: if the gay scene sometimes resembles a market-place, the cottage is more of a betting-shop.

Of course the discovery of this activity by the wrong people, and in particular by the police, could be, and sometimes is, disastrous, so certain safeguards are provided. Firstly, the cottage tends to be used as such only when the general public is out of the way. Secondly, a cottage tends to develop a regular clientele who will know each other by sight and will cease any activity if a stranger enters.

According to a Home Office study,[8] the passing of the 1967 Sexual Offences Act led to a doubling in the prosecution rate for indecency between males, and an increase in convictions by 250 per cent. The most visible effect of this clamp-down, which has been combined with a more open discussion of homosexuality throughout the media, is that a substantial proportion of all press cuttings sent to gay organisations are court reports of cottaging cases. The least visible effect of the clamp-down is that many serious assaults go unreported to the police, as is apparent from the background to several of the cases in the CHE survey. It is in fact not uncommon for the police, defending the enforcement of 'gross indecency' laws, to assert that by arresting men for cottaging they are 'protecting' those men from assaults by members of the general public. Actual cases of assault by arresting officers, cited in the CHE survey, do call that argument into question. Where cases are reported, the police response varies widely, depending on the relative weight the officers give to the criminality of acts of violence and acts of homosexual lovemaking.

Coming out

Coming out is a vital part of gay resistance to violence. Although it may lay people more open to attacks, it also makes for easier self-protection and stronger mutual support. It is essential to break down anti-gay stereotypes, to re-educate the whole of our society to accept that homosexuality is an ordinary part of the lives of a substantial minority of otherwise very ordinary men and women. Only as gay people come out and organise will it become easier for people to be open about the fact of their homosexuality at work, with members of their families, at school. This has, of course, been a central theme of the politics of gay liberation. As Andrew Hodges and David Hutter wrote in 1974,

> Gay Pride is the concept formed in opposition to the shame that all gay people are conditioned to feel, a shame that society demands as the condition for its limited tolerance; to deny this shame is to demand unconditional acceptance. It is pointless to limit coming out to 'those who will understand'; only by public, indiscriminate, indiscreet self-disclosure can this shame be denied.[9]

It is often said that gays who do come out are 'asking for trouble': such an attitude blames the victim for the offence, and makes victims of all gay people, implying that anyone identified as 'homosexual' deserves to be attacked.

Self-defence

Self-defence has from time to time surfaced as an issue among gay people. Self-defence training groups certainly have a role in opposing anti-gay and anti-woman violence, but it is not necessarily a direct role. By their very nature, they will not appeal to the closeted gays who are actually most at risk of violence. Those people will become safer as they come out, as their social involvement with other gay people increases. It doesn't matter whether the involvement is based on an interest in self-defence, sport, music, religion, train-spotting, shared political commitments or varieties of sexual excitement. The wider challenge of self-defence is to the expectation, shared by gays and queer-bashers alike, that anti-gay abuse will be passively accepted. When we do fight back, the results are encouraging. Publicity given to such action may reduce both the actual level of violence and, which is most important, the number of people who live in fear of it.

Postscript: the Lavender Panthers

I can still recall vividly how I first read these words, then re-read them privately, as a 14-year-old feeling desperately isolated and vulnerable, in the process of convincing myself that Yes, I was gay.

Four San Francisco teen-agers recently got the surprise of their young lives. Tooling around in their souped-up car looking for a little fun, they spotted two homosexuals leaving the Naked Grape, a well-known gay bar. The youths roared to a stop, jumped out of their car and began to push the homosexuals around. Suddenly a brawny band, led by a man in a clerical collar, leaped from a gray Volkswagen bus and lit into them. 'We didn't even ask questions,' said the Rev. Ray Broshears, 38.

Formed by the Rev. Ray, a Pentecostal Evangelist and known homosexual who himself was once beaten severely outside his gay mission center, the Panthers patrol the streets nightly with chains, billy clubs, whistles and cans of red spray paint. Their purpose, as the Rev. Ray candidly puts it, is to strike terror in the hearts of 'all those young punks who have been beating up my faggots.'

The basic band numbers 21 homosexuals, including two lesbians who are reputedly the toughest hombres in the lot. Besides their goal of halting the attacks, the Lavender Panthers want to gainsay the popular notion that all homosexuals are 'sissies, cowards and pansies' who will do nothing when attacked. All of the Panthers know judo, karate, Kung Fu or plain old alley fighting. For gays without defensive skills, the Panthers hold training sessions with instruction from a judo brown belt and a karate expert.

. . . But Ray insists that his Draconian measures are necessary. 'Middle America has always had a little tinge of homophobia,' he says. 'But I've had it up to here. All this queer bashing has simply got to stop.' (*Time*, 8 October 1973)

During the next five years, in which I was unable to discuss how I felt, either with adults or with people of my own age, this was one of the images to which I clung as an alternative to the bizarre fantasies transmitted by the press, the radio, and the school playground. For all its defects, I believe that story had some positive effect.

Notes

1 A. P. Bell and M. S. Weinberg (1978), 'Homosexualities: a study of diversity among men and women', London, Mitchell Beazley; also

G. Westwood, (pseudonym of Michael Schofield) (1960), 'A minority: a report on the life of the male homosexual in Great Britain', London, Longmans.

2   The quotation is taken from the full text as circulated by the archbishop's secretary, and held in The Hall-Carpenter Archives.

3   J. T. Meldrum (1980), *Attacks on Gay People* (2nd edn), London, Campaign for Homosexual Equality.

4   See also F. Pearce (1973), 'How to be immoral and ill, pathetic and dangerous, all at the same time: mass media and the homosexual', in S. Cohen and J. Young (eds), *The Manufacture of News, Deviance, Social Problems and the Mass Media*, London, Constable.

5   For a British account of the 'battered wife' syndrome, see R. E. Dobash, and R. Dobash (1980), 'Violence against wives: a case against the patriarchy', London, Open Books.

6   P. Marsh and A. Campbell (1979), 'Aspects of violence and aggression in community contexts', London, Whitbread Foundation.

7   L. Humphreys (1970), 'Tearoom trade: a study of homosexual encounters in public places', London, Duckworth.

8   R. Walmsley and K. White (1979), 'Sexual offences, consent and sentencing', Home Office Research Study no. 54, London, HMSO; see also R. Walmsley (1978), 'Indecency between males and the Sexual Offences Act 1967', *Criminal Law Review*, pp. 400–7.

9   A. P. Hodges and D. Hutter (1974), 'With downcast gays: aspects of homosexual self-oppression', London, Pomegranate Press, and Toronto, Pink Triangle Press.

5 PARLIAMENT AND THE LAW
Nigel Warner

071 – 278 –
1496 – 35 9
1 2 11 .
833 - 3912 CHE .

'I find nothing in the [1967 Sexual Offences] Act to indicate that
Parliament thought or intended to lay down that indulgence in
these practices is not corrupting.' Thus did an eminent judge sum
up, in a House of Lords ruling,[1] the thinking which underlies
discrimination against gays in contemporary criminal law. This
chapter sets out the historical background to this discrimination
and some of its consequences for gay people in Britain. It then
examines recent developments in the long process of establishing
full legal rights for gays.

The criminal law subdivides illegal homosexual conduct between
males into two principal offences: buggery (or anal intercourse)
and gross indecency (which broadly covers all other genital
contact). Sexual relationships between lesbians have never been
criminal except in the case of members of the armed forces, who
are subject to the provisions of the armed services' discipline acts.
Homosexual *orientation* (as opposed to homosexual *conduct*) has
never, of itself, been criminal. A summary of discriminatory
aspects of the criminal law is given at the end of the chapter.

Developments up to the Second World War

Male homosexual conduct first became the subject of the criminal
law in 1533 when buggery was made an offence with a maximum
sentence of death. Prior to that date 'the detestable and

abominable vice' had been dealt with exclusively by the ecclesi-astical courts.[2] Its enactment into statute law was a spin-off from Henry VIII's moves to limit the role of the church and does not appear to have marked any significant increase in hostility towards homosexual behaviour.[3]

For the next 350 years there were no changes in the law relating to male homosexual conduct except that the death penalty was abolished in 1861[4] (the last execution for buggery was in 1836). Thus, throughout this period, all consensual homosexual acts other than buggery remained legal. However total prohibition came with the passage of the 1885 Criminal Law Amendment Act. This act was put forward by the government in response to an energetic campaign against prostitution and its principal measure was to raise the age of consent for women to 16.[5] At the committee stage of the bill an MP called Henry Labouchere introduced an amendment making it an offence for a male person to commit, in public or private, 'an act of gross indecency with another male person'. Considerable uncertainty surrounds Labouchere's intentions with the amendment, which, as drafted, had no connection with the aims of the bill. There is evidence to suggest that he intended only to penalise homosexual acts with boys under 16 and the fact that the amendment also covered such acts between adults was a consequence of faulty drafting and inadequate scrutiny in Parliament.[6] Whatever Labouchere's and Parliament's intentions, no attempt was made subsequently to amend the legislation. On the contrary, it was soon to be enforced by the police and courts, the most notable of its early victims being Oscar Wilde.

If the Labouchere amendment resulted in all male homosexual acts being made criminal, the advent of the 1898 Vagrancy Act allowed matters to be taken a stage further by making it an offence for a man 'persistently to solicit in a public place for immoral purposes'. In fact this clause was designed to make illegal soliciting by pimps and it seems that there was no intention by the legislators that it should be used against homosexuals. It is an interesting comment on contemporary attitudes that the police and courts interpreted the clause as covering homosexual soliciting, and it was soon applied almost exclusively in this context, a practice which has persisted to this day. The range of punishments for soliciting included flogging, which was used against homosexual

offenders in the years before the First World War, particularly in London. Support for its use in such cases came from the highest levels. The Lord Chief Justice commented, when refusing an appeal against a sentence of fifteen strokes of the birch,

> If ever there was a case for corporal punishment it is for that particular class of offence of which the applicants have been found guilty − soliciting for immoral purposes. The sentence was not too severe and possibly, in another case of the same kind, it might be necessary, in the event of an appeal, to consider whether such sentences should not be increased.[7]

In view of the degree of homophobia prevalent at this period, it is perhaps not surprising that the Labouchere amendment was followed in due course by an attempt to criminalise lesbian sexual relationships. An MP called Macquisten introduced an amendment to the 1921 Criminal Law Amendment Bill which sought to punish 'any act of gross indecency between female persons'. It was supported by a substantial majority in the House of Commons (148 v. 53) on the basis of all the traditional arguments: the danger of national decline, the interference with child-rearing, the threat to marriage, and the corruption of young girls. However, when it was debated in the House of Lords it met with strong opposition and was withdrawn without a vote. This turn of events did not mark any sudden change in attitudes towards lesbian relationships: on the contrary, there was universal condemnation for this 'most disgusting and polluting subject'. It was due both to the weight of those opposing it − who included the Lord Chancellor and a former Director of Public Prosecutions, Lord Desart − and to the force of their arguments. One of the most vehemently advanced of these was that to make lesbian sexual relationships an offence would risk spreading the knowledge of lesbianism, and thus encourage its practice. Underpinning this was the view that lesbianism was virtually unknown to the majority of women. Thus the Lord Chancellor commented, 'If you accept a sophisticated society in a sophisticated city, I would be bold enough to say that of every thousand women, 999 have never even heard a whisper of these practices.' But prosecutions of lesbians would change all this. For Lord Desart, if there were a prosecution 'it would make public to thousands of people that there was this offence, that there was such a horror.' As far as he was concerned, the results of any prosecution would be 'far more appalling' than any 'good' the amendment might do.

It is likely that there was, by today's standards, much ignorance of lesbianism. The extent of prejudice, and the fact that the great majority of women had little or no economic independence, meant that overt lesbian relationships were exceedingly rare. But even making allowance for this, it seems probable that the degree of ignorance attributed to women in the debate was greatly exaggerated. The speakers were, of course, all men. The views which they put forward almost certainly tell us more of what they thought women should know about lesbianism than what women actually knew. If this is so their refusal to criminalise lesbian relationships would owe not a little to their acceptance of the passive sexual role traditionally ascribed to women. One of the sponsors of the amendment, Sir E. Wild, had consulted many 'asylum doctors' who assured him that 'asylums are largely populated by nymphomaniacs and people who indulge in this vice.'[8] Whatever the real facts, it is striking that the two categories of women whose positive sexual roles should challenge the passive one traditionally ascribed to women were seen as fit inmates for the lunatic asylum.

Lord Desart, in pointing to the dangers of 'spreading' lesbian sexual conduct by making it a criminal offence, drew support for his argument from the aftermath of the Oscar Wilde trials. These had 'attracted very great public attention' and were followed by 'a perfect outburst of that offence all through the country'. While this increase in the level of male homosexual offences was more probably due to a greater degree of police action than to any increase in the level of homosexual activity, Desart's argument of the dangers (as he saw things) of publicising homosexual conduct, did have a point which perhaps he did not appreciate: it seems probable that the publicity surrounding the application of the gross indecency law, and particularly the Oscar Wilde trials, contributed to the creation amongst homosexual males of a sense of identity, and to the foundation of the early homosexual rights movement. Prosecutions of lesbians might easily have had a similar consequence. Indeed, the prosecution in 1928 of Radclyffe Hall's lesbian novel, *The Well of Loneliness*, and the attendant publicity, had just this effect.[9]

The Wolfenden report and the 1967 Sexual Offences Act

It was to be more than thirty years before Parliament again debated the issue of homosexuality. The years after the Second World War saw a gradual increase in pressure for a relaxation of the laws affecting male homosexuals. There were two important elements of this change: the generally more relaxed attitudes towards sex, and the concern over a large increase in the number of prosecutions of homosexuals. The number of indictable homosexual offences known to the police increased sixfold between the late 1930s and the mid-1950s (from around 1,000 each year to 6,644 in 1955).[10] This increase, which was particularly marked from the mid-1940s onwards, coincided with the appointment of a number of senior officials of markedly homophobic disposition. Notable amongst these were the Director of Public Prosecutions, Sir Theobald Matthew, appointed in 1944, the Home Secretary at that time, Herbert Morrison, and the Home Secretary in the first post-war Conservative administration, Sir David Maxwell-Fyfe (later Lord Kilmuir). The Burgess and Maclean scandal, and pressure from the US government (then in the middle of the McCarthyite purges) gave added impetus to this trend.[11]

Public concern at the effects of this trend reached a peak in the mid-1950s, after the trials of a number of well-known figures, particularly Lord Montagu and Peter Wildeblood, the diplomatic correspondent of the *Daily Mail*. The latter published an account of his experiences, entitled *Against the Law*, which had a considerable impact on public opinion. These events led to debates in both Houses of Parliament and prompted the Church of England Moral Welfare Council to issue a pamphlet supporting the argument for reform. Faced with this pressure the government appointed a committee under Sir John Wolfenden to consider the law and practice relating to homosexual offences. (Its terms of reference also included prostitution.) It reported some three years later, its most significant recommendation being that consensual sexual acts between males over 21 should be decriminalised.

Seen from the perspective of the 1980s the Wolfenden Report leaves a somewhat confused impression. Its assessment of the facts was generally good, particularly when 'debunking' many of the traditional myths, for instance that homosexuality is a disease, a threat to the stability of the nation, the so-called 'seduction theory' (see page 91), the supposed dangers of anal intercourse. But its conclusions did not always follow logically from the facts as they were established. This arose from a lack of objectivity which was hardly surprising in view of contemporary attitudes to homosexuality and the broadly based membership of the committee. Thus, although its definition of the function of the criminal law sought to avoid any equation of the 'criminal' with the 'sinful' or 'immoral', the committee could not resist making it clear that it considered homosexuality to be just these: the proposed change in the law was 'not to be taken as saying that society should condone or approve homosexual behaviour';[12] the assumption that the average male homosexual tended easily to anti-social behaviour was reflected in the following admonition: 'It is important that the limited modification of the law which we propose should not be interpreted . . . as a general licence to adult homosexuals to behave as they please.'[13]

Two examples of inconsistency in logic stand out particularly: on the male age of consent, having dismissed the 'seduction theory', the committee opted for 21 because to fix the age lower would lay young men 'open to attentions and pressures of an undesirable kind'.[14] And yet, four paragraphs earlier, the committee had commented, 'there comes a time when a young man can properly be expected to "stand on his own feet" and we find it hard to believe that he needs to be protected from would-be seducers more carefully than a girl does', clearly implying that 16 was the appropriate age. As regards buggery, the committee decided to recommend the retention of the legal distinction between this and other forms of homosexual behaviour, together with a higher maximum penalty under certain circumstances. No specific reason was given, and as was pointed out by a significant dissenting minority of the committee, the report's analysis led to the opposite position to that adopted.

The committee's treatment of soliciting was similarly inconsistent. It supported the retention of homosexual soliciting as an offence, together with a relatively heavy maximum penalty, while refusing to tackle one of the more blatant forms of soliciting by heterosexual men, kerb crawling, on the basis of the 'difficulties of proof' and the 'possibility of a very damaging charge being levelled at an innocent motorist',[15] considerations which applied with equal or greater force to homosexual soliciting.

Some ten years elapsed between the publication of the Wolfenden Report and the enactment of its proposals in England and Wales. During this time the issue was raised repeatedly in Parliament. Between 1957 and 1962 there were four debates, in December 1957 in the House of Lords, and in 1958, 1960 and 1962 in the House of Commons. The Tory government was against change, the official explanation being that public opinion was not ready. It was supported in this view by the one parliamentary vote, in the 1960 debate, in which a motion calling for early implementation of the Wolfenden proposals was defeated by a majority of more than two to one.

The turning point came in May 1965. Following the change of government Lord Arran initiated a debate on the Wolfenden proposals, for which, to his surprise, there was very strong support. Encouraged by this he moved quickly, and two weeks later introduced a bill to implement them. This was the start of a parliamentary marathon in which the Arran bill was introduced three times into both Houses of Parliament before finally being enacted. It met with fierce opposition, particularly in the House of Commons, where it was initially defeated by a narrow margin in 1965, and was very nearly the victim of filibustering in 1967. Important factors in the success of the bill were the tacit support of the Labour government, who provided parliamentary time, and the support of the Church of England hierarchy. Another important ingredient was the work of the Homosexual Law Reform Society and of its North Western Committee in educating public opinion; the former also performed much of the 'leg-work' for the bill's sponsors.[16]

If the view that homosexuality was inherently immoral and anti-social was implicit in the Wolfenden Report, it became a major theme of the main parliamentary proponents of law reform. Their concern was to stress that decriminalisation of adult homosexual conduct was in no sense to be taken as acceptance or approval of it. For Lord Longford it was 'nauseating'. 'Never let it be thought for a moment,' he said, 'even by the ignorant and ill-disposed, that if we bring our law into conformity with what is general practice in Europe, we are condoning homosexuality. We are doing no such thing . . . we condemn it as utterly wrongful.'[17] Towards the end of all the debates Lord Arran was able to claim (with only a little exaggeration) that, 'in all the discussions we have had, and in all the speeches, no single noble Lord or noble Lady has ever said that homosexuality is right or a good thing. It has been universally condemned from start to finish, and by every single member of the House.'[18] The major themes of the reformers' arguments underscored this approach: the protection afforded by the Sexual Offences Bill, particularly for young people, was stressed repeatedly; homosexuality was a lesser evil than the blackmail which its prohibition encouraged; relaxing the law would make it easier for homosexuals who wished to be free of their practices to seek help from the caring ministries or would enable the community to concentrate on 'the preventive action which might possibly save a little boy from the terrible fate of growing up homosexual'[19] (Leo Abse).

Given the negative attitudes of those leading the reform campaign, it was hardly surprising that concessions were made, with the result that the 1967 Sexual Offences Act ended up even more restrictive than Wolfenden's proposals. A very narrow definition of privacy was adopted (Wolfenden had favoured the same definition for homosexual and heterosexual conduct), while restrictive provisions for merchant seamen were also introduced. Scotland was omitted from the scope of the bill to avoid increasing the opposition to it, and because the Scottish rules of evidence meant that in practice prosecutions were very rare.[20] (For the position on Northern Ireland see page 89.)

The devalued status which the reformers attributed to homosexual relationships found its parallel in the legal philosophy implicit in Arran's bill. Because the bill was merely amending the earlier legislation which had prohibited homosexual conduct, rather than repealing it, homosexual conduct remained broadly unlawful, except in the specific circumstances covered by the bill. During the debates on the bill several MPs underlined this point. Quintin Hogg (now Lord Hailsham) commented, 'Although it may be immoral, the heterosexual act is not illegal in the sense of being criminal. Broadly speaking, under the 1885 act, which the bill does not seek to repeal, the homosexual act is illegal in the sense of being criminal.'[21] Norman St John Stevas, a sponsor of the bill, said 'This Bill would create no recognised status for homosexuality. It would remain contrary to public policy. Homosexual relations would give rise neither to rights nor duties.'[22] While to the lay person such a distinction may seem arcane, its importance for gay people is considerable: in any legal issue affecting our sexuality, we start with diminished rights, having to contend with the basic assumption that our behaviour is essentially unlawful and tolerated only in very specific circumstances.

So it was that, both in terms of the criminal law and of the social attitudes promulgated within Parliament, the passage of the 1967 Sexual Offences Act left gays as second-class citizens, stigmatised as immoral and anti-social, and therefore acutely vulnerable to any future increase in the levels of intolerance.

The 1967 Sexual Offences Act in practice

During the 1970s the full implications of the discriminatory philosophy inherent in the 1967 Sexual Offences Act became apparent. The first important case in which it was put to the test was the prosecution of *International Times* (*IT*) magazine for conspiracy to corrupt public morals because it had published gay contact advertisements. The case is crucial both because in it the House of Lords set out unambiguously the implications of the 1967 Sexual Offences Act, and because it showed just how tenuous were the rights in law of gay people to contact one another and to engage in the sort of activities essential to the development of a gay community. Lord Reid, one of the judges, commented,

> There is a material difference between merely exempting certain conduct from criminal penalties and making it lawful in the full sense. Prostitution and gaming afford examples of this difference. So we must examine the provisions of the Sexual Offences Act 1967 to see just how far it altered the law. It enacts subject to limitation that a homosexual act in private shall not be an offence, but it goes no further than that. . . . I find nothing in the act to indicate that parliament thought or intended to lay down that indulgence in these practices is not corrupting.

Since homosexual conduct was corrupting it followed that to encourage it was to conspire to corrupt public morals. He went on,

> I read the act as saying that, even though it may be corrupting, if people choose to corrupt themselves in this way, that is their affair and the law will not intervene. But no licence is given to others to encourage the practice.[23]

The vagueness of the concepts inherent in the *IT* case have left considerable uncertainties as to the legality of a whole range of activities which form an important part of the gay community. While a number of the advertisements in *IT* magazine were explicitly sexual, the scope of the conspiracy laws taken with the legal status of homosexuality could allow in a future case for the prosecution of people engaged more generally in bringing gay people together, particularly where they were under 21. Thus gay clubs, social groups, counselling services and telephone help lines all, in theory, risk prosecution under the conspiracy laws. While such a prosecution would seem improbable in the present climate of opinion, the use of these laws against the Paedophile Information Exchange in 1981 shows that they are by no means a dead letter.

Another consequence of the status of homosexual conduct in law is that it has been impossible to establish charities explicitly for the benefit of gays. For example, the August Trust, which seeks to promote the welfare of elderly gays, has been refused charitable status, as has the theatre group, Gay Sweatshop. In refusing charitable status to gay organisations, it is clear that the Charity Commissioners have relied heavily on Lord Reid's statement in the *IT* appeal quoted above. In correspondence with Gay Sweatshop in 1978, the commissioners commented that, in the light of this and other cases, 'there can be no doubt that the law still regards such acts as contrary to public policy and immoral.'

Developments in the 1970s

While throughout the 1970s the legal establishment confirmed the oppressive philosophy of the 1967 Sexual Offences Act, successive governments made no effort to improve it, nor even extended it to Scotland and Northern Ireland.[24] The first full-scale attempt to change the law in Scotland was made by private member's bill in 1977 with the introduction of Lord Boothby's Sexual Offences (Scotland) Bill in the House of Lords. It passed through the House of Lords with only one vote, which was carried by 125 to 27. It was then introduced as a ten-minute rule bill in the House of Commons, but failed to receive a hearing.

Legal change finally came to Scotland in 1980. The vehicle was a government bill, the Criminal Justice (Scotland) Bill, to which

Robin Cook tabled an amendment identical with Boothby's bill of three years earlier. During the debate only two MPs spoke against the amendment and it was carried by 203 to 80. In the House of Lords, however, there was considerably more opposition and the amendment was carried by the rather small margin of 59 votes to 48.

The process of changing the law in Northern Ireland took even longer than for Scotland. Prior to 1972 the Northern Ireland parliament had responsibility for law reform in the province. Given the extent of prejudice against homosexuals in the churches and political parties, it was hardly surprising that no reform proposals were tabled at Stormont. The years immediately following the introduction of direct rule from Westminster in 1972 also saw no progress, the official view being that legislation on social issues should be left in abeyance pending the re-establishment of the Northern Ireland parliament.

This position became untenable in 1976 following the collapse of the Labour government's attempts to end direct rule. The pressure was intensified in May of that year when Jeffrey Dudgeon of the Northern Ireland Gay Rights Association began proceedings against the government under the European Convention on Human Rights. His principal claim was that the illegality of homosexual behaviour, together with a police investigation of his sex life arising from this, violated his right to respect for his private life (Article 8 of the convention). In July 1978 the government published a draft order in council, which would, if passed, have implemented the 1967 Sexual Offences Act in Northern Ireland. This met with vociferous opposition, particularly from the churches and Ian Paisley, with his 'Save Ulster from sodomy' campaign. In a minority position in the Commons, and dependent at times on the votes of Ulster MPs who were mostly against reform, the Labour government was unwilling to take the political risks involved in implementing the order.

No such difficulties faced the new Conservative government following the May 1979 general election. However, far from proceeding with reform, it contested the Dudgeon case (officially on the grounds of public concern), despite the support of the European Commission on Human Rights for it. As a result, the case was referred to the European Court of Human Rights. In October 1981 this ruled that the Northern Ireland law was in breach of Article 8 of the convention. The government could no longer resist change, and in October 1982 Parliament passed an order in council reforming the law in Northern Ireland. It had taken a quarter of a century for the proposals of the Wolfenden committee to be enacted in the main territories of the United Kingdom.

The European Court's judgment was of outstanding importance. By ruling that the Northern Ireland law was in breach of the convention, it acknowledged that the right to homosexual relationships was a fundamental human right. Moreover in making its judgment, it specifically rejected the much-used argument that hostile public opinion could justify a denial of this right.

No other legislative changes have taken place since 1967. However the first step in the direction of amending the 1967 act occurred in 1975 when the Home Secretary, Roy Jenkins, instructed the Criminal Law Revision Committee (CLRC) to review the whole field of sexual offences and established the Policy Advisory Committee (PAC) (the majority of whose members were not lawyers) to provide advice to the CLRC on medical, sociological and other non-legal issues, including an assessment of lay opinion. This step followed pressure from a number of organisations, including the Sexual Law Reform Society and CHE.

The PAC and CLRC have, to date, published a number of reports.[25] How far do these represent a development from the position of the reformers of the 1950s and 1960s? The clearest indication of their general thinking comes in the PAC's discussion of the male age of consent. It acknowledges that 'the law has a part to play in bringing about acceptance of homosexuals by not discriminating unnecessarily'.[26] The idea that homosexuals should be *accepted* is indeed an advance from the position of the 1960s when even the advocates of law reform were against *condoning* homosexuality. But that is as far as things go. The PAC recommended an age of consent for male homosexuals of 18, as against 16 for heterosexuals and for lesbians. Its main argument for discriminating in this way (apart from the state of public opinion) rested on two premises: the first was that 'in the vast majority of cases the homosexual way of life is less likely to be satisfactory than heterosexual relationships and more likely to lead to unhappiness';[27] thus did the supposed relative *unhappiness* of homosexual life-styles take over from their supposed *immorality* as a grounds for discrimination. The second premise was the notion of heterosexuality as an overriding sexual norm, against which other forms of sexuality should be discouraged, where possible. 'Most people feel that the natural and proper fulfillment of human sexuality is heterosexuality.'[28] Hence, the argument was seen not in terms of the rights of two groups within society (to each of whom their own different sexuality is natural and satisfying), but in terms of one group's way of life being abnormal and less conducive to happiness than that of another, and therefore to be discouraged. Nowhere did the PAC address the damaging effect on gay teenagers of a discriminatory law, nor consider their right to equality in law.

All this would have been irrelevant to the question of whether the age of consent for male homosexuals should have been 16 or 18 but for the PAC's revival of the so-called 'seduction theory'. This holds that some (in this case 16- and 17-year-old) boys of a basically heterosexual or bisexual disposition can be 'seduced' into a homosexual life-style and is based on the view that a person's sexual orientation is not necessarily fixed until about the age of 18. As already noted, this theory was discounted by the Wolfenden Committee; similar government comittees in Holland, Denmark and Switzerland have also discounted it,[29] as did the Royal College of Psychiatrists in its evidence to the PAC. It is hardly surprising that the PAC itself was unsure of its argument, stating no more strongly than that it 'was not convinced that there does not exist a vulnerable minority of young men aged 16–18 who may be in need of protection';[30] nor that a significant minority of the committee (five out of fifteen) dissented from this view.

The armed forces

The provisions of the 1967 Sexual Offences Act did not cover the armed forces and hence homosexual conduct by gay service women and men remains a breach of the military discipline acts even where the behaviour is in no way a threat to military discipline, for example where it takes place off duty and with a civilian. In April 1981, during the debate of an amendment sponsored by CHE designed to give gay services personnel the same rights as heterosexuals, the minister, Philip Goodhart, justified the discriminatory provisions of the existing laws as follows:

> Members of the Armed Forces are often required to serve in conditions where, both off and on duty, they are unavoidably living in closed communities, sometimes under stress. Such conditions, and the need for absolute trust and confidence both within and between all ranks, require that the potentially disruptive influence of homosexual practices should be excluded. It is, above all, necessary to ensure that those in authority over younger or junior men do not use their position to coerce or persuade those in their charge to perform acts in which they would otherwise not engage.[31]

Arguments such as these are based on a refusal to accept that, just as for heterosexual behaviour, a distinction can be drawn between homosexual behaviour which is disruptive of military discipline and homosexual behaviour which is not.[32]

In response to a parliamentary question the Ministry of Defence has published the figures for the number of gay servicemen and women discharged from the armed forces during the period 1976–80. Nearly 200 were dismissed following a court martial from the Army and Royal Air Force over this period (of whom over half served a prison sentence before discharge); no statistics were available for the Royal Navy. A further 500 were dismissed administratively (i.e. without a court martial) from all three services over the same period. Thus, on average over the five-year period, three gay people were losing their livelihood and being subjected to an investigation of their private life by the military police every week.[33]

In 1981 one victim of these discriminatory laws, John Bruce, decided to challenge them, and commenced proceedings under the European Convention on Human Rights.

Aspects of the civil law[34]

Legislation in the field of civil law has, until recently, ignored the existence of gay relationships. Given that they were illegal until 1967, and regarded as immoral and corrupting by the legal establishment at least until the late 1970s, this situation is hardly surprising. As a consequence gay couples face a situation in which the validity of their relationship is not recognised and it therefore carries none of the rights which attach to heterosexual relationships, whether common-law relationships or marriages. Some examples of the areas affected are discussed below.

Immigration A British national with a foreign lover has no right to have her/his lover settle in the United Kingdom. This contrasts with the rights ascribed to heterosexual couples under the immigration rules: generally speaking a foreign husband or wife may settle in this country, while in the case of an unmarried couple the rules provide for the exercise of ministerial discretion where an English man wishes to bring in his foreign lover (but not vice versa). Successive Home Office ministers have refused to exercise their discretionary powers in favour of foreign gay lovers.

Public housing Under the 1980 Housing Act the right of succession to a local authority tenancy is granted to both married and unmarried heterosexual couples. An attempt by CHE to amend this act to include gay couples was rejected by the government.[35]

Money Current tax rules provide particular benefits to married couples where both partners work. A wife is eligible for a pension on her husband's national insurance, or his employer's pension scheme. Neither of these benefits arise in the case of gay couples.

In 1982 Parliament recognised the existence of gay couples for the first time despite government opposition. An amendment to the 1982 Mental Health Bill provided that people of either sex who had lived together for five years or more would be regarded as 'next of kin' for the purposes of the Mental Health Act. The amendment was introduced specifically with gay couples in mind, but later extended to cover all cohabitants.[36]

The political parties

From the 1950s the main political parties adopted the position that homosexual law reform was a matter of conscience for individual MPs. This meant that the political parties maintained (in theory) a position of neutrality while they left individual MPs and peers to initiate legislation through private member's bills, on which a free vote was permitted. In reality matters were never so clear-cut: the process of legislating via a private member's bill is so precarious that, for any controversial issue, the tacit support of the party in power is essential. It follows that in practice there is no such thing as government neutrality: to remain neutral is to block change.

The Liberal Party was the first to break with this tradition. In the 1960s it officially supported the Wolfenden proposals; then in July 1975 it went beyond this with a commitment to the eradication of all discrimination against gays in the law, and reaffirmed this position in the run-up to the 1979 general election with the issue of a separate mini-manifesto on gay rights. The Labour Party's position on gay rights is evolving much more slowly: at the official level the Wilson/Callaghan administration stuck rigidly to the traditional line of neutrality. Since the 1979 general election, however, Labour has made progress towards adopting a position on gay rights. In March 1981 a discussion document (prepared under the auspices of the Human Rights and Race Relations subcommittee of the National Executive Committee) called *The Rights of Gay Men and Women* was published. This supported equal treatment in law (including the more controversial areas such as the male age of consent and the treatment of gay members of the armed forces), protection from discrimination, and a fairer approach in such areas as housing and immigration. Disappointingly, when it came to adopting an official position, in the Labour National Executive Committee's document 'Labour Programme 1982' (which was subsequently endorsed in the 1983 general election manifesto), these proposals were much watered down, with the male age of consent proposal raised to 18, and no mention of reform of the law in the armed forces. None the less the document represented an historic step forward: for the first time the Labour Party was officially committed to law reform; moreover that commitment included one of the most important issues, employment protection.

At the time of writing the SDP has had relatively little opportunity to develop a gay rights policy. An attempt in that direction failed in February 1982 when a move to incorporate gay rights in the SDP's constitution, which had the backing of the party's National Steering Committee, was rejected by area party delegates by 147 votes to 116. However, the SDP's *Citizens' Rights White Paper* published in the summer of 1983 incorporates a rather vague commitment to a comprehensive measure 'prohibiting all forms of unfair discrimination' against a variety of minorities, including gays.

The Conservatives, by contrast, are the only major party in which no attempt has been made to adopt a positive stand on law reform: on the contrary, it is arguable that on all issues where it has been challenged, the Conservative government has tended to hostility rather than to the official line of neutrality. Over the 1980 change in the Scottish law the Secretary of State, while making the traditional declaration of neutrality, gave his MPs a strong lead to vote against the change;[37] over Northern Ireland the government contested the Dudgeon case, and when subsequently changing the law, made it clear that it was motivated only by the need to meet the nation's obligations under the European Convention on Human Rights.[38] It has also opposed outright amendments to bills introduced to give gay couples succession rights in publicly financed housing (1980 Housing Act), to give gay servicemen and women equal rights to their heterosexual counterparts (1981 Armed Forces Act), to remove the penalty of imprisonment for male importuning (1982 Criminal Justice Act), and to make gay partners who have lived together for five years or more next of kin for the purposes of the Mental Health Act (1982 Mental Health Act).[39] On another important issue, employment, the government has similarly shown hostility to any move towards providing protection for gay people. In a letter to the National Council for Civil Liberties the Secretary of State for employment commented:

> there could arise cases in which it would not be unfair to dismiss an employee for the principal reason that he or she was homosexual, and therefore any legislative provision would need to make clear that an employee's homosexuality did constitute a valid reason for dismissal if it were relevant to the circumstances of that employee's employment and to the performance of his or her job.[40]

It is becoming ever clearer that the present government's official 'neutrality' applies (at best, grudgingly) to the minimal reforms of the 1960s, and that on many current issues it makes no pretence to neutrality.

Conclusion

The letter and spirit of the law as it affects homosexuals violates one of the fundamental principles of law in a free society: the law, both in its content and application, should treat all citizens with impartiality. But gays are subject to discrimination in numerous areas of the criminal law and are also frequently denied the protection and benefits of the civil law.

It is a measure of the prejudice against homosexuals that, in an age when the concept of universally applicable human rights is widely accepted, our parliamentary and legal establishment has such difficulty in recognising that these rights apply no less to gays than to others. This testifies to the powerful social and psychological forces which homosexuality confronts: sexual and religious taboos, together with the whole question of sexism and the traditional roles of men and women. The fact that male homosexual relationships were illegal for centuries, and up to the very recent past, compounds the problem: the law defines male homosexuality in terms of specific sexual acts, to which it attaches emotive and pejorative names. Henry VIII's statute made punishable the 'vice of buggery', Labouchere's amendment 'gross indecency'. Thus one effect of centuries of criminal status has been to dehumanise the legal establishment's view of homosexuality. It sees homosexuality in terms of 'unnatural' and 'immoral' physical acts, as though these acts had some distinct and separate existence, and as though the context of the acts, the relationship of which they are an expression, indeed the fact that they involve *human* beings with fundamental rights, were all irrelevant.

There are, however, many indications that the idea of gay rights as human rights is becoming more widely accepted. In contrast to the parliamentary debates of the 1960s, those in the 1980s have seen regular references to human rights. Even more significant have been two developments within the framework of the Council of Europe: the judgment of the European Court of Human Rights in the Dudgeon case has already been referred to. Only weeks before that judgment the Parliamentary Assembly of the Council of Europe passed a recommendation entitled 'on discrimination against homosexuals' which, after restating its firm commitment to human rights and the abolition of all forms of discrimination, recommended *inter alia* that member states should apply the same age of consent for homosexuals as for heterosexuals, and that they should assure equality of treatment in employment.[41]

While the impact of a resolution such as this will inevitably be slow, that of the Dudgeon judgment has already been considerable.

This can be demonstrated by comparing the voting record of the MPs who opposed the extension of the 1967 Sexual Offences Act to Scotland in 1980 with their record in the equivalent vote for Northern Ireland in 1982. Excluding Ulster MPs, some seventy-seven MPs had voted against changing the law in Scotland. Two years later only five of these opposed the equivalent legislation for Northern Ireland, while twenty-one actually supported it. While the circumstances peculiar to each vote (and especially the fact that the Northern Ireland Order was initiated by the government) in part explain this change, it seems clear that the educational effect of the European Court's judgment was also important. MPs who had previously seen the issue in the traditional dehumanised terms were forced for the first time to see it in the context of human rights. It was a small step forward in a process of change no less radical than that which transformed society's view of the slave trade from a legitimate commercial undertaking to a gross violation of the rights of the individual.

What actions are necessary to ensure that gays achieve equality in law? It should be evident from this chapter that major legal changes are likely to materialise only by gaining the support of the political party in power, or through a successful challenge to discriminatory laws under the European Convention. Other important areas of work are the monitoring of new legislation to ensure that the needs of gay people are considered, and the lobbying of MPs by their gay constituents as a contribution to the process of changing parliamentary opinion. In all these areas pressure groups are established and working with some effect. Each of the political parties has its own gay group (the Conservative Group for Homosexual Equality, the Liberal Gay Action Group, the Labour Campaign for Gay Rights, and the SDP Gay Group), while CHE, the Scottish Homosexual Rights Group and the NCCL Gay Rights Committee also work with the political parties and with individual MPs. CHE's Law Reform Committee is sponsoring three cases under the European Convention (covering the armed forces, male age of consent and privacy), and also monitors new legislation, while members of CHE and the political party gay groups lobby MPs at the constituency level. It is clear that the campaigning infrastructure necessary to achieve change exists. The only question is whether the groups and individuals concerned have the energy and resources to sustain and heighten their campaigns in the years ahead. There is no greater spur than the first signs of success. The developments in the Labour Party and at Strasbourg could provide the necessary stimulus.

Appendix 1: some discriminatory aspects of the criminal law

1 The age of consent for male homosexuals is 21, that for heterosexuals and lesbians 16.
2 Privacy is defined restrictively for gay men. Specifically, gay sexual acts involving men are not 'in private' if more than two men take part or are present, or if they take place in a lavatory to which the public have access.
3 Male or female members of the armed forces who engage in homosexual acts commit an offence under the armed services discipline acts, whatever the circumstances. (Specific provisions to this effect existed prior to the Arran bill, which left them unchanged).
4 It is an offence for a merchant seaman to have sex with another merchant seaman when on board his ship.
5 All male homosexual conduct remains a criminal offence in the Isle of Man and Jersey. (These have their own parliaments which have never adopted the 1967 Sexual Offences Act.) (In March 1983 Guernsey legalised homosexual acts in private between two consenting males over 21 for a trial period of three years.)
6 It is an offence for a man 'persistently to solicit or importune in a public place for an immoral purpose' (s.32 of the 1956 Sexual Offences Act). Homosexual behaviour is deemed an 'immoral purpose' by the law. While in theory s.32 can be applied to both homosexual and heterosexual soliciting, in practice it is applied almost exclusively to the former. It need take the form of no more than smiling at another man a couple of times.
7 Maximum penalties for homosexual offences are generally very much more severe than for equivalent heterosexual offences.

Appendix 2: ages of consent for gay men in West European countries

France, Sweden, Denmark, Turkey	15
Switzerland, Holland, Italy, Norway, Portugal	16
Greece	17

Austria, Belgium, Luxembourg, West Germany, Finland	18
United Kingdom	21

In Cyprus and Eire homosexual relationships between men remain totally illegal. In Spain the position is rather complex: there is no law specifically banning homosexual relationships. However homosexual acts between freely consenting adults can be punished under clause 431 of the penal code as an offence against public decency or good customs 'involving deeds of serious scandal or consequence'. Additionally, consensual acts involving a person under 23 may be punished under clause 452 of the penal code which punishes those who 'promote the prostitution or corruption of anyone aged under 23 years'. Corruption is considered to have occurred when more than one sexual act has taken place.

Lesbian relationships are not, it appears, referred to in the age of consent legislation of the above countries.

Sources: The Committee on Social and Health Questions of the Parliamentary Assembly of the Council of Europe, *Report on Discrimination Against Homosexuals*, Strasbourg, 1981; Robert Howes, *The Situation of Homosexuals in Spain in 1979*, London, 1979 (unpublished); Paul Crane, *Gays and the Law*, London, Pluto Press, 1982.

Notes

1 Lord Reid in the *IT* judgment, see p. 87.
2 See H. Montgomery Hyde's *The Other Love* (St. Albans, Mayflower Books, 1972) for a detailed account of the early development of the law.
3 See John Boswell's *Christianity, Social Tolerance and Homosexuality* (University of Chicago Press, 1980).
4 The death penalty was abolished in 1861 in England and Ireland and 1889 in Scotland.
5 See Jeff Weeks's *Coming Out* (London, Quartet Books, 1977) for a detailed account of the 1885 Criminal Law Amendment Act and the 1898 Vagrancy Act.
6 See H. Montgomery Hyde's *The Other Love*, pp. 153–6.
7 Quoted in the Commons Hansard for 12 November 1912, col. 1856.
8 Commons Hansard for 4 August 1921 and Lords Hansard for 15 August 1921. For more general information, see L. Faderman, *Surpassing the Love of Man*, London, Junction Books, 1981.

9 See Jeff Weeks's *Sex, Politics and Society* (Harlow, Longmans, 1981) Chapter 6.

10 Quoted in the 'Wolfenden Report' (*The Report of the Committee on Homosexual Offences and Prostitution*, London, HMSO, Cmnd 247) p. 130.

11 See Jeff Weeks's *Coming Out*, Chapter 14.

12 Wolfenden Report, para. 22.

13 Ibid., para. 124.

14 Ibid., para. 71.

15 Ibid., para. 267.

16 H. Montgomery Hyde's *The Other Love* gives a full account of the progress of the Arran bill.

17 Lords Hansard, 14 December 1957, cols 733 and 743.

18 Ibid., 16 June 1966, col. 160.

19 Commons Hansard, 5 July 1966, col. 262.

20 Lords Hansard, 10 May 1977, col. 166.

21 Commons Hansard, 3 July 1967, col. 1453.

22 Ibid., 19 December 1966, col. 1120.

23 Knuller v. DPP, 1973, AC 436, p. 457.

24 In Scotland there had been no prosecutions of homosexual acts which would not be an offence in England and Wales since 1967 and successive Lord Advocates had stated that this was policy. In Northern Ireland prosecutions had ceased at least by the early 1970s. There was, however, no publicly stated policy to this effect.

25 The PAC has published two documents on the age of consent, a working paper in June 1979 and its report (Cmnd 8216) in April 1981. The CLRC has published a working paper on sexual offences (October 1980) and another on prostitution and soliciting (December 1982, HMSO).

26 PAC, *Working Paper on the Age of Consent in Relation to Sexual Offences*, para. 56.

27 Ibid., para. 57.

28 Ibid., para. 59.

29 The Report of the Speijer Committee (Holland, 1969); the Report of the Danish Criminal Law Council (1975); *The Initial Proposals of the Committee of Experts for the Review of the Criminal Code*, Federal Department of Justice and of the Police (Berne 1981).

30 PAC *Working Paper*, op. cit., para. 53.

31 Commons Hansard, 19 May 1981, col. 251.

32 This distinction is drawn by the authorities in European countries such as Holland, Sweden, Denmark and Norway, who do not discriminate against gay services personnel.

33 Commons Hansard, Written Answers, 16 June 1981, col. 346.

34 See Paul Crane's *Gays and the Law* (London, Pluto Press, 1982) for a fuller account of this subject.

35 Commons Official Report of Standing Committee on the Housing Bill, 28 February 1980 (morning).

36 Commons Official Report of Special Standing Committee on the Mental Health Bill, 25 June 1982 and 27 May 1982.

37 Commons Hansard 22 July 1980. The Secretary of State expressed his concern that there had been inadequate time for discussion of the measure. However the precise issues had been widely debated for a quarter of a century.

38 Commons Hansard 25 October 1982, col. 836.

39 See notes 35, 31 and 36 for the references to the Housing, Armed Forces and Mental Health Acts respectively. For male importuning, see the Commons Official Report of the Standing Committee on the Criminal Justice Bill, 30 March 1982 (afternoon).

40 Quoted on page 10 of the Labour Party's *The Rights of Gay Men and Women*.

41 Recommendation 924 of the Parliamentary Assembly of the Council of Europe, 1 October 1981.

6 THE POLICE AND THE COURTS
Bruce Galloway

Introduction

> The British Police are the best in the world
> I don't believe one of these stories I've heard
> 'Bout them raiding our pubs for no reason at all
> Lining the customers up by the wall
> Picking out people and knocking them down
> Resisting arrest as they're kicked on the ground
> Searching their houses and calling them queer
> I don't believe that sort of thing happens here.
>
> (Tom Robinson, 'Glad to be Gay')

No body is so resented by homosexuals as the police. The feeling seems to be strongest among men over 35 — for obvious reasons. Before 1967, criminal sanctions against male homosexuality were imposed. Fear of exposure as gay in a fiercely disapproving society created suspicion of the police. Emotion has survived legislation. Most gays feel threatened by the police. An employer, priest or doctor may make your life unpleasant. The police can put you behind bars.

This chapter reflects two years' research by the CHE Police Group. I recommend readers to their forthcoming report, and record my gratitude for access to their records. I also thank John Alderson, former chief constable of Devon and Cornwall, ex-vice-president of the Liberal Gay Action Group, for the three-hour interview from which the quotations and views ascribed to him below are taken.

Police attitudes

> The police generally represent very conservative views, and are in fact a very conservative organisation. (John Alderson)

British police have traditionally had an enviable reputation for fair play. This has increasingly been questioned, following investigations into corruption and conflicts with various political and minority groups. Conflicts with the coloured community (for instance, in Brixton in 1981) have resulted in judicial allegations of racism, supported by independent academic research.[1] Other surveys have registered police antipathy to several 'troublesome' groups, including squatters, cannabis-users, the unemployed, and radical political groups.[2] This is relevant to lesbians and gay men. The archetypal police personality is 'conservative, dogmatic and authoritarian', valuing order and conformity.[3] Policing is a quasi-military job requiring the exercise of force to impose social rules. Those rules are laws; but personalities most attracted to rule enforcement and a regimented occupation typically support social conventions even where unconventionality is not illegal. Policemen subscribe to a conscious view of women which sees them as feminine and dependent, admiring the monogamous, parental family as an institution. Unattached women, especially feminists, elicit uncertainty and suspicion. The 'permissive society' is deprecated: divorce, abortion and illegitimacy are linked to the supposed increase in adolescent crime and disobedience. Homosexuals share with women an imputed inferiority, and with ethnic minorities a social stigma. Their apparent threat to the family, and therefore society, alienates policemen. Gays are dangerous, and behave unconventionally. The former criminality of male homosexuality and residual legal discrimination allied to the circumstances in which contact occurs between gays, as victims of crime, or offenders, and the police perpetuates the police view that all gays are actually or potentially criminal. It is the job of the police to fight crime.

Empirical evidence of antipathy is strong. It is something which John Alderson has experienced during his career:

> I think there is a macho self-image about the police. I often wonder whether the police macho doesn't somehow feel itself threatened by homosexuality.

Cases discussed in this chapter support this thesis. Typical police epithets when meeting gay men are 'queen', 'poof', and 'fairy' – the implication being that they are not *real* men. One excellent example comes from Alderson's own authority. A police chef in Camborne was exposed during a trawl of the gay community, and charged with minor sexual offences. Acquitted by judicial direction, he returned to his canteen with an unblemished character. What followed is significant precisely because it occurred outside the context of law enforcement. The man was sacked, police protesting that they found his homosexuality 'revolting, and would therefore not be able to eat food prepared by him.'[4] Unsurprisingly, there are few openly gay police officers in Britain, despite many covert homosexuals especially in the women's service. 'Coming out' would jeopardise any career.

Antipathy is strengthened by official strictures against homosexuality. The Police Federation reacted moralistically to proposals by the Law Revision Criminal Committee to reduce the gay male age of consent.

> The Federation . . . deplores the way official thinking on this subject appears to be surrendering to the pressure groups who try to persuade society that homosexual conduct is perfectly normal.[5]

Training manuals advise constables to watch out for homosexuals, as suspicious persons, presenting a range of sometimes hilarious stereotypes as representative.[6] A Scottish manual of 1980 is remarkable:

> It is a sad reflection on modern society that there are still to be found in our midst persons who are so lewdly disposed that they will stoop to the most revolting and almost unbelievable acts of indecency. The terms 'sodomy', 'indecent exposure' etc which are used in law give but little indication of the nature of these offences; the manner in which they are usually committed, and the evils they are liable to bring in their train. It is perhaps no exaggeration to say that many innocent children fall victims of the foul activities of moral degenerates to the detriment of mind and health of body. . . . Consequently, no effort is spared by the Police to suppress this insidious form of evil whenever and wherever it may occur.[7]

Personality, training, official opinion, experience and law thus combine to stigmatise homosexuals. The consequences are predictable.

Police actions towards gay people

A word of caution
Law enforcement inevitably involves conflict between police and members of the public. Coming into conflict with the police does not necessarily mean they are discriminating against you, particularly if you belong to a group against which the law itself discriminates. Police operations to enforce laws against certain varieties of homosexual behaviour cannot as such be considered discriminatory. Further evidence is required, e.g.:

> antagonism by police off duty
> unreasonable (e.g. violent, abusive) behaviour towards gays 'on the beat' or in police stations
> over-concentration of resources on homosexual offences
> attempts to invent new homosexual offences by charges under previously unused laws
> failure to act appropriately to offences against gays.

These are the charges examined below. The cases cited are a small but representative selection from many. Even one case would be excessive!

Queer-bashing

> Earl's Court, London. Two policemen appeared in court
> charged with offences arising from an off-duty 'queer-bashing'
> spree near a gay pub. They drove around hurling racist abuse at
> passing blacks and anti-gay abuse at men they took to be gay.
> One of the latter took offence and — thinking the policemen
> were just ordinary hooligans — took a kick at the car. The
> policemen stopped the car at once, pinned the man down on the
> bonnet and charged him with being drunk and disorderly.[8]

Violence and abuse off-duty is clear evidence of prejudice. In another example, two policemen infiltrated a gay party in Camberwell and assaulted two men, kicking one in the face and smashing a glass over another. Violence on duty is even more reprehensible. A Northern Ireland Gay Rights Association picket in 1978 was attacked by police, its leader left streaming blood in a police landrover. Assaults on men 'cottaging' are documented from areas as geographically and socially diverse as Glasgow, Surbiton, Shepherd's Bush and Merseyside. Abuse is commonplace. A police evacuation of the London Gay Workshops disco in Islington late in 1982 was accompanied by cries of 'pansies', 'poofters', and by 'humorous' remarks ('I'm standing with my back to the wall with all these queers around') and verbal intimidation ('We don't want any gross indecency here', to two men holding each other).

The police reaction to assaults on gays varies. In many cases, police have acted courteously and diligently upon complaint. Many, however, have occasioned indifference or hostility. A CHE convenor in Nottingham who had been assaulted, abused and robbed on leaving a gay club complained to the police. 'What do you want us to do, then?' was the response.[9] There have been similar cases in Central London, Putney, and again in Nottingham. Homosexuals reporting assaults have even been arrested for 'wasting police time'! The contrast with assaults upon heterosexuals is well illustrated by the following:

> Kensington: Holland Walk, a well-known gay cruising area, was the scene of a brutal stabbing which left a young Thai hospital worker with permanent injuries. . . . *Nineteen* plain-clothes officers were posted to the area, waiting for the attackers to return, posing as gay men waiting to be picked up. It appears that this decisive action took place because the victim was *not* gay, but simply using the road as a short cut home.[10]

Some police regard gays as 'legitimate targets', especially if assaulted in 'cottages' or 'cruising areas'. This is predictable, given their own operations there.

Cottaging and cruising

Police behaviour towards gays often suggests a strange sense of priorities in the enforcement of the law. In South London, the few dozen gay men who turn up after dark at a hidden cruising spot among the trees on Clapham Common have been forced to flee several times nightly . . . as police cars drive among the bushes — often at dangerously high speeds. Officers questioned on the Common . . . claim variously that they are investigating an attack and that complaints have been received from the public. But one gay man who was attacked on the Common had cause to doubt their peacekeeping role. After staggering on the road in front of a police car he was himself arrested.[11]

The greatest source of conflict between police and gay men is public sex — 'cottaging' or 'cruising'. It is illegal to have sex or make sexual advances in a 'public place', which includes parks, woods, toilets, etc. Police attention to these offences has increased since 1967; the annual rate of prosecutions for importuning has doubled, convictions more than tripled. Simplified trial procedures contributed to these increases, but the police decision to devote more time and manpower to detection created them. How far is such a concentration of resources justified? The offences are relatively trivial, normally meriting a two-figure fine. (The social consequences may be dire; see below.) They are 'victimless crimes'. The central issues are complaint, and reaction. Police should act primarily upon public complaint. Given increased acceptance of homosexuals generally, one would expect fewer complaints and *less* police activity. The inference is that police often initiate operations without complaint. The pattern of prosecutions confirms this. A 'cottage' may be ignored for years, then systematically investigated over months. The arrival of a new officer may change the priority given to such operations. Newspaper cuttings refer specifically to such new brooms.[12] One excellent example was in Stockport, where convictions rose 700 per cent in a year.

The police operations are correspondingly heavy-handed. Alderson considers the following reactions appropriate:

> uniformed patrols warning people of complaints and the illegality of public sex
> cautions for first-time offenders
> involvement of gay groups, to publicise complaints and act as referral agencies for first-time offenders.

These methods would follow official police emphasis on prevention before punishment. The reality is different. Motorised patrols playing round-up on Clapham Common are rare, although nearby Barnes has used mounted constables.[13] Uniformed foot patrols are however also rarely used, while the cautioning rate is lower than for any other sexual offence save rape and incest.[14] A referral scheme established in Cambridge after pressure from CHE and the Liberal Party was never used by police.[15] Standard police tactics are surveillance and entrapment. Entrapment by plain-clothes *agents provocateurs* is a tactic officially condemned by the Home Office but widely used. Newspaper cuttings frequently refer to plain-clothes men operating within conveniences, and to special training given to selected young constables.[16] Arrested men have complained of such incitement too often for coincidence. Covert surveillance is even more common, and measures used are remarkable for ingenuity and time involved. Police install spy-holes, mirrors, false grids and airvents, hidden compartments in cubicles, broom-cupboards and toilet roofs, erect ladders, photograph men leaving toilets and list car registration numbers nearby.[16] One convenience in Bournemouth was staked out four nights a week, over several months.[18] Gays preventing offences by warning of police surveillance have been arrested for obstructing police duty. These actions are altogether more appropriate to serious crime than public nuisance. Moreover, there are many cases where police have apparently falsified evidence.[19] One turned on a policeman's ability to see round two corners! Many believe that such operations are particularly attractive to police; not merely are they against homosexuals, but they have a high arrest rate, elicit ready confessions and guilty pleas, and little resistance. Recently, police have sought to make convictions easier still by bringing charges not under the 1956 Sexual Offences Act but under the 1936 Public Order Act, as 'behaviour likely to cause a breach of the peace'. This act was originally passed against street riots. This attempt to 'stretch' the law failed in court.[20]

Affection in public

The issue of public sex raises hackles among homosexuals and heterosexuals alike. In practice, cottaging and cruising are private activities, sexual exchanges (predominantly between married men) interrupted instantaneously by the arrival of third parties. The risk to children cited by police is chimerical, since most 'cottaging' occurs at night. A claim of public nuisance can however be made to justify police operations of some kind, if not of the kind and scale habitually employed. Harassment of gay couples publicly showing affection is less justifiable. Kissing, hugging, even walking hand in hand have led to trouble with police, usually abuse or injunctions to desist, occasionally arrest under the Public Order Act. Recent acquittals leave it uncertain whether such behaviour is 'a breach of the peace', but the threat is still used by police officers. No heterosexual couple has ever been arrested for such behaviour, under that charge. The discrimination therefore lies in the police mind, not the (in this case neutral) law.

Parties

The same excessive zeal can be seen in treatment of gay parties. The best example is Acton in 1982. Again, it is not the legality but scale of the reaction which is significant. Police were told of the party by a member expelled for drunkenness. A squad was detached to investigate possible infringements of the 1967 act. The intrusion was sudden, in force. A West German present described it as 'the sort of thing that happens in East Berlin', another as 'a Gestapo raid without the searchlights'.[21] Thirty-seven partygoers were arrested and held overnight, without charge. No heterosexual party would be disrupted thus. Such cases are not common, but highlight the vulnerability of gay men to police operations under the criminal law.

Gays in custody

Gays of both sexes suffer discrimination in police stations. Standard police tactics (denying the right to see a solicitor, alternating 'hard' and 'soft' interrogation, failure to notify detention to third parties) are more readily applied to 'sex offenders' than other criminals.[22] Other discriminatory practices are:

> violence and abuse
> semi-compulsory anal examinations of men
> gratuitously informing a suspect's employers, family and friends of his/her sexuality.

> West London. A 28-year-old wearing a gay badge . . . was first subjected to verbal abuse and then pushed around by a

policeman at a police station. When he tried to defend himself he was allegedly kicked and punched by three officers.[23]

The cases of gays abused and intimidated in stations are numerous and widespread geographically. In one disgraceful example, a lesbian was intercepted at Waterloo Station, taken to a station, examined bodily 'for drugs', locked in a room and subjected to a series of grinning PCs asking questions about her sex life. No charge was brought at any time, nor indication given of suspicion. The implication, of heterosexual policemen using their power to 'have fun' at a gay woman's expense, is profoundly unpleasant.[24] Young gay men, lacking confidence because of age and legal position, have also become frequent targets of abuse. This has included stripping, physical inspection and anal investigation, with comments such as 'You'll like this. You'll come back for more.'[25]

The most important maltreatment concerns the giving of information. Police have revealed a subject's homosexuality to friends, family and even employers, even before placing a charge.[26] This has led to gays released without charge or acquitted by the courts facing ostracism at home, or dismissal at work. Alderson considers this 'an abuse of police information . . . and totally unacceptable'.

Police actions towards the gay community

The examples above *are* selective. By no means every homosexual encountering the police will experience prejudice. The evidence is however that many police officers regard gays *per se* as criminals. Alderson emphasises the influence of the old sanctions:

> There was criminal legislation, which even in my time as a young recruit was drilled into us. It was regarded as a very serious crime, and a lot of time was spent prosecuting in this field.

Such attitudes colour police treatment of the gay community as a whole. The formation of Crawley CHE produced instructive warnings from local police officers: 'Break the law and we'll prosecute.'[27] Congregation, apparently, meant criminality. In practice, there is considerable harassment of the community, e.g.:

unreasonable operations towards pubs, clubs and sex shops
gratuitous investigations into the local gay community
infiltration of gay meetings, tapping of telephones and
interception of mail belonging to gay activities
exploitation of vulnerable homosexuals by security services,
and persecution of gay police officers.

Clubs, pubs, sex shops
Gays in Huddersfield issued a broadsheet in 1981: (see below)

A CRY FOR HELP

1984 has arrived at last in Huddersfield three years early.

POLICE HARASSMENT.

A minority group - the gay community - is being hounded by members
of the West Yorkshire Metropolitan Police Force.

Gay men are : - being taken from their homes and places of work,
- being stopped on the street and questioned,
- being forcibly medically examined,
- being refused legal advice whilst in police custody,
- being reported to employers for being gay,
- suffering physical injury whilst in police custody,
- having diaries and address books confiscated.

PERSONAL INVOLVEMENT BY SENIOR POLICE OFFICERS.

Particular Police Officers leading the persecution are openly anti-gay,
believing that recent changes in the Law to be morally wrong and that
homosexuality should be completely illegal at any age.

These are the Officers in charge of licencing matters in Huddersfield
and reliable sources from within the Police Force inform us that the
Chief Constable of West Yorkshire and even Home Office Directives have
little or no influence in Huddersfield - that Huddersfield will be
'policed' as they themselves see fit.

LATEST MOVE.

The latest move is to object to the licence of the Gemini Club - the
main meeting place for gay men and women in Yorkshire.

THIS IS 1981 NOT 1891.

We do not ask that we be allowed to break the Law. If criminal activities
have occured then let justice be done.

We do ask for basic human rights. To be respected for our individual
worth and not persecuted for our sexual preference.

We ask for freedom of assembly according to the dictates of our conscience.

ABOVE ALL WE ASK FOR A POLICE FORCE CAPABLE OF DISCRETION AND
UNDERSTANDING, PREPARED TO MOVE WITH THE TIMES, AND ONE WHICH
WILL UPHOLD THE LAWS OF THE LAND AND NOT BE A LAW UNTO ITSELF.

In December 1980 police raided the local Gemini Club, arresting twenty men for alleged sexual activities in a yard. Investigations followed into the backgrounds of more than a hundred members, and a major police trawl began involving repeated visits to the club. Protest spread, involving CHE and the gay movement. The 1981 Gay Pride March was eventually transferred to Huddersfield, with effect; almost all the criminal charges were withdrawn, and the Gemini kept its licence.

This incident is only the most celebrated in a series of episodes involving harassment in gay pubs and clubs. Police raids on such venues before 1967 were routine, and the Act has not deterred operations against the burgeoning 'scene'. Police have in some places sought the entire abolition of gay social venues, including one successful prosecution for 'running a disorderly house' and threats of another under 'licentious dancing' bye-laws.[28] The law is unclear. Gay discos survive, without security. The commonest reason for interference is under licensing laws. These give police comprehensive powers to enter and inspect places selling alcohol. Again, it is not the fact of enforcement but the scale and methods used which discriminate. Gay pubs and clubs in London are raided much more frequently than heterosexual ones. Simultaneous raids against several gay venues throughout the capital are common. They are often accompanied by intimidation of customers: lengthy questioning, abuse, threats of prosecution under licensing or sexual laws, name-taking, even forcible photographing for police files. Similar cases are known in Blackpool, Northampton and Brighton.[29] Venues in Scarborough and Bristol have been refused licences after police complaint, for being 'too blatant'.[30] Discos run by political or alternative gay groups are particularly prone to interference; London Gay Workshops and Icebreakers are examples.[31] Certain establishments receive more regular after-hours attention. The most famous is the Coleherne, in Earl's Court. Police patrol surrounding streets, moving on clients 'obstructing' the highway. Force, abuse and *agents provocateurs* seeking arrests for importuning are frequent complaints. The police are again acting within the law, after public complaint; but the frequency and scale of such operations is inappropriate to the degree of nuisance.

The clientele of gay saunas and sex shops are also harassed. 'Bath-houses' have a special place in gay life across the Atlantic.

Exclusively gay, they provide secure venues for social and sexual contacts. In Britain, they are defined as 'disorderly houses', and violate the privacy clauses of the 1967 act. Surveillance, infiltration and raids are used, keeping the scene small and ultra-discreet.[32] Operations under obscenity laws affect homosexuals unequally. Gay porn shops are more likely to be raided, and gay material in any shop more likely to be confiscated. The same mentality accepts *The Joy of Sex* in W. H. Smith but prevented the equally anodyne *The Joy of Gay Sex* from entering Britain. This discrimination between gay and other material lies not in the law but in the minds of police and customs officers.

Police trawls

There can be no excuse for building up dossiers on people who are carrying out sexual practices which are not illegal. The keeping of this kind of information is offensive. It is wrong to collect information on legal activities just because you may disagree with them. (John Alderson)

The most worrying aspect of police operations is the desire of some forces to build and retain on file a complete profile of the gay community: social and sexual networks, with names and photographs, meeting-places, sexual habits, leading figures. This perpetuates police work standard before 1967, when the gay male community was by definition criminal and suitable for investigation. The Act should have left gays no more worthy of gratuitous investigation than other groups, gardeners or Young Conservatives, for example. Police 'trawls' are discriminatory in themselves, and in the way they operate.

Trawls begin in many ways. Raids on clubs and pubs produce names and photographs for the files. Meetings can be infiltrated, and car numbers listed.[33] Interrogation of men cottaging or cruising is another starting-point. This low-grade intelligence becomes the basis for systematic investigation. A Huddersfield trawl is typical. Two youths were interviewed about their sex lives; they provided names and addresses of acquaintances, who were in turn interviewed and a network established. Diaries and address books were inspected, statements demanded involving explicit 'confession' of homosexuality, details occasionally leaked to friends, families, employers. The justification given was detection of under-age offences. The time spent and extraordinary detail of the questions asked suggest a wider interest in the gay community.

The pattern of trawls is instructive. There have been about twenty since 1967. The longest was ironically in Cornwall, part of Alderson's authority. South and West Yorkshire seem particularly vulnerable: Doncaster, Bradford and Rotherham have shared Huddersfield's experience. Greater Manchester, under control of Chief Constable James Anderton, has seen several witchhunts. The 'liberal' south-east is not however exempt; Brighton has suffered trawls, and harassment of the local club and social groups.[34]

One justification frequently used for trawls is investigations into murder. These murders usually have no homosexual element. In Northampton, more than two hundred gays were interrogated in a case where homosexuality was irrelevant. The crime's seriousness has led interviewees to co-operate too freely; people 'helping the police with enquiries' have been charged with sexual offences, despite police assurances beforehand. Information gathered is not returned or destroyed, remaining on police computers. Such operations are particularly dangerous for gays in the closet, or in vulnerable occupations. Relations between the police and the community after such trawls are usually so bad that the gay movement advises against direct co-operation even in murder enquiries. Homosexuals with useful evidence can pass it to the police through an intermediary, for example, GLAD (Gay Legal ADvice).

State security and gay liberation

Police dislike radical political groups, and homosexuals. Gay political groups are therefore doubly suspect. CHE and other groups have been investigated, their meetings infiltrated, their actions accused of criminality and revolutionary intent. Local campaigning has been discouraged, with, for example, the disruption of pickets in Reading and Brighton.[35] The gay movement is considered a pressure group seeking to destabilise society, and receives its share of surveillance. This has included photographing Gay Pride rallies, monitoring meetings, tapping telephones and opening mail of gay activists. Circumstantial evidence for the last two charges (strange noises, voices, 'feed-back', letters delayed and tampered with) has been strengthened by checks run by gay telecom/post office workers, and the public admission of Harold Salisbury, former chief constable of West Yorkshire, that gay activists were regularly monitored as 'a danger to the family'.[36] Raids upon radical gay premises such as the old Gay Liberation Front's headquarters in Caledonian Road have taken place.

Security services equally discriminate against gays in their own ranks, and exploit vulnerable gay politicians. The myth that all traitors are homosexual arises from the Vassall/Burgess-and-Maclean period, receiving support from the exposure of Anthony Blunt. The number of heterosexual traitors (Philby, Crabbe, the Pragers, Prime and others) has not denied this convenient fiction. Its greatest victim was the Queen's bodyguard, Michael Trestrail, forced to resign after years of service in 1982 because a male prostitute revealed their relationship. Subsequent investigations exonerated Trestrail, acknowledging his loyalty and dedication. His removal shows discrimination at the highest level in the police and security services. The latter may have compelled homosexuals, especially closeted politicians, to act as spies. Tom Driberg's alleged post-war experiences are matched by the blackmailing of gay Protestant leaders in Ulster during the 1970s to obtain information about Loyalist groups.[37]

Discrimination and the courts

Attitudes

> If you have but a passing acquaintance with the Bible, you will know what happened to Sodom when Jehovah called forth fire and brimstone to punish the inhabitants for their unnatural practices. It has always been in this country, and in every civilised country, a serious offence to commit sodomy, which is punishable by life imprisonment. It is as serious as committing manslaughter or grievous bodily harm. (High Court Judge, 1974[38])

> Those who frequent public toilets for homosexual purposes are in themselves a menace to society because of their destruction of locks and making holes in the doors they are making the public service utterly useless . . . these young men in chastising

those who do that committed a public service. (Defence lawyer in a queer-bashing case[39])

I am not going to waste public money by sending you to prison. At least make sure you do not pick up any young men in the streets of London . . . the fact that you were faced with this gun may teach you a lesson in the future. (Mr Justice Caulfield, sentencing a gay man held up at gunpoint by an under age heterosexual hustler. The gay man got a suspended prison sentence; the hustler was put on probation[40].)

One of the difficulties which judges have in sentencing offenders of this type is their own reactions of revulsion to what the accused has been proved to have done. Right-thinking members of the public have the same reactions. . . . There is a widely held opinion that homosexual offences involving boys lead to the corruption of the boys and cause them severe emotional damage. Judges of experience are of this opinion. (Lord Justice Lawton[41])

Cases such as these are all the more grave because some years ago Parliament committed itself to pass a Bugger's Charter which enabled perverts and homosexuals to pursue their perversions in private if their partners are over 21. (Mr Justice Melford Stevenson, 1978[42])

Such statements reveal attitudes and indicate areas of discrimination. Lawyers and judges frequently use words like 'unfortunate', 'unnatural', 'immoral' and 'repulsive' to describe homosexual acts. They adhere firmly to the seduction theory: that young men are seduced by older homosexuals, that this makes them homosexual, that the experience is inherently corrupting. This makes homosexuality itself corrupt. The legal profession shares the police's conservative, conformist assumptions about people and society. Their personality profile and equation of homosexuality with criminality − even more pronounced than that of the police, since the overt homosexuals they see are usually in the dock − prejudice them against gays. Such prejudices take several forms.

Leniency towards queer-bashers
The third quotation above is not the only case in which potentially

murderous attackers received leniency in court. A young man who battered a middle-aged homosexual to death in his kitchen escaped with an eighteen months' suspended sentence: 'I think there is a great deal of good in you and if I send you to prison I might forever stop the good from developing,' said the judge. The same day, he imprisoned a teenager for seven years for man-slaughter of 'a decent, hard-working man'.[43] A lesbian was murdered by her husband after demanding a separation. The man was first accused of manslaughter rather than murder, and sentenced to two and a half years; on appeal, he was released, the judge referring to the 'enormous provocation' he had received.[44] Sentences given to queer-bashers are generally shorter than those for comparable assaults, and more likely to be suspended, particularly if the defence allege 'provocation' by sexual advances.

Discounting homosexual testimony

The commonest conflict of evidence in homosexual cases is in cottaging, between a police *agent provocateur* claiming an advance and a defendant denying it. Invariably, defence testimony is discounted, however good the defendant's character or supporting evidence. This bias towards police testimony is more apparent than in non-homosexual cases. This implies that judges equate homosexuality with criminality, discounting gay testimony accordingly.

Failure to permit anonymity

A man facing a charge such as soliciting will be tried twice: once in court, and again in the newspapers. The 'trial by publicity' carries social penalties altogether disproportionate to the offence or trivial fine imposed. Mental breakdown, ostracism, the collapse of a marriage or loss of a job are well known, and suicide not infrequent.[45] This second trial could be prevented by allowing defendants anonymity. This never happens. Often, magistrates encourage lurid reporting by expressions of revulsion, thus prejudicing dispassionate administration of the law.

Interpretation of the law

Judges can modify, extend, even effectively nullify statute law by interpretations in court. These have since 1967 been generally hostile to homosexuals. Judges have established the principle implicit in the Sexual Offences Act, that homosexuality is not fully lawful, and extended it; homosexuality is now officially immoral and corrupting, in the eyes of the law. They have decided that it is illegal to publish gay contact ads,[46] or a poem depicting a homosexual fantasy about Christ.[47] They have supported the revival of offences for centuries forgotten, such as 'blasphemous libel' and 'corruption of public morals'. Tom O'Carroll of the Paedophile Information Exchange was imprisoned for 'conspiracy' to do the latter, for publishing a non-pornographic members' magazine. Judge Leonard has speculated that proprietors of gay pubs and clubs could be prosecuted under the same heading. Other judicial speculation would extend the special 'privacy' provisions of the 1967 Act into homes and hotels. The willingness of judges to see special restrictions on the lives of gay people is clear.

Differential sentencing

The law discriminates against gays, categorising as illegal behaviour common among heterosexuals and stipulating higher sentences for homosexual offences than heterosexual 'equivalents'. Prosecution rates are also higher for gay offences, as is the percentage of convictions. Discrimination is most evident in under-age cases. Gays are treated very much more severely than heterosexuals. While under half those convicted of sexual intercourse with 12-year-old girls are imprisoned, and only 20 per cent where girls of 13–15 were involved, more than 90 per cent of men having sex with youths of 14 and below are gaoled. Of men having sex with 15-year-old youths, 55 per cent suffer imprisonment. This blatant discrimination demonstrates the hold that the 'corruption theory' has on the judiciary. Its obsession with homosexual paedophilia is the more notable given that over 75 per cent of all known paedophile offences are heterosexual.

The lack of comparable adult heterosexual equivalents for 'soliciting' and of cases involving public heterosexual sex make most other comparisons impossible. In practice, heterosexual soliciting and public sex is treated lightly, usually with an unofficial police caution.

Civil law and other cases

Judicial discrimination in civil law cases such as divorce, custody and adoption is examined in Chapter 1. It is practically impossible for a gay couple to adopt, for a lesbian mother to gain custody, and often difficult for gay fathers to gain access. 'Danger of corruption' and 'lack of socially acceptable role-models' are frequently cited from the bench. Even where custody or access is given, it may be subject to humiliating restrictions, accompanied by detailed, prurient questioning about the gay person's sex life. Judges are particularly antipathetic to feminist lesbians, and to gays of either sex living with a lover. The anguish caused by some judicial decisions can be extreme. One woman had to choose between her child and her lover. A gay father found his access denied, despite superficial acceptance by the judge that he constituted 'no danger'. Gay teenagers have been taken into compulsory psychiatric 'care', at the demand of parents. Industrial tribunals (see Chapter 3) consider it reasonable to sack homosexuals because there exists prejudice against them which might damage the employer's business. All these examples show the extent to which judicial interpretation of the law has served to restrict the life of gay people.

Conclusion: what needs to be done?

Like the law they enforce, the police and courts discriminate against gays. Ending discrimination may take decades, so entrenched is the prejudice and conformist personality of the two professions. Yet change must come.

Ending police discrimination involves four types of activity: educating, monitoring, protesting and legislating.

Educating the police to take discrimination seriously and understand the gay community requires action at many levels within each police force. Studies have shown that 'community relations' courses during recruit training have an initial effect in lessening racial prejudice, but that this returns within three months to almost as high a level. Getting a gay input into these courses remains essential. The production of distribution leaflets for recruits, of more sophisticated training material for police colleges, and participation of gay spokespersons during training were all advocated by Alderson. Similar measures would be needed for refresher courses, for instance of senior police officers. (CHE has already had some success in 'placing' training material, and an experimental participation programme was carried out in Derby.) Education must also be taken into the streets. Contacts between gay groups and 'community relations officers' have often proved useless, or counterproductive; direct contact with operational officers, in the Vice Squad for instance, is essential.

Monitoring police activities and reporting on abuses of police power are in the short term likely to be more effective than education. Monitoring is in progress in certain areas; CHE Police Group and NCCL have been doing this nationally, while GALOP (Gay London Police Monitoring Group) provides a model that can be copied anywhere. Monitoring requires good publicity within the gay community, knowledge of the law and of the police, and courage. It is a valuable weapon to correct malpractices, and encourage more enlightened views:

> It is important for the good police officers to have this monitoring, too, because they suffer from the abuses of their less particular colleagues, in public opinion. (John Alderson)

Protest by individuals and communities facing discrimination is a third strand. Gay people should know their rights and not allow them to be infringed.[48] If they are, they should complain. Most complaints are rejected, but a few are upheld, and all help to instil caution into police minds. One well-publicised complaint can bring home to others the discrimination that exists. Gay groups should protest against police trawls and witchhunts. Public demonstrations of opinion can influence police operations, as Huddersfield shows.

Legislation to alter the nature of policing and eliminate legal discrimination against gays provides the only permanent solution to harassment. Alderson's concept of 'community policing' has possibilities. By returning more constables to the beat, it both threatens greater police contact with homosexuals and makes those contacts potentially more productive. Its structure of consultation between police and local community groups could also be used productively by gay groups. A form of community policing specifically including the gay community, augmented by independent complaints systems and police operational accountability to elected local authorities, would help community relations generally and the interchange of views between gays and the police. This is Liberal, and in part Labour policy. Permanent solutions require changes to eliminate discrimination in the law.

This would include an equal age of consent for gay men, an end to special restrictions in the 1967 Act, and the replacement of laws on public sex by one stipulating 'public nuisance' as the criterion and applicable equally to heterosexuals. A bill of rights including the right to privacy and freedom of information would curtail police trawls, open files and prevent covert security operations against activists. Employment protection legislation would end the leakage of confidential information, and might bring some gay police officers out of their closets. Such changes are also the only sure way of influencing the legal profession. Court attitudes are improving. Juries, not judges, now define 'immorality' and 'privacy'. 'Similar fact' evidence (such as the fact of being a homosexual) is no longer admitted. But until homosexuals are acknowledged as equals before the law, courts will feel justified in their own discrimination – in sentencing, interpretation, testimony, and so on.

Most of these changes lie far ahead. As I write, a bill is being hurried through Parliament increasing police powers to stop, search and detain, permitting arrests 'to prevent an affront to public decency' – a phrase with spine-chilling implications. The trend is toward higher police powers unmatched by community accountability.[49] New complaints procedures will leave the system only semi-independent. This increases the need for action by gay people. The alternative?

> Sit back and watch as they close down our clubs
> Arrest us for meeting and smash up our pubs
> Make sure your boyfriend's at least 21
> So only your friends and your brothers get done.
>
> (Tom Robinson, 'Glad to be Gay')

Notes

1 See Lord Scarman, *Report on the Brixton Disorders* (Harmondsworth, Penguin, 1982). See also A. M. Colman and L. P. Gorman, 'Conservatism, dogmatism and authoritarianism in British police officers', *Sociology*, vol. 16, no. 1.

2 Ibid., and also P. M. Cook, 'Empirical survey of police attitudes', *Police Review*, no. 85, 1977; L. J. Potter, 'Police officer personality', (unpublished M.Ed. thesis, University of Bradford, 1977); M. Small,

'Investigation of the relationship between intelligence, interests, personality, characteristics and job performance of police constables' (unpublished M.Sc. thesis, University of Aston, 1969).

3   See Colman and Gorman, op. cit.

4   CHE, *What about the gay workers?* (1981), p. 9.

5   Press release, 10 April 1981, reported in the *Daily Telegraph*.

6   These are splendidly satirised in a short film, *Watch Out, There's A Queer About* (Oval Video, 1981).

7   Grampian Police, *Scottish Criminal Law, Police Duties and Procedures* (Aberdeen University Press, 1980), p. 7.

8   Julian Meldrum, *Attacks on Gay People* (London, Campaign for Homosexual Equality, 2nd edn, 1980), p. 3.

9   Ibid., p. 22.

10 Ibid., p. 30.

11 Brian Deer, 'Trust is a two-way street', *New Statesman*, 27 June 1980.

12 See *Edgware, Mill Hill and Kingsbury Times*, 16 April 1976; *Merton and Morden News*, 11 January 1974.

13 *Richmond Herald*, 23 August 1968.

14 *Sexual Offences, Consent and Sentencing* (Home Office Research Study no. 54), pp. 41–3.

15 *Cambridge News*, 12 October 1972 and 3 October 1977. I am grateful to Bernard Greaves of Liberal Gay Action Group for making his papers available to me.

16 *Essex County Standard*, 2 June 1978.

17 *Gay News*, no. 161.

18 *Bournemouth Echo*, 22 March 1978.

19 *Evening Standard*, 3 February 1964.

20 *Western Gazette*, 15 December 1978; see also Paul Crane, *Gays and the Law*, London, Pluto Press, 1982, p. 27.

21 *Guardian*, 20 December 1982; *Capital Gay, passim*.

22 Crane, op. cit., p. 51.

23 Meldrum, op. cit., p. 6.

24 Crane, op. cit., p. 48.

25 Ibid., pp. 38, 63.

26 Meldrum, op. cit., p. 29 and *passim*; *South Yorks and Rotherham Advertiser*, 18 August 1978.

27 *Gay News*, no. 86, p. 3.

28 Crane, op. cit., p. 31.

29 *Brighton Evening Argus*, 20 December 1980; *Northants Evening Telegraph*, 25 September 1980.

30 *Bristol Evening Post*, 15 October 1976; *Worthing Gazette*, 14 January 1976.

31 *Gay News*, 21 August 1980; see p. 107 above for the Pied Bull Incident.

32 *Manchester Evening News*, 16 May 1979.

33 *Morning Star*, 23 August 1978 and 13 October 1978; and *South Yorks and Rotherham Advertiser*, 18 August 1978; *Sheffield Star*, 13 and 20 October 1978.

34 *Brighton Evening Argus*, 3 January 1981. Crane, op. cit., p. 55ff. is definitive; see also CHE's Submission to the Royal Commission on Criminal Procedure for details of the Cornwall trawl.

35 *Brighton Evening Argus*, 30 September 1980; *Reading Evening Post*, 17 May 1976.

36 This amazing admission was on national television, in 1980, with the author watching. The reference is lost.

37 *The Sunday Times*, 12 December 1982.

38 Quoted in Crane, op. cit.

39 Meldrum, op. cit., p. 34.

40 Ibid., p. 28.

41 Quoted in Crane, op. cit.

42 Ibid.

43 Ibid., p. 12.

44 S. Cohen *et al.*, *The Law and Sexuality*, Manchester, Grass Roots Books, 1978, p. 94.

45 *Gay News*, no. 145; *What About the Gay Workers?*, op. cit., *passim*.

46 *International Times* trial; see Cohen, op. cit., p. 88.

47 *Gay News* trial; see ibid., p. 89.

48 The NCCL leaflet 'Homosexuality and the Criminal Law' is the best short guide.

49 Cf. the 1982 Criminal Justice (Scotland) Act.

7 IN PRISON
Nick Billingham

The gay prison population

The position of gay people in prison is a subject on which very little information has come to light. In part this is because of the secrecy which surrounds the whole subject of prison life and treatment in Britain. But it also springs from the very understandable desire on the part of gays who have experienced periods of imprisonment to put the experience behind them after release and their consequent reluctance to participate in public discussion. Nevertheless, enough information is available from official sources to indicate that many of the problems and inadequacies that exist in our prison system generally place gay prisoners, and particularly gay sex offenders, in a position of especial difficulty. It must be said at the outset that most of this evidence relates only to male gay prisoners; the position of lesbians in prison in Britain is even less well documented. Young gay prisoners in borstals and detention centres are only partially covered by it; their position deserves a special study which it has unfortunately not been possible to attempt here.

Despite this lack of hard evidence — or perhaps partly because of it — a number of popular misconceptions, often of a sensational kind, exist about prison life. It is sometimes suggested that closed single-sex institutions such as prisons provide an environment in which homosexuality is widely practised as the only form of sexual release available and that therefore they should be more congenial for gay people than for others. It is a disciplinary offence for a

prisoner to be 'indecent in language, act or gesture',[1] although the way in which this rule is enforced depends on the approach adopted by individual prison governors. But whatever may be the extent of homosexual behaviour in a prison, the idea that this places gay people at some sort of advantage does not stand up to examination.

The single most important feature of prison life is the lack of privacy and when this is coupled with a general atmosphere of mistrust between individual prisoners and between prisoners and prison staff it is only with the greatest difficulty that any very close and mutually supportive relationships between individuals can develop whether or not they are based on a sexual relationship. Being gay in a male prison is more likely to provide one more category to which a label can be attached which reinforces the divisions within prison society.

The Home Office, which through its Prisons Department is responsible for running the prison service in England and Wales, does not keep any central record of the number of gay people in prison. In some prisons, however, particularly those to which prisoners are sent after sentence for assessment and allocation, a questionnaire covering personal details is compiled on each prisoner and sexual orientation is one item which can be covered, particularly in the case of long-term prisoners. The total prison population has exceeded 40,000 for a number of years (in 1979 the average number of inmates was 40,762 males of which 7,027 were young offenders in borstals and detention centres, and 1,458 females of which 161 were young offenders in borstals.)[2] It is reasonable to infer from this that at least 2,000 gay people are in prison and the actual total may well be significantly higher.

The great majority of gay prisoners are there for offences which have nothing to do with sex at all. The number of people sentenced to immediate imprisonment for all sexual offences is around 1,300 per year.[3] Of these probably between 200 and 300 are likely to be men convicted of gay offences under the Sexual Offences Acts.[4] There are of course no specifically lesbian offences under these acts and it is impossible to say from the statistics whether there are any offences for which lesbians are particularly likely to be imprisoned.

The group of male gay sex offenders is therefore not large in relation to the total (though it may well be a higher proportion of the male gay prison population than is the number of straight sex offenders to the male straight population), but it is an important one from the point of view of examining the treatment and experiences of gays in prison to which we shall return below. Here, however, it is worth noting that the Home Office research study already referred to found that the 'vast majority' of persons convicted of a homosexual offence had been involved in consensual behaviour while a majority of heterosexual offences had involved behaviour in which the victim or partner was not a willing participant.[5] To the extent that this is reflected in the prison population — and the differences in the laws applying to gay offences and in police and court attitudes discussed elsewhere strongly suggest that it is — it follows that many of these gay sex offenders find themselves in prison for acts which they do not regard as dangerous or harmful at all. In short they do not see themselves as criminals in the same sense as the majority of other inmates or even as the majority of heterosexual sex offenders such as men convicted of rape and actual indecent assaults on women.

Before completing this preliminary survey of gays within the general prison population, it is worth noting that gays are also represented among the significant proportion of the prison population which, it is now widely recognised, are there not because they constitute any real danger to society but because there is no alternative form of help available to them. While these are often portrayed as social inadequates, closer examination usually reveals that they are as much victims of external circumstances which have labelled them as outcasts as of any personal inadequacies. Many gay people still experience the type of isolation and feelings of desperation that lead some people into behaviour that brings them into conflict with the law. When this happens, the 'cause' is not the fact of being gay itself but strains set up by the actual or perceived reactions of others. It has been common for some people in authority to assume a link between what they see as sexual deviance and anti-social behaviour even where the evidence for this is slight and in such cases prison sentences represent a reflex moral judgment as much as any positive concern either for the individual or for the protection of society generally.[6]

Prison conditions

Leaving aside remand centres, adult prisons in England and Wales are divided into local prisons, closed training prisons and open training prisons. After conviction and sentence a prisoner will be sent first to a local prison for assessment and allocation and in the case of short sentences (up to six months) the whole of the sentence may be served there. Prisoners with any record of violence or of sexual offences are barred from open prisons and this means that any gay sex offender will usually have to serve the whole sentence in a closed prison even if the offence was consensual and there is no suggestion of a danger to the public at large. Other gay prisoners may be sent to open prisons, although it appears that some governors may regard openly gay people as unsuitable for prisons having dormitory accommodation. Furthermore, factors which determine the priority with which prisoners are allocated to training prisons may include marital status and the perceived stability of a prisoner's background and such considerations can tend in practice to militate against gays.

The most serious cases of overcrowding and poor conditions are to be found in local prisons. This results partly from deliberate Home Office policy to ensure that conditions for long-term prisoners in training prisons should remain tolerable and to minimise any risk of outbreaks of trouble in these institutions. But as the problem of overcrowding grows pressure is increasing for changes in this policy.[7] The worst prisons for overcrowding, such as Oxford, Leeds, Leicester, Bedford, Birmingham, Gloucester, Holloway, Lincoln, Liverpool, Manchester, Brixton and Wormwood Scrubs,[8] have prisoners sharing two or three to a cell. They also tend to be the prisons with the poorest facilities for work or educational and recreational activities.[9] If it is true, as suggested above, that some gay prisoners find it more difficult to be allocated to training prisons, they will have to endure these conditions longer than average; it seems to be not uncommon for prisoners serving quite long sentences to have to wait six or nine months for allocation. This is the general background which must be borne in mind when we come to consider the specialist units.

Actual evidence of abuse and physical mistreatment directed against gays within the general prison system is anecdotal and inconclusive, which is not to say that it does not occur. Other cases, however, suggest that it is possible to survive as an openly gay person in prison. Evidence to support this can be seen in the fact that prisoners are now generally allowed to subscribe to *Gay News* and to correspond with some gay organisations. But survival on such terms requires personal qualities of strength and self-reliance at least as great as are needed in the outside world. What is not disputed is that prisoners who fall, or are believed to fall, into the category of sex offender, which is usually equated with child molester under the general prison slang term 'nonce', are particularly at risk from their fellow prisoners. This risk is recognised by the existence of Prison Rule 43(1), which provides:

> Where it appears desirable, for the maintenance of good order or discipline or in his own interests, that a prisoner should not associate with other prisoners . . . the governor may arrange for the prisoner's removal from association accordingly.

Rule 43

There are Rule 43 landings in several prisons and in addition to these there are now separate long-term segregation wings in three prisons — Maidstone, Gloucester and Wakefield — to which prisoners needing to be segregated for all or most of their sentences may be allocated. The 1981 report of the Chief Inspector of Prisons gave the total number of prisoners in England and Wales in July 1981 on Rule 43 for their own protection (as opposed to disciplinary reasons) as 714.[10] Prisoners in this category are segregated at their own request and it has not been suggested that they are under any official pressure to seek segregation: indeed, the attitude of the prison authorities seems to be motivated by a desire to keep the numbers as low as possible. Prisoners seeking long-term segregation are made up of two main categories — police informers and sex offenders — and while there is no officially published breakdown of the figure anecdotal evidence from one specialist wing suggests that around two-thirds of the inmates were sex offenders and half or so of those were gay. It is impossible to generalise from this with any confidence, but it seems probable that the number of gay sex offenders on Rule 43 is a significant proportion of the total number of gay sex offenders in prison and that gay people are highly represented on most Rule 43 wings and landings. Some may seek this status in order to have the company of other gay inmates, but sex offenders in prison are more often thought to prefer to keep themselves to themselves; the reason for their being on Rule 43 is more likely to be real fear for their own safety.

Two detailed accounts of the conditions in which Rule 43 prisoners live have been published recently. One is contained in the 1981 report of the Chief Inspector of Prisons.[11] The other is a study of the first separate Rule 43 wing which was established at Shepton Mallet (now replaced by the three already referred to) conducted over a two-year period between 1966 and 1968.[12] The latter gives an account of the experiences of a rather small sample of sex offenders and others which led them to seek segregation and puts forward a number of sociological and psychological theories to explain why the prison system results in some categories of prisoner being cast as scapegoats; it shows that such is the need for scapegoats within male prison society that a hierarchy of different categories of offender can be seen even within the Rule 43 wing. The former concentrates more on the actual physical conditions and regimes to which Rule 43 prisoners are subject and is consequently less theoretical and more directly relevant to this chapter.

The chief inspector's report recognises that Rule 43 prisoners are 'often among the most vulnerable members of the prison population' and comments that the fact of their segregation does not diminish the hostility of other inmates:

> There remains a residual threat of physical or verbal assault.
> Because of the design of many prisons it is rarely possible
> totally to prevent any contact with other inmates, nor is it
> possible to maintain a separate kitchen in which to prepare the
> food for Rule 43 inmates to exclude the risk of deliberate
> adulteration of their meals by an inmate from the kitchen
> working party.

Special steps have had to be taken in some prisons to move Rule 43 prisoners around by routes and at times which minimise any chance of an encounter with other prisoners and to prevent adulteration of their food. And while the inspector's report finds no specific evidence to support allegations of ill-treatment of certain prisoners at the time of reception in prisons, it implies that special arrangements are necessary to prevent the possibility of such incidents occurring. Coming from such a source, these comments strongly support the contention that there are real problems facing Rule 43 prisoners, many of whom, as we have seen, are gay. And while the number of gay prisoners who experience physical ill-treatment may be small, the knowledge that it can and does go on pervades the whole atmosphere of prisons and must add to the feelings of fear and isolation experienced by other gay prisoners who can have no absolute confidence that they will not be categorised with the scapegoats whatever their offence.

This is not to say that efforts are not made in some Rule 43 wings to make life as tolerable as possible, often on the initiative of a few prison officers directly responsible for them who may come to have the best appreciation of the pressures bearing down on the inmates. The Thanet wing at Maidstone and the special wing at Gloucester have been singled out for praise although any steps to provide a relatively civilised environment have to stop short of creating conditions which may excite jealousy or resentment among other prisoners.

But elsewhere the position is much less satisfactory. The chief inspector's report describes it as follows:

> While at some prisons we visited Rule 43 prisoners occupied a reasonably large area separated from the prison, at others they were held in the punishment cells or suffered particularly from over-crowding. This was especially so in local prisons: at Leeds for example, 83 prisoners shared 29 cells. Because of the limited size of the area set aside, association with other Rule 43 prisoners and other out-of-cell activities were often not possible.
>
> Moreover, the general facilities and regime of the prison could not be made available because it was not practicable to make separate provision away from the general prison population. Thus, at Leeds, there were no facilities for evening or weekend associations; often the only employment available was hand sewing mailbags; there was no opportunity to take any form of physical recreation other than the statutory exercise period; and the only education available to these 83 inmates was a 2 hour class each day for eight prisoners. Almost half the population of this wing had endured these conditions for six months or more, and eight had lived like that for a year or longer.

Such a spartan and depressing regime, taken together with the low esteem in which this group of prisoners is generally held and the isolation often suffered because family and friends have disowned them, makes these prisoners' sentences drear in the extreme. It is curious that Rule 43 prisoners seem, by and large, to accept their lot: this may well be because the prospect of a return to the normal prison population is even less welcome. Nevertheless, we are in no doubt that conditions such as these are unacceptable. No matter how despicable a man's crime, equity and humanity demand that he should serve his prison sentence in circumstances broadly similar to those encountered by other inmates.

This official indictment of present-day prison conditions is remarkable both for its candour and for the fact that it has so far elicited such little concern among the general population. We do not maintain that these conditions apply only to gay prisoners, nor to more than a small proportion of them. But the evidence does suggest that gay people are more than proportionately represented among prisoners who do suffer such conditions and we fear that general lack of concern for gay people may contribute to the attitudes that tolerate them.

Medical treatment

The subject of medical treatment of gay sex offenders in prison is touched on in Chapter 9. One of the most wide-ranging surveys of the specialist treatment given to sex offenders in British prisons appears in a recent issue of the quarterly journal of Radical Alternatives to Prison, *The Abolitionist*.[13] Drawing on published articles from the *Prison Medical Journal* and on a paper presented by the senior psychologist at Wormwood Scrubs psychiatric unit to the 12th Cropwood Round-Table Conference held at Cambridge in December 1979,[14] the survey provides a rare insight into an area normally totally hidden from lay eyes.

The techniques described include behaviour modification — ranging from crude aversion therapy to more positive attempts to redirect sexual drive known in America as 'orgasmic reconditioning' — and anti-libidinal drug treatment. The special psychiatric unit at Wormwood Scrubs has played a part in the development of both; behaviour modification is also practised at Winson Green prison, Birmingham. The psychiatric unit at Grendon Underwood largely confines its activities to psychotherapeutic treatment and the more serious criticisms do not apply to these.

Tests involving particularly crude-sounding aversion therapy techniques carried out at Wormwood Scrubs are described in the Cropwood paper already referred to. They involved ten men, all in their twenties, eight of whom had been convicted of offences involving boys, one of offences against young girls and a tenth who 'was a transvestite imprisoned for burglary − he habitually broke into houses in order to acquire female underwear.' The aim of the treatment for eight of these men is stated to have been 'to achieve an exclusively heterosexual orientation'. The technique involved administering a series of electric shocks through terminals attached to the subject's wrists every time that measurable signs of sexual arousal were evident in response to 'a series of deviant stimuli, in most cases erotic pictures of young boys'. The results state that after release from prison only one offender had subsequently reappeared before the courts and was found not guilty. Five of the subjects are said to have reported 'a satisfactory outcome' although it is unclear whether this is to be interpreted as meaning simply no reoffending or, in the case of the gay subjects, conversion to a heterosexual life. The description concludes:

> The actual number of treatment sessions required were few −
> an average of 7 − and the number of shocks administered also
> few − in most cases less than 30. Perhaps for this reason none of
> the subjects displayed anxiety, depression or anger during the
> treatment period. The treatment package is still being applied
> and has proved most suitable for a prison setting.

The use of drugs to suppress sexual drive (not always the same thing as desire) has been partly pioneered at Wormwood Scrubs. In addition to surgical hormone implants, which were prescribed for older recidivist sex offenders between 1963 and 1980, tests involving two oral anti-libidinal drugs (Benperidol and Cyproterone Acetate) have been carried out. As described in the Cropwood paper these involved nine men who had committed sexual offences involving young boys and others committed for offences of unlawful sexual intercourse, rape and murder; their ages ranged from 23 to 59. The purpose of the tests was to compare the effectiveness and suitability of the two drugs for use by prisoners 'and also to establish objectively the time required for each of the treatments to take effect and, perhaps more important, how long they took to wear off.' In the case of Benperidol there are known adverse side-effects which have to be controlled with other drugs and it is believed that its use for sexual control has now been largely discontinued. Cyproterone Acetate is still used. To be effective the drug has to be taken regularly throughout life and while it is claimed that it will certainly prevent recurrence of sexual offences it also prevents a man 'achieving a socially acceptable sexual life'. The use of such a drug within prisons — where presumably there are no opportunities for committing sexual offences — when there can be no guarantee that it will be continued after release raises doubts as to the purpose of the whole exercise as well as the serious ethical questions that surround the use of such drugs in any context.

The supposed justification for these 'treatments' — which might rather be called experiments since the dividing line between the two in the cases reported is impossible to discern — is that they are applied only under strict supervision and in the case of persistent offenders who would otherwise be condemned to a life of successive terms of imprisonment and have themselves sought treatment as the only way out of their compulsions and anxieties. Even if it is accepted that there is a possible justification for the use of such treatments in extreme cases, it is difficult to be satisfied that the circumstances in which someone serving a long prison sentence opts to accept them can truly be said to allow a rational, free and informed choice. Gays can also not help remarking on the very high proportion of gay offenders included in the reported tests.

The fear of many gay people is that these reported tests may be only the visible part of a much more extensive iceberg. One ex-prisoner has reported to us being prescribed drugs which produced side-effects very similar to those associated with hormone treatments outside any of the special psychiatric units. The underlying problem with medical treatment in prison is the secrecy with which it is surrounded and the divided and potentially conflicting responsibilities of the Prison Medical Service towards the well-being of patients and the demands of the system.

The end product

As a further twist we are aware of complaints that it is more difficult for openly gay people to obtain parole than for other prisoners, but there is no documentary evidence to enable this to be verified. Even if it is true, it would be difficult to know whether the reason lay in the deliberate policy of parole boards or the attitudes of those officials within the prison service whose reports form the basis of individual parole decisions. But none of the evidence that has been quoted is principally a criticism of ordinary prison officers; it is rather an indication of the way in which the inhumanity of a system which devotes more energy to categorising and controlling people than to helping them works to the particular disadvantage of one group.

When all this has been said and we return to the position of the ordinary gay prisoner we are faced again with the central problem of isolation. Prison Rule 31 provides that special attention shall be paid 'to the maintenance of such relations between a prisoner and his family as are desirable in the interests of both', and that a prisoner shall be encouraged and assisted to establish and maintain 'such relations with persons and agencies outside prison as may, in the opinion of the governor, best promote the interests of his family and his own social rehabilitation'. The wording hardly suggests that this rule was framed with any particular understanding of the circumstances and needs of most gay prisoners. Whether or not a gay prisoner is encouraged and assisted to establish and maintain links with gay friends and gay organisations will depend on the attitude of prison governors and staff and their interpretation of the prisoner's best interests and of social rehabilitation.

In some prisons local gay organisations and self-help groups are allowed to play a role in providing links with the outside world for gay prisoners. But there is little evidence of any encouragement given to gay prisoners to take steps to establish such contacts themselves and the attitude of the Home Office Prison Department to suggestions that these contacts should be officially recognised as potentially valuable has been one of deep suspicion. The reality of life for a young gay prisoner inside for a non-sexual offence is best summed up in two extracts from letters written while he was serving his sentence:

Today is the completion of my first six months here which is equal to nine months (with one-third remission) of my sentence or 1½ years if I get parole next year. I'm still without a boyfriend though. I hope it won't have a drastic effect on me when I get out; being lonely for such a long period in here.

Twelve months later he wrote.

The thing which antagonises me more than anything else about this set-up is that if I couldn't cope outside before then how has all of this supposed to help me cope when I'm finally released? If I was a vindictive person or a ruthless criminal or even somebody who enjoyed a little dabble in crime then I suppose this would help to tame me. If I was tamed even more than I have been these past 23 years then I'd be scared of living in case I made a mistake, therefore scared of working in case a judge was to condemn that respectable act as inappropriate. It could be that they think that loneliness cures all loneliness and that a sincere and conscientious worker becomes even more so when deprived of such abilities for very long periods. I should be out within the next 30 weeks but I know when they do eventually let me out that I'll be completely lost. Who are the vindictive people then?

Notes

1   The Prison Rules 1964 Approved by Parliament in Statutory Instrument SI 1964, no. 388.
2   Report on the work of the Prison Department, London, HMSO, 1979, Cmnd 7965.
3   Criminal statistics England and Wales, London, HMSO, 1980, Cmnd 8376.
4   For an analysis of custodial rates for different sexual offences see Home Office Research Study no. 54: Sexual Offences Consent and Sentencing, Appendix C.
5   Ibid., p. 47.
6   One extreme example of how this can work is provided by the case of Bruce Lee (see the *Sunday Times*, 18 July 1982). After a horrifying but apparently motiveless case of arson in which three people died, the police decided to search for suspects within the local gay community. Lee was arrested and subsequently tried and convicted

on the basis of a confession about which serious doubts have since been raised. The supposed connection between gay people and motiveless arson (the potential seriousness of which is obvious but not central to the argument) appears to be recognised within prison subculture according to evidence from one prisoner, but a closer investigation of this fascinating subject is outside the scope of this chapter.

7   See Report of Her Majesty's Chief Inspector of Prisons for England and Wales 1981, Cmnd 8532, paras 3.15 to 3.19.

8   See Report on the work of the Prison Department, op. cit., Appendix 3.

9   Report of Her Majesty's Chief Inspector of Prisons, op. cit., paras 3.04 to 3.08, 4.21 and 4.34.

10   Ibid., para. 6.03.

11   Ibid., Chapter 6. The extracts quoted are all from this chapter.

12   Philip Priestley, *Community of Scapegoats — The Segregation of Sex Offenders and Informers in Prisons*, Oxford, Pergamon Press, 1980.

13   'Medical treatment of sex offenders', *The Abolitionist*, no. 9, Autumn 1981, obtainable from Radical Alternatives to Prison (RAP), 97 Caledonian Road, London N1.

14   Reprinted in D. J. West (ed.), *Sex Offenders in the Criminal Justice System*, Cropwood Conference series, no. 12, 1980, University of Cambridge, Institute of Criminology.

8 THE CHURCH
Robin Green

Either I might enjoy the ruler in heaven,
or one must regard as a crime
Something which the providence of fate
has made necessary.

Ganymede and Helen, twelfth century

A gift of God gladly to be accepted,
honoured and enjoyed.

*Statement of Conviction of the Gay
Christian Movement*, 1976

In the last two centuries some gay people have both expected and
been led to expect the seeds of their own liberation in the trust
deeds of the Christian church. Most have been profoundly
disillusioned. The ecclesiastical wind has blown low on the
personal and corporate history of gay people. History endows
certain institutions in any society with the unique function of
making and keeping that society whole. The church is one of those
institutions. But between its trust deeds of faith, that is, the story
and the tradition of Jesus, and its institutional behaviour there is
always a *trahaison des clercs*.[1] It has betrayed its role especially in
relation to minority groups. It is possibly the greatest moral charge
that can at present be laid against the church as an institution.

It is a common fallacy within the Christian church to account for
that destructive behaviour by the individual acts of men and
women. But the *trahaison des clercs* cannot be excused so easily. I

will argue in this chapter that sexism, like racism, functions as a process within the structures of the institutional churches. By sexism I mean discrimination on the basis of either sexual gender or sexual orientation. The essential problem is not that gay women and men are oppressed but rather that the churches perpetuate at many levels a process of structural sexism, which becomes the seed bed for individual oppression. I do not believe that any of the major churches, with the possible exception of the Quakers, escape this charge. Because I am a reluctant priest within the Anglican church, that is the place from which I view this bleak landscape. I have tried to take into account the public statements of the other major churches. In the case of the black neo-Pentecostal churches, there are no public statements. It is, therefore, extremely difficult to judge accurately what appears at first sight to be extreme hostility to gay people. I am also very conscious of not being able to take account of the other major religious traditions in multi-ethnic Britain.

The church, by its trust deeds, should be playing an extremely dynamic role in combating the evils that oppress gay people. Its response over the last two centuries has been extremely variegated. At the time of the Wolfenden report, some churches actively encouraged a change in the law whereas fifteen years later, Christian MPs were still arguing for no change in the law with regard to Northern Ireland. The reaction of some churches to the *Gay News* blasphemy trial was for a change in the law to take account of multi-faith Britain whilst other churches simply repeated the classic homophobic arguments. My contention is that the major churches are inhibited from taking part in a dynamic struggle for justice precisely because a number of strands are subtly interwoven into a process of institutional and structural sexism. Those strands are:

the meaning of gay people communicated through biblical and theological statements
the development of particular social values
the blessing of popular moralities
the imposition of certain social institutions as norms
discrimination against clergy
special 'professional' provision
indirect reinforcement of political homophobia.

The positive identity of some gay people within the churches has begun to challenge the churches to reflect on their traditional position. But that change means that a more radical transformation has yet to take place. If there is a process of structural sexism at work, the more fundamental task is to address the social environment within the churches and to act for change in that. It is that structural sexism that continues to pose the basic threat to the homosexual identity of many people. Unless a radical transformation is effected, the churches will continue to practice inequality in love.

Christianity and the meaning of gay people

The homosexual revolution has challenged all the major churches to re-examine their position in relation to the *meaning* of gay people. The public statements that the churches have made in response to that revolution have the most immediate impact on the majority of gay people (see Appendix 1). Although that majority is not involved in the day-to-day life of the Christian church, it will, nevertheless, to a greater or lesser degree feel the impact of those public statements. The churches remain to some extent social vehicles through which the meaning of human nature is transmitted. Certainly the churches understand themselves to be in the business of refining and redefining what human nature, including sexual nature, is. The homosexual revolution has accelerated that process.

The challenge of that revolution has led to a plurality of response. I will examine first the historical position, and pay particular attention to the way in which the churches' attempts at redefining the *meaning* of homosexual people either deepens their oppression or promotes their liberation.

Unrefined religion and hard porn have much in common! They both attempt to define the meaning of human sexual behaviour by genitalia rather than by internal perception and feeling. The unrefined religious position, evasive and heavy with uncritical biblical language, focuses on outward and physical actions rather than the fun and sensibility of interior desire. The obsessional pursuit of religious authority rather than truth which frequently accompanies such an unrefined position is itself a sign of deep sexual insecurity and suppression. Nevertheless, the insistent preoccupation with four or five biblical texts as the props for their perception of homosexual people has long-term effects on individual lives. The following was heard in the course of a counselling interview:

> I went to this conference in Bristol. The minister said first of all that touching was forbidden. Touching could lead to all kinds of unsuspected desires. Then he launched into an attack on gay people. They couldn't exist because the bible condemned them. I felt terrible. I couldn't join in for the rest of the weekend. How could it be? I knew inside that I was gay but everything outside said, 'It's not possible for you to exist.' I existed and I didn't exist.

It is impossible here to analyse in detail the biblical passages which have led people to adopt the traditional, but unrefined, position in respect of homosexual people. But there is an increasing amount of critical evidence to suggest that the exegesis from which meaning has been derived has been less than careful in the degree of attention that it has paid to the social, historical and cultural contexts of the passages under dispute. In addition those who accept the authority of these passages appear to pay scant regard to the fact that Jesus makes no reference whatsoever to homosexual people. There are further inconsistencies in the position of many who adopt the traditional position: they tuck in cheerfully to their prawn cocktails followed by pork chops, condemning homosexual people, apparently oblivious to the fact that the texts they claim offer the authority for the condemnation equally forbid the eating of shellfish and pork! It is an intellectually indefensible position.

There appears to be an increasing weight of critical evidence that the New Testament, which might be thought to carry greater weight for Christians, takes no demonstrable position on homosexual people. The references in St Paul's epistles appear to be about heterosexual people committing homosexual acts. That is a radically different matter to same-sex relationships. Paul is condemning people who are acting against their own truth. To suggest that heterosexuals denying their own truth is normative for the Christian churches' position on homosexual people has been a castration of both the body and the soul for literally thousands of gay people. For that is the effect of such a position; like compulsive porn it forces individuals into a divorce between inner perception and external behaviour.

But mercifully more truth has emerged under the impact of the homosexual revolution than is officially allowed. Both the Anglican and Methodist churches have had commissions meeting about the nature of human sexuality. The British Council of Churches sponsored a group that produced 'God's Yes to Sexuality' in 1981. All the major Christian denominations have within them groups struggling to understand afresh the dynamic of human sexuality, including homosexuality. The reports published by the Anglican church in 1979 and the Methodist church in 1982 are themselves indicators of a fresh intellectual struggle to interpret Christian truth in the light of psychological, anthropological and sociological studies. The Anglican report falls lamentably short of what gay people could legitimately demand and led to gay people being defined by the Archbishop of Canterbury as *handicapped*. But the Methodist report does seem to constitute an advance in thinking not least because it sets homosexual people in the context of human sexuality in general. It admits that there are markedly different positions about homosexual people within the church and argues for that plurality of approach for many years to come. It recognises the traditional approach but says with equal force that a judicious historical perspective on the effect of the Scriptures on attitudes towards homosexual people is that they had no effect at all.

This divergence of views has increasingly characterised the pronouncements of Christian churches about homosexual relations. They present a shift in the limits of tolerance and even if the inherited meaning that has shaped so much homophobia remains deeply within the consciousness of the churches, still forming props of prejudice, nevertheless the limits of tolerance are not fixed for ever. This comment could not have been written by a major church commission ten years ago:

> . . . for some homosexual people (as for some heterosexual people) celibacy is a vocation, and that for others a choice between a partnership without physical expression and one that includes genital expression within a committed relationship is to be accepted as a choice which Christians may responsibly make.[2]

The shift is, however, a shift in the limits of *tolerance* and many gay people would want a much less ambiguous statement from the churches about the meaning of their sexuality. Within the struggle for truth and meaning gay Christians have been making their contribution and they represent a third strand in that plurality of response to the homosexual revolution. Their liberating impact can be heard in this echo:

> When I was a child I used to say the traditional morning blessings. If you were a man you said, 'Blessed are you, Lord our God, King of the universe who has not made me a woman'. If you were a woman you said: 'Blessed are you, Lord our God, King of the universe, who has made me according to your will'. If you knew you were gay, you had a long think, for you knew you were not wanted.
>
> In a new revision of the liturgy, everyone now says: 'Blessed are you, Lord our God, King of the universe, who has made me according to your will'. It is the only response which goes beyond the sociology of the past.[3]

In any debate about homosexual people and their meaning those of us who are gay argue that the most creative starting-point for a deep investigation of our sexuality is Jesus himself. Christian orthodoxy, understood in all its fulness, has always claimed that human meaning finds its fulfilment in him. We forget too easily that Jesus was a marginal person whom Christians claim took human meaning into the meaning of God. By that action the meaning and value of those who experience themselves on the margins of human society was changed for ever. Life which had taken the brunt of prejudice and discrimination was restored at the centre of God's life. By that action all the categories by which people are defined and labelled were challenged and the status of marginal people transformed. We do well to set up Jesus as the normal person because by doing so we do not exclude or label anyone as 'abnormal', 'handicapped', 'sick', 'perverted' or by those other pernicious labels that the Christian churches have bandied around for too long. Gay people in the churches believe that the humanity of Jesus, properly understood within the fulness of Christian orthodoxy, will not allow any human being to be devalued without it being an affront to the dignity of God because the humanity of Jesus has made an irreversible difference to God himself. By that struggle to re-understand Jesus as the proper norm for an understanding of what it means to be human, including sexually human, gay Christians are seeking to redress the balance in meaning that has constituted the Christian churches' position for too long.

Other cultures and other religious systems have developed radically different perceptions of gay people to Christianity: the Christian churches have to the very recent past transmitted interpretations of gay people which have oppressed them and distorted the meaning of their lives. Those voices are always in the ascendant when the churches experience revivalism and charismatic 'renewal'. Gay people need always to be on the alert, therefore, not only to public pronouncements about their meaning but also to revivalist movements within the churches. As I write, the debate is very finely poised within all the major churches: the shifts in tolerance could move in any direction. There remains, however, the challenge of exorcising from the public imagination definitions of what homosexual people are not: for the sum total of nearly a thousand years of negative meaning has not been holy truth but the silence of embarrassment interrupted by shrieks of opportune falsehood. In relation to gay people, the church is escaping very slowly from being a past master at the penalising of courageous meaning.

Christianity and social values

For many gay people those worlds of meaning have become interior words shaping their *values*. This is experienced most immediately at a personal level, although it has immense social implications. Because of the church's traditional stances about the nature of gay people, the sense of identity in many gay people is already encumbered with the marks of death. It has led them to make self evaluations like, 'I'm an ineffective priest,' or 'I'm a rotten lover'. This process of self-devaluation rose to the level of public statement in these words, which were part of a speech in the Anglican General Synod's debate in 1981 on 'Homosexual relations': a priest, who 'came out' in the debate, is speaking:

> I am telling the Synod that homosexuality, however inevitably some men and women and boys and girls belong in that

condition, is a disability. It is part of the fault of things. Homosexuality is a cheat. So it is no business of the Church or any other group to make equal what is not equal.[4]

I shall deal later with the ways in which the church idealises marriage and the family by imposing them as social norms. But it is worth noting here that in many ways the family has become the primary source in western society for value systems. In so far as it has become that, it has assumed a religious connotation. Within the complex psychological kaleidoscope that forms the inner life of each family, individuals internalise all kinds of evaluations about themselves, their roles, their status, their worth and their values. The church too often sanctifies family life without recognising the ways in which that process actually heightens the shadow side of human sensibility. The loneliness of too many gay people is partially accounted for by the dissonance between their interior world of values, positive or negative, and the values embodied in the institution of the family and, to some degree, within the institution of the church.

That interaction between the family as institution and the church as institution focuses something of the process by which Christian values are transmuted into general social values. It can be argued that both Christian theology and Christian values are not only determined to some extent by society but also determine, again to some extent, that society, and therefore, its values. Socially determined values may prove to be socially significant. Christian values may then act as both a dependent and independent variable within society. But there appears to be a subtle variation on that theme. Society also has a way of absorbing into itself values which were once the independent province of the Christian church and giving them a currency for which no *a priori* Christian theology is required. I would want to argue that in many ways society has transmuted the negative values that the church has ascribed to gay people and made them a social norm. In that way gay people, who have no Christian belief, have been influenced by the negative value judgments of the Christian church. This has led to the perpetuation of a self-image within the gay community of gay people as devalued and denigrated. It may also account to some degree for the internalised oppression of some gay people. Within some of us there are whispers, which sometimes become screams, like, 'Don't bother attempting it because you know from the word go that you'll never bring it to fulfilment.'

Christianity and popular morality

This process of the church's values being transmuted into general social values finds its mirror image at the level of *popular morality*. In a masterly study of the position of gay people in the first 1,400 years of the Christian church, *Christianity, Social Tolerance and Homosexuality*, John Boswell has analysed the ways in which the Christian church adopted ethical and moral positions. He shows that they did not arise from the trust deeds of faith but reflected the hostility to gay people and their sexuality which became noticeable in periods of social change. John Boswell concludes:

> Neither Christian society nor Christian theology as a whole evinced or supported any particular hostility to homosexuality, but both reflected and in the end retained positions adopted by some governments and theologians which could be used to derogate homosexual acts.[5]

The disappearance of urban subcultures plus increased governmental regulation of personal morality and the inability of society to deal with deviant minority groups all seem to have led to an acceleration in social homophobia, which the church as a social institution also internalised and made its own.

John Boswell's argument seems to me to be particularly important because the church has always publicly claimed that its dilemma about homosexual people and their sexual life-style was based on the historical trust deeds of Christian faith. But by a critical-analytical examination of not only the biblical material but also the writings of major Christian authors for the first 1,400 years of Christianity, Boswell demonstrates that significantly different perceptions of homosexual people, with a very positive affirmation of their life-style, have been current at many stages of Christian development. He also points up the contrast between a biological sex ethic, which only became normative at a late stage in the development of sexual ethics, and what he calls a transcendent sexual ethic in which both gay and straight love were celebrated in all their fulness. He demonstrates that gay people were prominent, influential and accepted for their contribution to society at many levels, including the church.

He also demonstrates how public hostility and prejudice developed during the thirteenth and fourteenth centuries with a general increase in hostility towards minority groups. This intolerance was reflected in and perpetuated by its incorporation into the theological, moral and legal compilations of the late middle ages and became normative for Christian thinking for many centuries. It played a definitive role in the formation of homophobia within the Christian church.

This dynamic between church and society both in terms of *values* and of *popular morality* illustrates well the ways in which the church as a social institution both forms and is formed by socially 'acceptable' values and morality. It also begins to explain how some of the other groupings analysed in other parts of this book, like politicians, judges, police, media pundits, can lay claim to 'Christian' values as supportive of their homophobia. Popular moral judgment and homophobic behaviour both have their roots in a dual process: firstly, the church through its general ethical statements actually shapes and influences socio-ethical norms; and secondly, the church as a social institution assimilates into itself, and then sanctifies, intolerance of deviation from social norms in the corporate state. Neither of those processes have necessarily anything to do with the teaching of Jesus or with the trust deeds of Christian faith. In fact there is an increasing degree of critical evidence that those patterns of intolerance are themselves deviations from Christian orthodoxy. Nevertheless, they still continue to shape and determine the public attitudes of the servants of the corporate state as well as sharply defining eruptions of popular morality like the Festival of Light. It is persistently assumed in such movements that there is a necessary relationship between individual Christian morality and homophobia. They have assimilated a bogus comparison with a previous age, tarted up to satisfy the illusory security of their present social and religious position.

Christianity and social institutions

The fifth strand in this process of institutional and structural sexism, the seed bed of prejudice within the church, is closely allied to the previous two. The church promotes particular kinds of *social institutions as norms*. The two most obvious ones are marriage and the family. This is explicitly spelt out in the Anglican church's report on *Homosexual Relations*:

> We believe that Anglicans should continue to teach that the norm for sexual relationships is one of mutual love, expressed and nurtured in life-long and exclusive marriage based on the givenness of biological and psychological potential, and open to the future in respect both of permanence and procreation.[6]

There are others within the church who would want to claim that the proper Christian norm for all human relationships is friendship and that can take a whole variety of forms of which heterosexual marriage is one option, albeit the primary option for the majority of people. The objection to the church's position is that it is wholly inappropriate for at least one in ten of the human race.

I have experienced at first hand how deeply influential such a view can be and how subtly the church can manipulate a particular view of human relationships. The social pressures within the church towards marriage and family life are both insidious and powerful and it is easy to find oneself in 'the marriage trap' because of the unconscious processes that are prevalent and are brought to bear especially on the church's professional staff. The extremely painful consequences of that are spelt out in this case history:

> Over 20 years, marriage became emotionally more and more difficult, though sexual activity occurred — without much sense of fulfilment.
>
> Husband and Wife grew apart psychologically and theologically. From a sense of commitment, and to find space, husband moved from parish ministry to a specialist post. As the children of the marriage grew up, husband could face more honestly the wife's longstanding accusation, 'You don't need me'.
>
> Neither in youth nor adult life had there been any practice of homosexual acts. Now — without the emotional support of parish friendships, and under the strain of overwork — occasional homosexual phantasies became something more. Husband tried for a year to hold the marriage together, and be true to himself by meeting once a week without sexual

engagement one of several male friends who could accept him as a gay person. This was not acceptable to the wife, who believed that one's gayness should be rejected, healed or exorcised.

A redundancy situation led to a secular job away from home. After a few months of mutual cruelty at weekends, husband moved out. Shortly thereafter he met his present partner, who now lives with him.

The case history well illustrates how a Christian minister can find himself trapped between a growing inner perception of himself as gay and the church's idealisation of marriage and the family as norms. Some of the reasons for that idealisation are wholly healthy and positive but the churches have to re-understand that the biological sexual ethic which underwrites such a position has not always been normative for Christians. It is also sometimes difficult not to escape the conclusion that the political concern about the family is in fact a way of reasserting traditional forms of power and authority within the church and avoiding questions about a different kind of society that is emerging. Mirages of consultation have not actually deflected attention away from the ways in which real political power is still exercised in both the church and other major and minor social institutions.

An inability to deal with the fact that the Janet and John nuclear family is not the final word in human relationships all too often leads the church to suppress its own ambivalence, actually there in its trust deeds, about the real status of marriage and the family. It also coincidentally makes it ill equipped to deal with the shadow side of both those social phenomena. The church has to struggle much harder with the contemporary paradoxes of human friendship if it is going to claim to have any ministry to real human need. It will also need to reassess radically the notion of friendship as a proper norm for the assessment of human relationships. In fact I think that it could be argued that the whole of our society needs to engage in an urgent re-evaluation of friendship because friendship allows space for a rich variety of human relations that stretch far beyond the boundaries of the natural family. We need to take enormous risks in exploring new ways and new norms for being human.

Christianity and the church's clergy

I want now to turn to the ways in which prejudice and discrimination take root in individual lives and especially with the ways in which the church sometimes deals with its professional staff who are gay. I think it is easy to deal with prejudice in the church simply in terms of *professional discrimination*: that is why up to now I have tried to illustrate the ways in which the churches' sexism affects the wider gay community. However, we must now turn to the question of *professional discrimination* because it is there that the prejudice is earthed and finds its most vicious expression. I want to illustrate the nature of that process by a number of stories.

> A. worked as an assistant priest in an Anglican parish in the south of England. He lived in a clergy house. His parish priest suspected that he was in love with B., a priest from another Anglican diocese. One day the parish priest, believing that he had evidence, entered A.'s flat without notice, tried the bedroom door which was locked and waited in the next room to interview A. He suspended A. from all priestly functions, having reported the matter to the bishop. A. had to live outside the parish initially.
>
> The bishop asked for intimate details of the friendship and said that the ending of the physical relationship was necessary for A.'s ministry to continue.
>
> A. was prevented from saying mass for 3 weeks but was unable to hear confessions for the rest of his time in that parish. He eventually moved to a parish in another diocese. When the time came for him to move from that parish, he discovered that he was on the Archbishop's list, a list of priests about whom special vigilance had to be taken. With the help of others, his name was cleared from the list.
>
> When he became a parish priest in a third diocese his bishop said, 'Anything that you do is your own affair before God but if you cause scandal to the church I will not support you.'

It is possible to discern within that case history a number of features about how discrimination operates in the church. Firstly, gays themselves have to face an uncomfortable fact. It is not always the straight world that exercises that discrimination but other gays. Homosexual people suffering from self-oppression, like A.'s parish priest, are one of the biggest threats to other gay people in the life of the church. It was a closeted gay who set this particular process in action. Men and women who are unable to own and be open about their sexual preferences are very quickly trapped into projections, fantasies, transferences and counter-transferences which radically affect and sometimes disastrously alter the direction of people's lives. One gay priest said to me recently, 'I'd rather work in a diocese with a straight bishop any day. If you work in one with a closeted gay anywhere in the hierarchy you know there will be trouble'. It may be a hard fact for some gay people to accept, but gay people can be the source of our own oppression.

Secondly, there is inconsistency in practice in the ways in which senior churchmen handle the gay question. Gay priests and other ministers can never be quite sure where they are. In the case study just quoted A. and B. had radically different reactions from their bishops and parish priests. In the second bishop's comment, it might be extremely difficult to define what he would mean by 'scandal'. Some bishops might interpret that to mean a parishioner's complaint that X. had had a young man staying in the vicarage for a week! I understand that some bishops use working for gay rights as a rule of thumb as to whether someone is forbidden to work in an Anglican diocese. It is extremely difficult to see how they justify such a position in terms of the church's public statements over several decades on the human rights issue and the rulings of the European Court on Human Rights on a number of gay issues. In the Anglican General Synod's debate in 1981 on 'Homosexual relations' I pointed out myself that the church was sailing extremely close to the wind in terms of the European declaration on human rights in relation to what its report said about the provisions for 'safeguarding' employment for gay people within the church.

Thirdly, the study reveals the extreme ambiguity within the church about private and public life. I think that it could be justifiably argued that priests and other clergy have a more publicly exposed life than any other professional group. Their life is open to constant scrutiny not least because the vast majority actually live right in the middle of the areas where they work. It is extraordinarily difficult, therefore, to 'hide' the nature of one's relationships. Many people within the church believe that a gay friendship lived under those conditions constitutes a scandal. Most gay people would obviously disagree.

But the case study reveals a much more sinister invasion of private life. Both the parish priest's invasion of A.'s flat and the bishop's inquisitorial questions demonstrate how the church feels it has a God-given right to probe that intimate, internal world which is, in fact, the divine affirmation of our own proper autonomy. It needs to be spelt out, if necessary in legal terms, that that invasion of privacy is in fact a violation of the dignity and rights of human beings.

Fourthly, A.'s story also illustrates the ways in which the church operates in a homophobic way without recognising it. The second bishop's comment equates homosexual behaviour with scandal. This story also vividly illustrates how homophobia operates:

> Albert Ogle was interviewed in 1982 for a post in one of the divisions of the British Council of Churches. At the time of the interview the Council was in informal dialogue with the Gay Christian Movement and had just published 'God's Yes to Sexuality', which contains a positive affirmation of gay relation-ships.
>
> Albert was recommended for the job by an appointing committee. When he met the General Secretary of the BCC, the Rev. Philip Morgan, he said in passing that he was gay but was not an active gay rights campaigner. 24 hours later the job was withdrawn.
>
> Other staff members have since raised the issue of the employment of gay people within the BCC. It is understood that the General Secretary has said off the record that the BCC will not employ gay people in executive positions. It is not clear on what authority such a statement is made. At the time of writing, the issue is still alive in the BCC.

Fifthly, the first history also illustrates the ways in which the church has its machinery for ensuring that one's name and future and promotion is 'blacked' unless one can prove otherwise. It should not need spelling out but perhaps it should be said that A. had committed no offence under secular or ecclesiastical law. He was simply in love with someone of the same sex. The archbishop's list and other mechanisms may be necessary protections against charlatans and counterfeiters. They are not necessary mechanisms to oppress men and women who are the victims of irrational prejudice and indiscriminate discrimination! Unfortunately the church has an appalling history when it comes to providing adequate facts and information to justify unjust and oppressive behaviour. Half-truths, innuendo, gossip, untested perceptions and biased decisions are all used to 'block' the personal and professional development of clergy, both gay and straight.

Finally, the study illustrates the ways in which the church puts ministerial practice and human integrity under severe strain. It demands celibacy whilst at the same time arguing that celibacy is a vocation for only some within the church. By saying that it demands celibacy, I mean that it attempts to suppress and discourage many forms of sexual partnership that do not conform to the marriage norm. One further story will illustrate what I mean. E. was training as a deaconess in the Anglican church:

> My journey towards ministerial practice was probably doomed from the beginning, but the prayer had to be acted out and personal integrity considered throughout. My sponsoring bishop on being informed by the college principal of my relationship with C. summoned me to interview. I was glad to share personal things with him because I knew that it did have influence on what I did and where I did it. I believed, and still do, that as ministry effected from within marriage and family life reaches only certain people so does ministry effected from within a gay relationship. The bishop saw otherwise. In November 1979 at the end of our interview I was told I could complete my training (I wasn't aware that this was in question) and it was intimated that the only difficulties would be the practical ones of placing C., a Methodist, and I together in a certain locality. In July 1980, having completed my training, and having done so with some merit on both academic and placement levels, the same bishop wrote to say he was sorry that he was unable to give me my Inter Diocesan Certificate because he had no intention of giving me a job 'due to my situation'. However, should my situation change, he would be pleased to see me again.

The position of women within the church is already severely disadvantaged and they are the victims of open sexism. This story illustrates how, equally, they can be trapped into violations of both their integrity and their vocation. In fact E. would argue that for many men in same-sex relationships ordination has and does offer a greater insurance policy than for women who are debarred from the security of such status by other clergy. I agree with her.

Having said all that, it has to be said in the cause of justice that the church is able to rise above its own institutional and structural sexism occasionally, at least in regard of men, and often offers a quality of affirmation and care that transcends anything offered comparably in the wider secular society. Although there are numerous cases of minor discrimination, with gay men and women being blocked from holding positions of authority within the church, nevertheless there are equally numerous instances of gay men and women being valued, allowed to go forward for ordination and encouraged to make a positive contribution to the life of the churches. That, at least, ought to be celebrated.

Christianity and special 'professional' provisions

The next strand relates very closely indeed to the previous one. Within the power structures of the church gay people suffer from prejudice by virtue of the fact that either it is seen to be necessary to make *special provision* for them or that their particular needs have to be argued for. I think this operates at two particular levels. Following the General Synod debate in 1981 on homosexual relations, the House of Bishops established a committee with the dual function of drawing up pastoral guidelines for gay ordinands and clergy; and reflecting on how the church might be much more active in resisting discrimination and injustice against gay people.

At a certain level, the question of homosexual people touches either guilt or conscience. It is often difficult to distinguish which! I am not clear whether the other major churches have anything akin to the Anglican committee. It is the kind of body that tends to be clouded in secrecy and it is comparatively difficult to establish clear facts about it. It was never made public that such a body had been established.

At the time of writing, the committee is preparing to discuss the pastoral guidelines with the House of Bishops. As far as it is possible to judge, they are not to be published. This may be an issue, then, for the gay community. Do the guidelines, for example, allow for campaigning for gay rights? The committee is believed not to have tackled the discrimination issue.

Secondly, the issue of special provision tends to be focused at the level of pastoral care. The issue of the pastoral care and professional development of the church's professional staff has only recently become a matter of vigorous debate. In those debates it is usually marriages under strain that receive attention. Almost invariably those conducting the debate need to be reminded that there are others within the church who may have particular needs of their own arising out of a different life-style or sexual preference. In one Anglican diocese recently an archdeacon managed to make passing reference to gay people in the final paragraph of his paper on pastoral care. In subsequent debate it was argued that younger gay priests are much more likely to break silence about their sexuality and that this will have very considerable implications for the church in the immediate future.

In this area gay people have to tread a difficult tightrope. At one level they need to resist being made recipients of special provision and given peculiar attention within the power structures of the church. But at another level we need to recognise that we do have special needs, arising out of centuries of oppression and sexism, and that the church has a particular responsibility to redress the balance and ensure that gay men and women are not only allowed to find their place within the structures of the church but are also given the right pastoral support to develop an effective ministry there.

Christianity and political homophobia

The final strand is more a logical outcome of many of these perceptions rather than a clearly defined strand in its own right. But it does seem to me that the church's institutional sexism does operate in terms of *indirect political reinforcement*. There are a whole number of political groups who use what they believe to be a 'Christian' system of belief and morality to perpetuate perceptions of political reality usually from an extreme right-wing stance. Some of those 'perceptions' have quite specific implications for gay people. One might cite as examples of the ways in which political groups latch on to Christian belief the 'Save Ulster from Sodomy' campaign, the anti-gay propaganda of the National Front, the 'Kill a queer for Christ' campaign of Anita Bryant, the Moral Majority's theological assumptions and the 'gay under the bed' syndrome that influences the thinking of at least some parts of the British political system. All that I want to note here is that different political groupings seize upon homophobia within the churches to sanction their own political stances about gay people. In that sense the churches' own compromised record on the issue of gay people feeds and indirectly reinforces some of the most destructive anti-gay propaganda and some of the most violent political perceptions that exist within constitutional democracies.

Christianity and the gay response

It will be obvious to the reader by now that the gay revolution has forced this institutional and structural sexism into the arena of public debate within the Christian churches. For the best part of two decades the different churches have been making a wide variety of responses to the homosexual revolution. In some, perceptions have shifted from condemnation to ambiguity and ambivalence. In the extraordinary case of the Quakers there has been tolerance, acceptance and positive affirmation for many years. In the Roman Catholic church, at least at the level of public statement, there seems to be no recognisable shift from the condemnation of homosexual people. But the last thing that one must assume with the Christian churches is a necessary correspondence between public statement and private practice. I realise that is an astonishing statement about an institution that claims to believe in 'a Word made flesh'. The problem with the churches is that they spend a great deal of time turning flesh into words!

As I have indicated already there are divergent attitudes within all the major churches towards homosexual people and that is likely to be the case for many years to come. Within a very rich plurality of reflection and thought at the moment it is extraordinarily difficult to see how any major Christian denomination would reach a consensus about the status of gay people. Nevertheless the shifts that have happened can be partially accounted for by the gay liberation movement. We might, therefore, ask: what can gays expect from the churches in the immediate future? Numerous gays will regard that as a wholly irrelevant question because they will regard the church as an irrelevant institution. In one way I respect their atheism but if the analysis of this chapter holds I doubt whether it is actually in the best interests of the gay liberation movement as a whole to ignore the influence and limited power of the churches as institutions. Certainly gay people should not expect much from the churches in the immediate future although I think we might demand much from individual Christians and be surprised at what we receive! But that does not mean that gay people and others should not continue to challenge the institutional and structural sexism of the churches. I will return at the end of the chapter to ways in which that might be effected.

I want to turn now and describe briefly the strategies that gay Christians and sympathetic allies have been using to challenge and change this process of institutional and structural sexism within the churches. There is no doubt that the strategy employed by a significant majority is that of accommodation. Because for many gay Christians their experience of being human remains fragmented, they are paralysed into silence. There are thousands of gay men and women who are completely tacit about their sexual orientation within their Christian congregations and there are too many gay clergy whose sexual lives are lived out in the hidden corners of gay pubs and public lavatories. Elaine Willis caught this accommodation beautifully in the Gay Pride week service on 27 June 1982:

> Our faith is silent about our sexuality and our sexual selves disown our faith. And we feel that there is a Great Silence in heaven about who we are; and we are tentative, we are cautious, we are self protective. And the gay experience, yours and mine, is one of aloneness and isolation, self-despising and dispossessing.[7]

Accommodation can obviously only be a short-term strategy if it is not to wreak havoc with that human sensibility and sensitivity which makes us truly sexual beings.

Thousands of other gays have opted for the strategy of alienation and exile. It is a strategy, often not self-chosen, too well known to all minority groups. But many gay people see no hope within the institutional church at all and either pursue an individual Christian discipleship or disown their Christian faith altogether. The problem is that this can sometimes turn them into oppressors of Christians, and there are rather too many gays who operate their own subtle forms of oppression and prejudice. Or it can mean that they never quite disown their faith and live in considerable personal anguish for many years. But perhaps what many who have opted out have never really recognised is that most gay relationships achieve what stability they possess not through external religion but through the inner primacy of love. The question always remains: how in the painful struggle to sustain this relationship against all that stands against it is the primacy of love to be nurtured and sustained?

The third strategy has been for individual sects to grow up committed totally to a ministry to gay people. The Metropolitan Community church is the largest such grouping in Britain and performs an extremely valuable ministry amongst gay people. It is an open criticism of the inability of the major Christian churches to minister effectively to the gay community. As a sect it also runs all the risks of becoming insular and inbred and of not setting gay people free for the rest of the human community. But it may be a useful staging post for some gay Christians in their individual struggle to put together the fragmented elements of their experience.

The fourth strategy has been the development of groups within all the major churches who have taken the brief of gay Christians as their particular contribution. 'Quest' within the Roman Catholic church and the Friend's Homosexual Fellowship are two examples of that. But I want here to focus specifically on the Gay Christian Movement, not least because it is an ecumenical organisation but also because it seems to me to have made the most dynamic contribution to the reconciliation of the two words 'gay' and 'Christian'. It was formed on 3 April 1976 and has always had two perspectives to its work. Firstly, it has created a network of care and support for gay Christians throughout the country. It has a scheme of local groups as well as befriending and counselling schemes. In addition to that it has always recognised the need for a continuing theological reflection to enable gay Christians to reconcile the different parts of themselves. But, secondly, it has also recognised from the beginning the institutional sexism with which this chapter has been concerned. It has, therefore, seen itself as having an important political lobbying and campaigning role within the churches as well as allying itself with other elements in the gay liberation movement, working with and from the gay community. Its statement of conviction about the possibility of being wholly gay and wholly Christian remains one of the most formative documents in this country for gay Christians.

GCM has been extremely influential partially because of its ecumenical nature but also because it has provided a focus for creative Christian reflection from within the gay community and by gay people. I think it could also be argued that it has been extremely influential in changing public consciousness and shifting the limits of tolerance within at least the major Protestant churches. It also remains a vitally important place to stand for a Christian critique of the gay community.

It may be important for gays who are not Christians to understand that many gays who are would themselves want to make a critique of the gay community. At this point of dialogue it may be necessary to argue vigorously about what is prejudice and what is genuine critique. For there is no doubt that many of us who are Christian and gay would want to argue that there are aspects of the gay community, which the Christian, by her trust deeds, has to question radically. This may be heard by some gay people as a new outbreak of prejudices but in so far as it is with and for the gay community, I would argue that it is a legitimate exercise. Gay Christians would certainly want to raise questions about the increasing pressure that capitalism makes on gays: about the depersonalisation of the gay scene and the stereotyping of human personality that characterises much of the classified ads in *Gay News* and many other journals; about the use and abuse of gay pornography and especially the violent elements within it; about the male sexism that pervades whole areas of the commercial gay community; about ageism and the gay community's difficulties about older gays; about the whole range of issues that women have been pressing on the gay community. At all those points gay Christians would want to claim a necessary freedom because there are authentic Christians values and beliefs that question that institutional sexism, which sometimes seems to be developing within the gay community itself. There is a necessary ambivalence, judged against the Christian trust deeds, about many forms of gay culture. Questioning those forms is not prejudice or discrimination but an attempt to create those conditions in which gay people can be fully themselves in the whole of their humanity.

Discrimination and prejudice against gay people within the church and by the church has to be resisted by Christians in the name of a God of justice and truth. I believe that the institutional and structural sexism analysed here offers to society a mirror image of the way it operates itself. From that it is clear that discrimination and prejudice remain powerful forces within the church and society. Public opinion towards minority groups has a perverse way of changing suddenly and there is evidence from America that this is already happening. Institutional sexism within the church, whilst it remains unredeemed, will always provide a context to accommodate such perverse changes of opinion. Gay people and their allies cannot afford not to go on resisting that sexism. There needs to be a widespread debate within the gay liberation movement about where it is heading and gay Christians have to play their part in that. Too many gay people, including gay Christians, prefer their comfortable hopelessness to that vigorous debate. Their comfortable hopelessness is a dangerous illusion! So how is this renewed debate to happen within the churches?

Christianity and Christian action

First of all, the influence of gays on the church will depend very much on freeing themselves from a ghetto mentality. Gayness can and does become an obsession. When that happens gay people have little chance of imaginatively educating public opinion. Gay Christians need to identify and to take initiatives about a responsible dialogue with church people at all levels. There is evidence that when gay Christians publicly own their sexual life-style, attitudes change. An unnecessary dimension of alienation will remain between gay people and society at large unless gay people come out of their closet and break the silence of the ghetto. Constructive dialogue cannot be engaged in by those who cut themselves off from society.

Secondly, gay Christians need to develop a much tougher theological and ethical dialogue within the churches themselves. There is a temptation for campaigners to engage in moral exhortation at the expense of really confronting the theological questions about their sexual life-style at an equivalent level.

Thirdly, the processes of discrimination within the churches needs to be monitored and analysed much more carefully. No organisation has taken seriously the task of gathering, compiling and analysing specific evidence about particular cases of discrimination. Is it too optimistic to imagine that the gay liberation movement can find new resources to practise this monitoring alongside its work in other fields? Perhaps GCM needs to re-orientate radically in order to be able to do more of this monitoring itself.

Fourthly, gay Christians and their friends will need to be vigilant at all the levels described in this chapter and be ready to campaign on precise and specific issues. Deep-seated and destructive fears and phobias can only be countered by empathy and truthful confrontation. Gay Christians should not be deceived by the uneasy silence that has followed the great debates about homosexual people in some of the major churches. In some ways the silence arises out of pathological guilt; in other ways, out of impotent fear. Both need to be dealt with by the compassion of truth.

We must not, however, become ensnared in the darkness of festivals of light. For what they forget, but we must not, is that darkness and light exist together within ourselves. We shall make no progress if we disown our own darkness and project it all on to the church. There is an oppressor within each one of us and that oppressor perpetuates its own forms of prejudice and discrimination. As a Christian I experience that from some gay people. There is at least one gay bookshop that will not stock GCM publications! In any oppression, the oppressed can take on some of the characteristics of the oppressor. Gay people need to be liberated from prejudice as well. Unless we are, we may unwittingly feed that prejudice which manifests itself as discrimination and oppression. Prejudice can only be conquered by a love, expressed in the responsibility of our solidarity with our neighbour. Gay people must never hesitate to remind the church that we are made for love by Love and that that Love gives to every individual, irrespective of sexual orientation and life-style, a dignity that is infinite and indestructible. Only that will finally transform centuries of inequality in love.

Appendix 1: Public statements made by the churches

ROMAN CATHOLIC CHURCH *An Introduction to the Pastoral Care of Homosexual People* (Roman Catholic Social Welfare Commission, 1979). The last two popes have also made a number of public statements on the question of homosexual people.

METHODIST CHURCH *A Christian Understanding of Human Sexuality* (Methodist Conference, 1982).

ANGLICAN CHURCH *Homosexual Relations* (London, CIO Publishing, 1979).

BAPTIST CHURCH There have been no official public statements.

UNITED REFORMED CHURCH A group is working on human sexuality and hopes to publish its findings late in 1983.

PENTECOSTAL CHURCHES No known public statements.

BRITISH COUNCIL OF CHURCHES Rachel Moss (ed.), 'God's Yes to Sexuality' (Collins Fount, 1981). The BCC Assembly passed six Resolutions based on the report.

QUAKERS *Towards a Quaker View of Sex* (Friends Home Service Committee, 1963).

A number of other Christian and 'pseudo-Christian' bodies have made public statements. They include the Evangelical Alliance, the Church Society, the Church Union and the Nationwide Festival of Light.

Notes

1 '*la trahaison des clercs*' is the treachery of the opinion-formers of a society, of whom one group is the clergy.

2 Methodist Church Division of Social Responsibility, *A Christian Understanding of Sexuality*, 1982, p. 11.

3 Rabbi Lionel Blue, *Godly and Gay*, Gay Christian Movement, 1981, p. 15.

4 General Synod of the Church of England, *Report of Proceedings*, vol. 12, no. 1, February 1981, p. 435.

5 J. Boswell, *Christianity, Social Tolerance and Homosexuality*, University of Chicago Press, 1980, p. 333.

6 General Synod Board of Social Responsibility, *Homosexual Relations*, London, CIO Publishing, 1979, p. 50.

7 Elaine Willis, *Gay Pride Week Sermon*, Gay Christian Movement, 1982 (published by GCM, BM Box 6914, London WC1N 3XX).

9 THE MEDICAL PROFESSION
John Marshall

The medical and psychiatric professions have played a crucial role in the social control and oppression of homosexuality. We have been told that we are sick, disturbed, emotionally immature, genetically flawed and many other things. As a result, many people with homosexual feelings have viewed their position with a deep sense of anxiety, inferiority and inadequacy.

These pathological conceptions of homosexuality have obviously been challenged in recent years and many authorities would now endorse a rather different account. But the sickness theory is still deeply entrenched in many orthodox psychoanalytic circles and experiments continue to be carried out in behaviour modification. In addition, among the general population it is quite likely that many still regard homosexuality as a legitimate subject for medical concern. Certainly, a number of young people are advised by their parents to seek out medical help when they first become aware of their homosexual identity.

The purpose of this chapter is to trace the main historical themes of medical and psychiatric debate on homosexuality and to indicate the social and political significance of such debate in shaping ideas about homosexuality. It should be stressed that most theories have been based upon a curious mixture of social prejudice, dubious science and idle speculation. As such, these theories have little intrinsic merit although some have been used in an interesting way to challenge gay oppression. It should also be stressed that most attempts to 'cure' homosexuality have a poor record and are usually unsuccessful.[1]

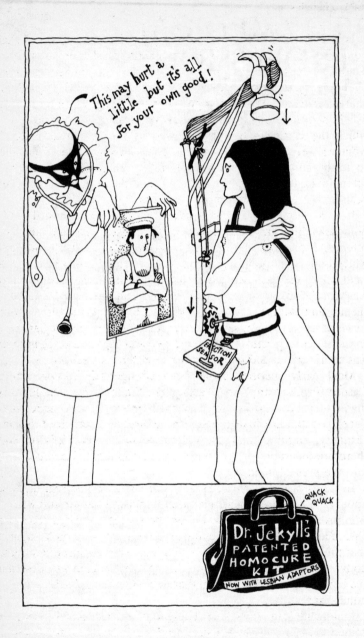

Early theories

It is important at the outset to recognise that our notion of 'the homosexual', as a specific type of person, is a relatively new idea. Traditionally, homosexuality was not even classified as a separate phenomenon and was certainly not regarded as the distinguishing characteristic of a particular type of person. Instead, homosexuality was lumped together with all other forms of non-procreative sex which the Christian tradition viewed as sin. All men (but not women) were thought capable of such sin unless carefully and judicially controlled. Sodomy was rather an ill-defined offence, often linked to fears about witchcraft, and the term was applied to both heterosexual and homosexual behaviour.[2]

It was only from the late nineteenth century onwards that homosexuality was increasingly defined as a separate kind of offence. Moreover, it began to be seen as a specific 'condition' which only some people possessed. As Jeffrey Weeks has argued (and others have shown), the emergence of the new conception was closely linked to the growth of medical science which, from the mid-nineteenth century, began to break down the various forms of non-procreative sex into a number of specific 'deviations'. In the process, homosexuality emerged as a separate category and was soon surrounded by a number of different theories.[3]

Most early theories came from continental Europe where Casper (in Germany) and Tardieu (in France) were the leading medico-legal experts just after the mid-century. It was Casper who developed the distinction between 'innate' and 'acquired' homo-sexuality, arguing that most homosexuality was inborn and therefore incurable. It was this view that dominated debates well into the present century.

In terms of initial ideas, however, the most influential theorist appears to have been Karl Heinrich Ulrichs, a lawyer and writer, who produced numerous works on the subject between 1862 and 1895. He accepted the congenital argument and went on to suggest that the male homosexual has a 'feminine soul enclosed in a male body'. Ulrichs coined the term 'urning' (or 'uranian') to describe the homosexual and he also elaborated a complex classification of homosexual types.

Meanwhile, in 1869, the Hungarian doctor K. M. Benkert coined the term 'homosexuality' to describe what he regarded as an inborn condition which it was foolish to punish as a crime. His term did not enter English usage until the 1890s and it took several decades before it was commonly employed. In the same year, 1869, Dr Karl Westphal adopted the phrase 'contrary sexual feeling' which he defined as a form of inborn moral insanity. This view had considerable influence and was taken up by a number of other theorists.

But the period's leading medical writer was Richard von Krafft-Ebing, a professor of psychiatry in Vienna, whose major work, *Psychopathia Sexualis: A Medico-Forensic Study*, first appeared in 1887. Initially, he argued that homosexuality was the result of hereditary weakness in the central nervous system which was always pathological. But by the end of his life he seemed prepared to accept that homosexuality was a harmless variation, compatible with psychic health. Following Ulrichs, he claimed that the male congenital urning was a feminised man (with 'feminine' interests) and that the female urning showed comparable 'masculine' traits. The condition was caused, he argued, by a genetic flaw in the human embryo which produced a peculiar form of psychic hermaphrodism.

During this period, various attempts were made to 'treat' homosexuality, notably in the work of Charcot and Magnan who claimed success with hypnosis. But by the end of the century the general opinion seemed to be that homosexuality was inborn and therefore incurable. Some writers, like the French psychologist Binet, disputed this claim and continued to argue that homosexuality was acquired by the influence of environment. But this argument was gradually defeated and homosexuality was largely explained by genetic predisposition.

These ideas were generally slow to be taken up in Britain but they did have a profound influence upon a number of different writers. The most influential English theorist of the period, Havelock Ellis, was cautious about the concept of an 'intermediate sex' but even he shared similar assumptions. His major statement on homosexuality, *Sexual Inversion*, first appeared in 1896 and it later formed the second volume of his *Studies in the Psychology of Sex*. Like most theorists, Ellis was keen to show that homosexuality was inborn, harmless and non-pathological. He was deeply committed to biological theories and was provided with a convenient explanation of homosexuality when hormones were discovered at the beginning of the century. In his later work, *Psychology of Sex* (1933), he summarised the main consensus of the period:

> In male inverts there is a frequent tendency to approximate to the feminine type, and in female inverts to the masculine type; this occurs in both physical and in psychic respects, and though it may be traced in a number of respects, it is by no means always obtrusive. Some male inverts, however, insist on their masculinity, while others are quite unable to say whether they feel more like a man or like a woman. Among female inverts, there is usually some approximation to the masculine attitude and temperament though this is by no means always conspicuous.[4]

Ellis also asserted the familiar view that male homosexuals are sensitive, above average intelligence, unable to whistle, and fond of the colour green.

Although many of these early theories were developed by people trained in medicine or psychiatry, it should be apparent that their general conclusions did not represent a 'sickness model' of homosexuality. As we have seen, some writers did accept a sickness theory but they were gradually defeated by the alternative stress on natural biological variation. However, the concept of an intermediate or 'third sex' did pave the way for extensive experiments in hormone treatment which continued throughout the twentieth century. In this sense, the liberal thrust of the early theories was ultimately undermined.

In terms of general ideas about sex and sexuality, however, the real significance of this early work was that it created, for the first time, a distinct notion of 'the homosexual' as a particular type of person. For scientists, at least, homosexuality was no longer seen as a widespread potential in all human beings but was seen instead as a definite peculiarity in a fixed and sometimes unfortunate minority. Even though the early theories were often positive, this conception of homosexuality does imply a basic acceptance of the heterosexual norm and it tends to avoid a genuine defence of homosexual experience. In addition, as Mary McIntosh argued in 1968, the categorisation has important consequences for the social control of homosexual behaviour.[5]

The social impact of Freud

By the mid-twentieth century, the major point of departure for theoretical and clinical research into homosexuality was Freud's *Three Essays on the Theory of Sexuality*, first published in 1905.[6] These essays, together with Freud's numerous other writings on psychoanalysis, established a new perspective on 'sexual deviations' and had a profound impact on popular notions of homosexuality.

Freud's early essay on homosexuality was a critical but tentative summary of the main themes to emerge from previous enquiries. In itself, it did not represent a fully fledged theory of homosexuality and it even showed a cautious respect for traditional biological assumptions. Nevertheless, the *Three Essays* did take the first few steps towards a new and dynamic psychological perspective on the subject of sexual inversion. Some important observations were added later, in the form of footnotes, and the theory developed as other ideas emerged from various writers.

One writer, Ferenczi, made a significant contribution towards these developments when he distinguished, in 1914, between 'subject/object homoerotics' and 'subject homoerotics'. The former, he claimed, are male inverts who think and behave like women and are usually sexually passive. The latter, by contrast, are completely masculine and usually take the active role in intercourse. According to him, it is only the first type who are true 'sexual intermediates' and their condition is likely to be irreversible. In the case of 'object homoerotics', however, he argued that we are dealing with otherwise 'normal' men who had merely changed their choice of sexual object. In such cases, he suggested, a change in sexual preference is always possible with psychiatric help.[7]

This distinction obviously cleared the ground for a radical change of emphasis away from 'third sex' theories. It was consistent with Freud's early views and encouraged theorists to concentrate more fully on the psychological determinants of sexual object choice. It also gave rise to a widespread distinction between 'active' and 'passive' male homosexuals which became very common during the 1950s and 1960s.

Within a rich web of emerging ideas, psychoanalysts usually argued that homosexuality is the product of unresolved psychic difficulties often associated with the oedipus complex. In brief, it was claimed that every boy has a close relationship with his mother and is unconsciously resentful and jealous of his father. This attachment to the mother has a sexual component which produces a powerful combination of incestuous desire and guilt. Those boys who grow up to be homosexual have been unable to resolve these oedipal difficulties. As a result, they become involved in a ceaseless flight from women who remind them, at an unconscious level, of their incest anxieties. Frequently, said Freud, narcissism plays a crucial role in the development of same-sex attachments. As he put it:

> In all the cases we have examined we have established the fact that the future inverts, in the earliest years of their childhood, pass through a phase of very intense but short-lived fixation to a woman (usually their mother), and that, after leaving this behind, they identify themselves with a woman and take *themselves* as their sexual object. That is to say, they proceed from a narcissistic basis, and look for a young man who resembles themselves and whom *they* may love as their mother loved *them*.[8]

Another factor arising from this scenario is an unconscious connection between women and castration anxiety. The point was emphasised by Fenichel in 1934:

> Psychoanalysis of homosexuals has . . . brought out the fact that homosexual men suffer from repressed memories, from castration anxiety arising from the perception of the female genitalia. . . . The sight of the female genitals may arouse in a boy a sense of disappointment or anxiety reactions connected with the castration complex in the following of two ways: first . . . the actual absence of a penis in a woman, i.e. the recognition that there are actually human beings without a penis, leads to the conclusion that one might also become such a being; in other words, old threats of castration may be revived by such observations. Secondly, the female genital, through the unconscious connection of castration anxiety with old oral anxieties, is perceived as an instrument which might bite or tear off the penis.[9]

As these views indicate, male sexual development was often the main focus of attention in psychoanalytic theory. In the early years, Freud seemed to believe that the theory of the oedipus complex, originally developed in connection with boys, could be easily translated in a similar way to girls. It was not until many years later that he became fully aware of the lack of symmetry between the sexes. Eventually, lesbianism was 'explained' by a complicated theory which emphasised an inverted oedipal complex and the added effects of so-called 'penis envy'.

One consequence of these theories was that sexual development came to be seen much more clearly as a psychological phenomenon and, as a result, the older biological theories were gradually superceded. This change of emphasis was due, in part, to the general development of psychology and the growing social tendency to explain 'deviant' behaviour as the complex outcome of psychological forces. In other words, many varieties of crime, delinquency and deviance were increasingly viewed as legitimate matters for psychological science rather than matters of morality.

In relation to homosexuality, this change of emphasis was also connected to several other factors. For example, during the first part of this century various experiments had taken place to test the 'third sex' theory. And by the early 1950s there seemed to be a general consensus that the theory was either wrong or inconclusive. As one writer put it:

> Instead of confirming the biological theory of homosexuality, studies of human intersexuals afford additional evidence that the direction of the sexual inclinations does not depend upon physical constitution.[10]

Similarly, experiments in endocrinology had failed to discover any significant relation between glandular disturbance and homosexuality. Reviewing the evidence for *The Practitioner* in 1954, Swyer concluded:

> The capacity for sexual response is not primarily dependent upon the sex hormones and the direction of sexual preference is influenced mainly by psychological and environmental conditioning.[11]

The same conclusion had also been reached by a number of other investigators. In this context, psychological theories increasingly filled the gap and they had the added benefit of appearing to explain the wide diversity of homosexual behaviour.

But there were also pressures which encouraged the spread of new psychological theories. During the 1950s Britain was hit by a 'moral panic' about male homosexual behaviour. The number of police prosecutions rose dramatically and there were a number of major 'scandals'. Earlier, in 1948, Alfred Kinsey had published his massive work *Sexual Behaviour in the Human Male* which showed conclusively that male homosexual conduct was much more widespread than had previously been believed. Consequently, the traditional tendency to ignore the subject had to be abandoned and there were also pressures to re-evaluate the older theories and stereotypes. Even newspapers began to break 'the last of the taboos' by discussing the issue openly and by challenging misconceptions.[12]

These developments served to heighten public awareness of male homosexuality and increased the pressure on the medical establishment to offer their own solutions. It was part of a discernible trend during the late 1940s and early 1950s to overcome what *The Practitioner* described as the 'reticence which has prohibited a frank discussion of sexual disorders, their cause and remedy, even in the medical press'.[13]

But the actual views being discussed in medical journals during the period were still rather confused. Writers often combined old ideas with a variety of new theories drawn mainly from psychoanalysis. In 1947, for example, Sir William Norwood East adopted crude psychoanalytic views when referring to a three-part process of personal growth (autoerotic, homosexual and heterosexual), and he felt that an arrest of development at the second stage was the most common cause of adult homosexuality. But he also referred to a 'general tendency towards perversion' (which exists in some people) and to the possibility that hereditary factors play some part. He also believed that seduction in youth was the most important environmental factor in male homosexuality and that such seduction may be encouraged if a boy is brought up in a 'girlish' manner.[14]

The influence of the psychoanalytic framework was also apparent in the numerous writings of Clifford Allen, a consultant psychiatrist, who seems to have been particularly important in promoting the trend. In his *Sexual Perversions and Abnormalities* (1949), for example, he outlined Freudian ideas and offered the following conclusion:

> From whatever point of view we regard sexual perversions we must admit that they are traceable, like the neuroses and psychoses, back to childhood and, far from being the result of an innate refusal to live normally and enjoy the sexual pleasures of the majority or an attempt to gain secret and sinister joys, they are the product of disease processes which have affected the mental life of the pervert.[15]

And he added:

> We shall see that in certain cases it is possible, by psycho-therapy, to reverse the process and allow the patient to return to normality.[16]

This emphasis on childhood inevitably led to a discussion of the oedipus complex and by 1958 (in *Homosexuality: Its Nature, Causation and Treatment*) Allen was listing the following four factors as the major causes of homosexuality: hostility to the mother; excessive affection for the mother; hostility to the father; and affection for the father when the father himself does not show sufficient heterosexual traits. Although these factors might appear contradictory, they were presented as different dimensions of the oedipal complex and amounted, in practice, to a single causal hypothesis which was often found in Clifford Allen's work. For example:

> One must admit that to grow up normally a boy must have a suitable man from whom he can learn normal reactions. The boy normally moulds his personality on his mother during the first few years of his life but then should unconsciously and even consciously copy his father. If he has no father, or his father is overshadowed by his mother, he cannot do so.[17]

This theory, which was frequently presented in this unsophisticated and unconvincing manner, was usually based on moral assumptions which regarded homosexuality as intrinsically undesirable. In various articles by Allen, his own value judgments were made absolutely clear, as in the following example:

> To the normal man a woman is such a desirable thing, so lovely in her shape and delightful in her ways, that it is incomprehensible that a man should reject her, and turn for his sexual pleasure to other men or even to grubby little boys.[18]

It is important to stress that this assumption of heterosexual superiority is not merely an example of incidental personal prejudice on the part of certain writers. It also indicates the main *theoretical* weakness of most psychoanalytic thought on homosexuality. For it was usually assumed that heterosexuality is so compelling that everyone naturally becomes heterosexual unless their psychosexual development is blocked or inhibited by oedipal anxieties or other factors. Homosexuality was thus defined in *negative* terms as an avoidance of heterosexuality or a 'ceaseless flight' from various unconscious fears. But as Tripp has argued, all sexual attraction is based on *positive* motives and positive sexual feelings. Unless this is clearly recognised, no theory can ever account for the enormous variety of human sexual response.[19]

Freud himself seems to have been aware of these complexities but his followers, like Clifford Allen, were usually naive by comparison. As a result, crude Freudian theories became part of popular opinion and persuaded many homosexuals that they really were the unfortunate victims of a serious sexual disorder.

Medical views and the struggle for law reform

The emergence of a moral panic in the early 1950s inspired repeated demands for an official enquiry into laws relating to homosexuality. By 1954 these demands were met when Sir John Wolfenden was appointed to chair a departmental committee on homosexuality and prostitution. It was the beginning of a widespread debate on homosexuality in which medical views were to play a crucial part.

Looking back at these debates, it is at once apparent that psychological theories – although extremely negative – actually provided the main rationale for 'progressive' views during the period. Despite their dubious quality, they allowed advocates of reform to challenge the view that homosexuality was a dangerous vice which ought to be punished as a crime. It was argued instead that homosexuality was a 'condition' (like being left-handed or colour blind, only worse) which deserves an element of sympathy and understanding.

The influence of psychological theories is seen most clearly in the progressive thrust of various religious publications which undoubtedly played an important role in creating a climate favourable to reform. The tone was set by an interim report in 1952 from the Church of England Moral Welfare Council, entitled *The Problem of Homosexuality*. It is significant that this report began by referring to 'the implications of psychological and other scientific knowledge about inversion in assessing moral guilt and in imposing punishment'.[20]

In the light of such considerations, the report managed to advocate reform whilst retaining its essentially conservative moral stand. It distinguished sharply between homosexuality as a 'condition' (which was held to be morally neutral) and homosexuality as a form of behaviour (which was thought to be always immoral but not justifiably criminal). It also covered a huge area of ambiguity by distinguishing between the 'genuine invert' (who was not responsible for his or her condition) and the so-called 'pervert' (who was basically 'normal' but nevertheless engaged in homosexual conduct). Needless to say, it was only the genuine invert who deserved a degree of help and understanding.

By 1956 the Church of England Moral Welfare Council had published a larger document, *Sexual Offenders and Social Punishment*, which was submitted as powerful evidence to the Wolfenden committee. Other religious documents, like *Towards a Quaker View of Sex*, were more outspoken and made a useful contribution towards the later spirit of reform. But in general terms, the real significance of shifts in religious opinion clearly lay in the capacity to use medical 'knowledge' as a means of re-evaluating traditional taboos without fundamentally departing from orthodox moral strictures. Homosexuality continued to be viewed as immoral but science allowed a small degree of tolerance for those individuals who were genuinely homosexual. It was this liberal compromise between 'new science' and 'old theology' that characterised the whole law reform movement and eventually ensured its limited success.

As part of this process, the direct evidence of the medical profession was obviously an important factor. Such evidence was presented to the Wolfenden committee from a number of different sources and was sometimes fairly progressive. But the report of the British Medical Association, entitled *Homosexuality and Prostitution*, probably offers the best indication of typical medical opinion. This report is interesting not only because it outlined the main themes of 'scientific' opinion but also because it drew heavily on religious perspectives and thereby showed the close mutual influence of the two most quoted professions.

The BMA report can hardly be described as progressive and it stubbornly resisted any pressures to advocate reform. Instead, it outlined the 'facts', reviewed the arguments and left the Wolfenden committee to draw its own conclusions. It distinguished between two types of homosexuality, essential and acquired, which was broadly similar to the invert/pervert distinction. Essential homosexuality was defined as either genetically determined or caused by early environmental influences such as an exaggerated emotional attachment to one parent. Acquired homosexuality included a range of casual homosexual behaviour which was not indicative of a basic predisposition.

The report acknowledged that the medical profession 'has no panacea to offer for the cure of homosexuality' but nevertheless offered much discussion about the various forms of treatment. It also recommended the establishment of special teams of workers to be available in both prisons and observation centres for the treatment and reformation of homosexual offenders. At certain points in the report, the underlying antipathy towards homosexuals was indicated by sudden moral outbursts. For example:

> Not only are their actual practices repulsive, but the behaviour
> and appearance of homosexuals congregating blatantly in
> public houses, streets and restaurants are an outrage to public
> decency. Effeminate men wearing make-up and using scent are
> objectionable to everyone.[21]

Despite this obvious hostility, it is quite clear that the main implication of the report was that male homosexual activities should be decriminalised, if only to avoid the undesirable effects of legal control and to encourage research and treatment. It was precisely in this spirit that the Wolfenden committee made its own recommendations in 1957, although it wisely avoided the contentious and sometimes melodramatic fervour of the British Medical Association.

It took ten years of struggle to implement the main proposals of the Wolfenden committee. Throughout the debates, medical opinion was always a crucial component of the reformist cause and this was nowhere more apparent than in the speeches of Leo Abse, one of the leading figures in the movement for law reform. In a speech to the House of Commons in 1966, for example, Abse adopted the following popular theory:

> A lad without a father, lacking a male figure with whom to identify, is sometimes left with a curse, for such it must be, of a male body encasing a feminine soul.[22]

In other speeches during the period, Abse elaborated the same theme and frequently gave the impression that he had been deeply influenced by the work of Clifford Allen. For all its weakness, it was an argument that eventually contributed to the Sexual Offences Act of 1967 and a limited degree of freedom for homosexual men.

The sickness theory

One consequence of medico-legal discussion about homosexuality appears to have been the widespread popular adoption of new forms of prejudice based upon notions of sickness. In October 1965, for example, a British National Opinion Poll published the results of a survey which showed that 93 per cent of those interviewed considered that homosexuals were in need of medical or psychiatric treatment. Despite this remarkable consensus, the same survey showed that a large minority (36 per cent) also believed that homosexual acts should remain criminal offences.[23] In this sense, for some people at least, the sickness theory seems to have compounded popular prejudice rather than to have offered a more 'humane' approach.

As we have seen, the sickness theory was advocated by some psychiatrists in Britain but its main international exponents were the American neo-Freudians, Edmund Bergler and Irving Bieber. In 1956 Bergler produced a hard-hitting, highly polemical work called *Homosexuality: Disease or Way of Life?* in which he argued that lesbians and gay men are the product of an 'unresolved masochistic conflict with the mother of earlist infancy'.[24] According to him, homosexuality is a 'neurotic disease' which is always accompanied by irrationality, psychic masochism, depression, malice and megalomania. He also claimed that for those patients who really want to change, a cure is possible through psychiatric therapy.

The main publication by Bieber and his colleagues, *Homosexuality: A Psychoanalytic Study*, appeared in 1962 and was a much more sober assessment. Nevertheless, it was deeply committed to the sickness theory and made strenuous efforts to prove it by detailed analysis of questionnaires given to 160 male homosexual patients. In typical fashion, the authors argued that homosexuality is caused by disturbed parent–child relationships which lead to 'hidden but incapacitating fears of the oppposite sex'.[25] Like Bergler, they also argued that many homosexuals can be cured.

This stress on sickness and disease was extremely influential and, as Wolfenden noted, was probably part of the general tendency to replace old concepts of immorality with new concepts of illness. But the sickness theory of homosexuality was not without its opponents. One such critic was Desmond Curran, a consultant psychiatrist and a liberal member of the Wolfenden committee, who carried out a survey in 1957 (with Denis Parr) of 100 male homosexuals seen in private practice. The results were published in the *British Medical Journal* and included the following observations:

> If homosexuality is a disease (as has often been suggested), it is in a vast number of cases mono-symptomatic, non-progressive, and compatible with subjective well-being and objective efficiency. In our series, both practising and non-practising homosexuals were on the whole successful and valuable members of society, quite unlike the popular conception of such persons as vicious, criminal, effete, or depraved.[26]

The influence of Desmond Curran was also seen in the Wolfenden report itself which flatly rejected the concept of disease.

Another significant critic of the sickness theory was Evelyn Hooker, the American social psychologist, who found no evidence of maladjustment in male homosexuals. In one study she matched small groups of homosexuals and heterosexuals (of the same age, education and intelligence), gave both groups standard personality tests, and asked two clinical psychologists to identify the homosexual in each pair. The judges were unable to do so and Hooker tentatively concluded that homosexuality as a clinical entity does not exist and that its forms are as varied as those of heterosexuality.[27]

But despite these challenges to the sickness theory, the mere fact that the medical profession was so deeply involved in discussion about homosexuality was sufficient to promote a public image of illness. After all, even doctors who rejected the sickness theory were regarding homosexuality as a 'problem' and were totally preoccupied by its psychological causes, its social abnormality and its therapeutic possibilities. If not a disease, homosexuality was at least seen as a legitimate subject for medical concern and an appropriate topic for medical expertise. For this reason it is significant that Michael Schofield, in a study published in 1960, reported that although 40 per cent of his respondents were too frightened or embarrassed to ask for help or advice, of those who did seek guidance, most went to a doctor.[28]

Clearly, once male homosexuality had been partially decriminalised in 1967, the main requirement was a fundamental challenge to the subtle forms of oppression which inevitably resulted from medical control. In Britain and America, this challenge arose in the late 1960s and early 1970s with the dramatic emergence of the modern gay movement.

Attacks on the medical model

Although the law has usually been the main focus of attention for homophile groups, it has often been recognised that major improvements are unlikely to be achieved by law reform alone. Consequently, gay activist groups in the United States (and later in Britain and elsewhere) began to attack other institutions which seemed to lie at the heart of our oppression.

An obvious target for this heightened sense of struggle was the psychiatric profession and its associated institutions which (as we have seen) claimed to be the ultimate authority on homosexuality. In America, from 1969, gay groups began to demonstrate at psychiatric conferences and they disrupted annual conventions of the American Psychiatric Association (APA). Largely as a result of these protests, a debate occurred within the profession which culminated, in December 1973, in an official decision of the APA to cease classifying homosexuality as a psychiatric disorder. A resolution was also passed which deplored all public and private discrimination against homosexuals, including the use of 'pejora-

tive connotations derived from diagnostic or descriptive terminology used in psychiatry' as the basis for such discrimination.[29]

These efforts in the United States were significantly influenced
by the broader intellectual climate which had produced a major
challenge to the whole concept of 'mental illness' and a powerful
critique of the psychiatric profession. R. D. Laing in Britain and
Thomas Szasz in America were among the most important writers
in what came to be known as the anti-psychiatry movement.
Thomas Szasz, in particular, was extremely influential in various
struggles against psychiatric concepts of homosexuality. In a book
published in 1970, for example, he compared traditional religious
mythology with the newer, but equally dangerous, secular mythology of psychiatric practice. He wrote:

> It is clear that psychiatrists have a vested interest in diagnosing
> as mentally ill as many people as possible, just as inquisitors had
> in branding them as heretics. The 'conscientious' psychiatrist
> authenticates himself as a competent medical man by holding
> that sexual deviants are mentally ill, just as the 'conscientious'
> inquisitor authenticated himself as a faithful Christian by
> holding that homosexuals were heretics. We must realise that in
> situations of this kind we are confronted, not with scientific
> problems to be solved, but with social roles to be confirmed.
> Inquisitor and witch, psychiatrist and mental patient, create
> each other and authenticate each other's roles.[30]

These views were important because they provided gay activists
with a strong intellectual rationale for their furious attacks on
psychiatry and they also forced psychiatrists to re-evaluate their
social role and to be more aware of their tacit value judgments. In
the United States, one consequence of these new debates was an
interesting shift in the publicly recognised 'experts' on homosexuality. In the 1967 edition of Freedman and Kaplan's textbook
on clinical psychiatry, for example, the chapter on homosexuality
was written by Irving Bieber, one of the leading advocates of the
sickness theory. But in the revised edition of 1975 the chapter was
written by Judd Marmor, a leading exponent of the 'alternative
life-style' viewpoint.[31]

During the early 1970s these developments began to have an
influence on the emerging gay movement in Britain. Anti-
psychiatry had been an important element in the general ideology

of gay liberation in America and this was reflected when these ideas were absorbed into Britain by a new generation of gays. This influence was seen most clearly when a gay Counter-Psychiatry Group was formed in London in 1971. It was an active group which, among other things, organised a Harley Street demonstration and also campaigned against David Reuben's book *Everything You Always Wanted to Know About Sex*. The group also published a pamphlet, *Psychiatry and the Homosexual*, which clearly illustrates the militant mood of the period:

> We are not in this pamphlet asking the medical profession for help. The sympathetic 'help' of liberal-minded psychiatrists can be as dangerous to our standing as human beings as was pre-Freudian condemnation. In fact we do not want a reformed medical attitude to homosexuality. We want there to be no medical attitude at all. Certainly GPs should have a better knowledge of gay people, but only in the same way as they should be informed on local housing and employment, fields where they claim no expertise. To call for medical schools to train doctors as experts on gay people is to ask for future generations of homosexuals to be stigmatised as objects of medical attention. In the same way, we do not want psychiatrists to *correct* their chapters on homosexuality, but to *omit* them. However tolerant their attitudes, the very presence of such chapters in psychiatric textbooks perpetuates the false connection between homosexuality and medicine.[32]

It was this mood which inspired gay activists to make occasional protests at medical or psychiatric conferences. In November 1972, for example, the London Medical Group held a symposium on aversion therapy as part of a two-part course on punishment and treatment. The meeting was not open to the public but one gay man, Peter Tatchell, managed to gain admission. In an angry mood, Tatchell intervened during speeches from Professor Hans Eysenck and Dr Isaac Marks and was eventually ejected from the meeting.[33]

Other protests occurred in 1974 at a conference in Bradford organised by the British Medical Association. About fifty members of the Gay Liberation Front and the Campaign for Homosexual Equality disrupted the meeting for an hour, complaining bitterly about negative medical responses to homosexuality. Reflecting the fashion for 'radical drag', Don Milligan, a member of Bradford GLF, wore a long blue velvet dress embroidered with sequins.[34]

Meanwhile, conventional scholars were joining the debate and in 1979 an important contribution was made by Masters and Johnson, the leading contemporary sex therapists. In their book, *Homosexuality in Perspective*, they stressed the functional equivalence of heterosexuality and homosexuality, as well as insisting that homosexuality cannot be classified as a psychiatric disease. The same theme was also echoed by a number of other writers.

Clearly, the combined efforts of liberal scholars, gay liberation and the anti-psychiatry movement has been sufficient to create a much more careful approach to homosexuality in recent years. There appears to be greater sensitivity to the social and moral issues involved in the diagnosis of deviant behaviour as illness and, as a consequence, the sickness theory is now less frequently heard. But there has also been an important element of resistance to these ideas, particularly in conservative areas of psychoanalysis. Likewise, behaviourists have largely been able to avoid the objections of the gay movement and have continued to experiment with various forms of behaviour modification.

Treatment perspectives today

The work of John Bancroft, a behaviourist psychiatrist, provides a good illustration of the way in which new ideas have failed to prevent some of the older methods of treatment. In his book, *Deviant Sexual Behaviour*, Bancroft begins with a clear assessment of medical prejudice and its role in the treatment of homosexuality. He acknowledges that attitudes towards homosexuality are culturally variable and that the medical profession in our own society has been deeply influenced by a long tradition of social hostility. To this extent, he is acutely aware of the newer critical responses to psychiatric practice. But despite this awareness, he argues that there will continue to be a number of individuals who are severely distressed by their sexual preferences and that doctors or clinical psychologists can help such people ('for impeccable reasons') to modify their behaviour.[35]

Bancroft goes on to describe different forms of behaviour therapy which he, and other practitioners, continue to use with varying degrees of success. Perhaps the best known form of behaviour modification is aversion therapy which actually includes a wide variety of methods. In some cases (for male homosexuals) an image of a male figure is combined with the injection of chemicals which produce a state of nausea and vomiting. The method is described by McConaghy:

> For the first treatment 1.5 mg of apomorphine were adminis-
> tered by sub-cutaneous injection, and after five minutes a slide
> of a nude or semi-nude male was projected on the wall of the
> room within the patient's vision. If the nausea produced by the
> apomorphine was not sufficiently unpleasant, the dose was
> increased with subsequent injections up to 6 mg. Severe nausea
> lasting about ten minutes without vomiting was considered a
> satisfactory response.[36]

A similar method involves the use of unpleasant electric shocks which act as the noxious stimuli. According to Bancroft, electric shock treatment has been the most common form of aversion therapy since the early 1960s. He describes some of the usual methods:

> The deviant stimulus (e.g. slide of the deviant sexual object) is
> presented to the subject and immediately followed by an
> unpleasant electric shock. This procedure is repeated many
> times. This is best exemplified in one of the methods of
> treatment of homosexuality reported by Feldman and
> MacCulloch. The patient watched a screen and at intervals a
> slide of an attractive male was displayed. In the last half second
> of the two-second period the subject received a shock. The slide
> and shock were terminated simultaneously. Approximately 24
> such trials were involved in each session which lasted about 20
> minutes.
>
> Mandel has used a form of classical conditioning procedure in
> which the noxious stimulus is more easily related to the deviant
> stimulus. Slides of an attractive homosexual partner were
> shown and, as soon as the subject indicated sexual interest a
> second slide, showing 'nauseous running sores', was super-
> imposed on the first. The procedure was contrasted with the
> projection of slides of attractive women unassociated with any
> unpleasant stimuli.[37]

Bancroft's own work has usually involved experiments which produce an electric shock in response to signs of sexual arousal in the penis. The procedure is as follows:

> The patient is shown a slide or picture of deviant sexual interest (e.g. an attractive man in the case of a homosexual), and is asked, while looking at the picture, to imagine himself in a sexually exciting situation with the person in the picture. Erectile changes are measured by means of a penis plethysmo-graph and when an erectile change reaches a predetermined level a shock is given . . . following the first shock a further burst of three shocks was given if after 15 seconds the erectile response was not acually falling and was still above the criterion level.[38]

There are numerous other methods of behaviour modification, all of which can be equally distressing for the patient. Although some success is claimed with such methods it is clear from the literature that many patients gain no apparent benefit from behaviour modification.

One distinguishing characteristic of behaviourist methods is that therapists need not regard the deviant behaviour as either pathological or intrinsically undesirable. As Bancroft tries to show, the therapist merely seeks to modify behaviour which, for whatever reason, is unwanted by the patient. In this sense, it is implied that behaviourism itself is morally and medically neutral. However, it should be apparent that this position is dangerously simplistic and does not absolve the therapist from crucial ethical questions. Yet such questions are not usually posed by researchers within this field.

Unlike behaviourists, psychoanalysts often continue to regard homosexuality not only as treatable but also as perverted and pathological. An American psychoanalyst, Charles Socarides, is probably the leading contemporary exponent of the sickness theory and he (along with Bieber) was extremely active in the debates which occurred within the American Psychiatric Association in 1973. Although he was ultimately defeated, Socarides continues to write about homosexuality from a sickness perspective. His latest major work on the subject, *Homosexuality*, appeared in 1978 and he has also contributed to a textbook on sexual deivation which was published in Britain in 1979. The following quotation is taken from the latter work and provides a clear indication of his views:

> . . . homosexuality of the obligatory type must be acknow-
> ledged as a psychosexual disorder, for which therapy is not only
> possible but necessary since the condition requires careful
> psychoanalytic attention. One's compassion for the plight of the
> homosexual, his responsiveness as a patient, and his value as a
> human being in interaction with the scientific challenge and
> fulfilment posed by his intrapsychic conflicts, leads to a
> mutuality of gratitude and satisfaction between patient and
> psychoanalyst, which well justifies the commitment to the
> attempted alleviation of this important and serious disorder.[39]

This view might appear rather eccentric but it does indicate the clear persistence of sickness theories within psychoanalysis. Fortunately, it is a view that is becoming less influential as the lobby to demedicalise homosexuality becomes increasingly successful.

Other methods of treatment have been used in the past as an alternative to prison for homosexual offenders. But since 1967, when adult male homosexuality was decriminalised, these methods tend to have been reserved for paedophile offenders. Although it has involved relatively few prisoners, experiments with hormone treatment have been carried out since 1963 in some British prisons and special hospitals. The usual procedure is for a small pellet of hormone oestradiol to be gradually absorbed into the body after being implanted under the skin. The result is a decline in sexual desire and eventual loss of potency. The implant has to be renewed every few months but whilst active it amounts to a form of chemical castration. An alternative method is surgical castration which usually involves the removal of part of the testes and the prostrate gland.[40]

Hormone treatment in England (as elsewhere) has often led to the development of breasts in men which have had to be surgically removed. Partly because of these side-effects it was reported in 1980 that this form of treatment has now been abandoned in London prisons.[41] A less dramatic method of treatment for sex offenders is group psychotherapy or individual psychiatric attention which is available at some penal institutions and special hospitals in Britain. Behaviour modification has also attracted some attention from prison staff but does not appear to have been widely used.

Attitudes of general practitioners

Although this chapter has been concerned primarily with the views of 'experts' or 'specialists' on homosexuality, the role of the general practitioner is often equally important. Such doctors are unlikely to have received special instruction on homosexuality but their moral and medical judgments can sometimes have severe consequences for homosexual patients. This was illustrated in the winter of 1979–80 when Geoffrey Brighton, a student at Leeds University, applied to train as a teacher. As a matter of routine the student was required to pass a medical examination before being accepted. His doctor found him physically fit but felt unable to issue a medical certificate because the patient's medical record indicated that he was homosexual. A certificate was therefore refused unless the student agreed to see a psychiatrist.

The case received considerable publicity and provoked some angry reactions. A representative of MIND, the National Association for Mental Health, expressed 'extreme disappointment' that the student had been referred to a psychiatrist 'as if homosexuality was a mental illness'.[42] In response to such criticism, the head of the student health service tried to justify the decision as follows:

> It's a question of trying to assess a person from a medical and teaching point of view. Is he a menace to the pupils? This is obviously a consideration, just as it would be if he drank like a fish.[43]

This reaction obviously reflects some widespread misconceptions about both male and female homosexuality. But how common are such attitudes among general practitioners? As an initial attempt to discover current opinions, I recently conducted a small survey of general practitioners in an English provincial town. The purpose of the survey was to find out, in a very general way, the different conceptions of homosexuality typically held by doctors. Do they consider it to be an illness, a perversion or a natural form of sexual variation? Does homosexuality *per se* require treatment? Should patients with problems related to homosexuality be referred to a psychiatrist or to one of the many gay self-help groups which now exist throughout the country?

In addition, an attempt was made to discover the general moral attitudes of doctors towards their homosexual patients. Do doctors feel that a person's homosexuality renders him or her unfit to be employed in certain occupations? Would doctors feel tempted to break the usual promise of confidentiality by informing a third person of a patient's homosexuality?

In order to find some tentative answers to these questions, a list was compiled of all general practitioners operating in a small town in the south of England. A brief questionnaire was then sent to each doctor. Of forty-five doctors contacted, thirty-two (71 per cent) completed and returned the questionnaire. Clearly, we are in no position to know the views of those doctors who failed to reply but it might be reasonable to suppose that non-respondents had less than favourable views. If this is the case, we should recognise that the results of the survey might be rather misleading. Nevertheless, the survey was interesting and produced some instructive answers.

Among those doctors who completed the questionnaire, it emerged that only one felt that homosexuality is a disease. The majority (75 per cent) felt that homosexuality is a natural form of sexual variation. Some doctors gave other answers and these are shown in Table 1.

Table 1: Conceptions of homosexuality

disease	1
maladjustment of psychosexual development	1
perversion	2
unnatural sexual variation	3
mental weakness	1
natural sexual variation	24

A similar size majority felt that homosexuality *per se* does not require medical treatment. Of six doctors who answered that homosexuality *does* require treatment, only three specified a particular form or forms of treatment. These included group therapy, hormone treatment, abreaction and 'advice and encouragement to act normally'.

Although these answers indicate what might be regarded as a generally favourable attitude towards homosexuality, it is significant that seventeen doctors (53 per cent) felt that a person's homosexuality might be a reason for exclusion from certain occupations. The occupations mentioned are listed in Table 2.

Table 2: Occupations potentially unsuitable for homosexuals

Occupation	Number of times mentioned
teaching	5
all work with children or young people	11
civil and diplomatic service	3
armed forces	2
police	1
security work	1
nursing	1
social work	1

Obviously, some doctors mentioned more than one occupation. A total of *fifteen* respondents (47 per cent) mentioned school teaching or other work with children. However, not all homosexuals were thought to be a danger to children: paedophiles, pederasts, and 'child-oriented' homosexuals were singled out in five cases where work with children was mentioned. In the other ten cases no such distinction was made. One doctor even offered the novel idea that homosexuals are likely to suffer great psychological traumas in voluntarily suppressing their homosexuality when working in jobs with children.

In another question doctors were asked about referral in cases where a patient has difficulty in accepting his or her own homosexuality. Various answers were given and some doctors understandably wished to keep their options open. However, a total of sixteen doctors stated a preference for referral to a psychiatric practitioner. A further nine doctors wished to keep this as an option. Only three doctors stated a preference for referral to a gay self-help group although eight other doctors mentioned this as a possibility.

On the issue of confidentiality, a large proportion of doctors reported that they would definitely not inform a third person of a patient's homosexuality. But eight doctors replied that they might consider disclosure. Of these, five stated that they might inform a third person if the patient is in a position of trust with children.

One doctor said that he would inform the patient's employing authority. Another replied that he would only inform a third person if there was a medico-legal problem.

In general terms, the survey seemed to indicate that although doctors are not particularly prone to the sickness theory, they have been deeply influenced by the strong association which wrongly exists between homosexuality and sexual attraction to children. Even when doctors made an explicit distinction between paedophiles and pederasts, and 'adult-oriented' homosexuals, the fact that these categories were mentioned is in itself revealing. Presumably, a questionnaire on heterosexuality would not produce warnings about 'child-oriented' heterosexuals, despite the fact that most sexual offences involving children are *heterosexual* offences. It is also significant that these fears about children could lead to a betrayal of confidence by a sizeable minority of doctors.

Summary and conclusion

In this chapter I have traced the main historical themes of medical and psychiatric debate on homosexuality. We have seen that the original theories, dating from the late nineteenth century, were largely positive although they conceptualised 'the homosexual' in gender terms as an 'intermediate sex'. It was largely the influence of Freud which created a break from this tradition and a new concept of the homosexual, defined in terms of sexual orientation. Although Freud was an imaginative theorist, many of his ideas have been crudely employed by numerous other writers who created a notion of the homosexual as a sick or disordered person. Such ideas were highly influential and even contributed, in an ironic way, to the spirit of law reform.

Since the late 1960s, the combined influence of liberal scholars, anti-psychiatry and the gay movement itself has created an important lobby to demedicalise homosexuality and thus pave the way for a major challenge to heterosexist assumptions. This lobby has been very successful but there remains a considerable element of resistance to these ideas. Gay men and lesbians can still suffer the crippling effects of aversion therapy or the humiliation of psychiatric treatment. In addition, our evidence suggests that discrimination still occurs within hospitals (see pp. 15–16) and that prejudice is still common among many general practitioners.

Clearly, the medical profession still occupies an important place in the maintenance of gay oppression. We must therefore emphasise the continuing need to challenge medical authority both by action within the gay movement and by the creation of debate within the profession itself. After a century of largely negative medical ideology, our task, as always, remains formidable.

Notes

1   See C. A. Tripp, *The Homosexual Matrix*, London, Quartet, 1975, ch. 11.

2   See Alan Bray, *Homosexuality in Renaissance England*, London, Gay Men's Press, 1982.

3   Jeffrey Weeks, *Coming Out: Homosexual Politics in Britain from the 19th Century to the Present*, London, Quartet, 1977. Other historical accounts appear in Arno Karlen, *Sexuality and Homosexuality*, London, Macdonald, 1971; Vern Bullough, *Sexual Variance in Society and History*, Chichester, Wiley, 1976; John Lauritsen and David Thorstad, *The Early Homosexual Rights Movement (1864–1935)*, New York, Times Change Press, 1974. For a full discussion of the emergence and character of the homosexual category see the essays in Kenneth Plummer (ed.), *The Making of the Modern Homosexual*, London, Hutchinson, 1981.

4   Havelock Ellis, *Psychology of Sex*, London, Heinemann, 1933, p. 199.

5   Mary McIntosh, 'The homosexual role', 1968, reprinted in Kenneth Plummer (ed.), *The Making of the Modern Homosexual*, London, Hutchinson, 1981.

6   Sigmund Freud, 'Three essays on the theory of sexuality', first published in 1905, in *On Sexuality*, Pelican Freud Library, 1977.

7   S. Ferenczi, *First Contributions to Psycho-Analysis*, London, Hogarth Press, 1952, Ch. XII.

8   Sigmund Freud, 'Three essays', op. cit., p. 56.

9   O. Fenichel, *Outline of Clinical Psychoanalysis*, London, Kegan Paul, 1934.

10 D. J. West, *Homosexuality*, London, Duckworth, 1955, p. 70.

11 G. I. M. Swyer, 'Homosexuality: the endocrinological aspect', in *The Practitioner*, vol. 172, 1954, pp. 374–7.

12 See Hugh Cudlipp, *At Your Peril*, London, Weidenfeld & Nicholson, 1962.

13　*The Practitioner*, vol. 158, 1947.

14　W. Norwood East, 'Homosexuality', in *The Medical Press*, 3 September 1947.

15　Clifford Allen, *Sexual Perversions and Abnormalities*, Oxford University Press, 1949.

16　Ibid.

17　Clifford Allen, *Homosexuality: Its Nature, Causation and Treatment*, St. Albans, Staples Press, 1958, pp. 47–8.

18　Clifford Allen, 'The meaning of homosexuality', *International Journal of Sexology*, vol. VII, no. 4, May 1954.

19　C. A. Tripp, *The Homosexual Matrix*, London, Quartet, 1975.

20　Church of England Moral Welfare Council, *The Problem of Homosexuality*, Church Information Board, 1952.

21　*Homosexuality and Prostitution*, British Medical Association, 1955.

22　Hansard, vol. 731, col. 262.

23　*Daily Mail*, 28 October 1965.

24　Edmund Bergler, *Homosexuality: Disease or Way of Life?*, New York, Hill & Wang, 1956.

25　Irving Bieber, *Homosexuality: A Psychoanalytic Study*, New York, Basic Books, 1962.

26　Desmond Curran and Denis Parr, 'Homosexuality: an analysis of 100 male cases seen in private practice', *British Medical Journal*, 6 April 1957.

27　Evelyn Hooker, 'Male homosexuality in the rorschach', *Journal of Protective Techniques*, vol. 22, 1958, pp. 18–31.

28　Gordon Westwood, *A Minority*, London, Longmans, 1960.

29　See Malcolm Spector, 'Legitimizing homosexuality', in *Society*, July/August 1977, pp. 52–6.

30　Thomas Szasz, *The Manufacture of Madness*, New York, Harper & Row, 1970.

31　I owe this point to Malcolm Spector: see note 29.

32　*Psychiatry and the Homosexual*, Gay Liberation Information Service, 1978 (first published 1973).

33　See *Gay News*, no. 11, 1972.

34　*Guardian*, 14 September 1974.

35　John Bancroft, *Deviant Sexual Behaviour: Modification and Assessment*, Oxford, Clarendon Press, 1974.

36　N. McConaghy, 'Subjective and penile plethysmograph responses following aversion-relief and apomorphine aversion therapy for homosexual impulses', *British Journal of Psychiatry*, vol. 115, 1967, pp. 723–30. Quoted by Bancroft, op. cit., pp. 33–4.

37　Bancroft, op. cit., p. 36.

38　Bancroft, op. cit., pp. 39–40.

39 Charles Socarides, 'The psychoanalytic theory of homosexuality with special reference to therapy', in I. Rosen (ed.), *Sexual Deviation*, Oxford University Press, 1979.
40 See Sean McConville, 'What fit punishment?' in Brian Taylor (ed.), *Perspectives on Paedophilia*, London, Batsford, 1981.
41 *Guardian*, 29 March 1980.
42 Quoted in the *Yorkshire Post*, 11 January 1980.
43 Quoted in the *New Statesman*, 11 January 1980.

10 THE MEDIA
Keith Howes

Introduction

Mae West thinks they are going to take over. Black American leader Huey Newton considers them more oppressed than the blacks. *They* are gay and 'Gay is Good' proclaims the slogan of Britain's 'fastest growing revolutionary movement' — the Gay Liberation Front.

This is the opening paragraph of an article entitled 'Don't Waste Your Sympathy!', which appeared in *She* magazine in February 1971. It remains one of the few pieces to have tackled the subject of the British gay movement — and the discrimination it seeks to remove — in a national mass circulation publication.

The article's words are supportive, challenging, even angry. Yet the writer treats the subject with the rapturous awe of an anthropologist discovering a lost Amazon tribe. Which is strange because the writer himself was — and is — gay. However, the 'I' directing the reader's attention and sympathies could not allow himself to become the 'me' and, in the process, possibly encourage active identification instead of breezy curiosity or morbid prurience.

'What Gay Liberation Front wants is acceptance for homosexuals — no more, no less', rang the sub-head; 'Keith Howes investigates.' It's only now, from the vantage point of eight years living as an openly gay man, that I can fully appreciate just how much I had been duped into believing that people like myself were something 'other', and how I, in turn, had short-changed and indirectly deceived gays and heterosexuals alike through a pretence of objectivity.

The justification for my 'friendly neutrality' towards a subject directly related to my own emotional feelings and experience was, apart from wanting to 'protect' my then lover (who was a child psychotherapist) that I was involved in quality journalism for an informed readership. Therefore there was no need to dot the 'i's and cross the 't's. Was there?

I now see that 'quality' and 'informed' were misnomers. The readership in this context was mainly ignorant; and by not aligning myself with my subjects I was further endorsing the media's view of life as being 99.9 per cent heterosexual. I was giving the public what it supposedly wanted: generalisations, simplifications and nonsensical divisions between groups of people. To enable them to respond to something that was new and complex, I presented them with the comfortable fiction that gays were a sub-species, abnormal in a normal world; Them not Us. A successful piece of sleight-of-hand fitting perfectly within the mythology Anna Durell describes so aptly in Chapter 1.

This chapter will attempt to describe, in a necessarily compressed form, the mass media's image and coverage of us over the past thirty years; and also how they have adapted their particular view of human behaviour to our more openly expressed needs and demands.

Stereotypes: good for a laugh

The titles *have* changed. For *Tea And Sympathy, The Third Sex, The Loudest Whisper, Serious Charge* and *Victim* now read *Coming Out, Making Love, Partners, Cruising* and *Another Way*. Where once we were *One In Twenty* (according to the title of Bryan Magee's 1965 book) we are now *One In Five* (if we are to believe Channel 4's 1983 gay entertainment show). Much has happened to effect this change, but as far as a large part of the mass public is concerned (and the media which serves it) the homosexual remains what he (rarely she) has always been − or rather what he became in the depressed, rigid, suspicious culture of post-war Britain.

To inspect examples of the 1950s-style 'queer' and 'dyke' you need do no more than go and see *The Mousetrap*, now in its thirty-somethingth year in London. There, on stage, is a tippy-toes homosexual: artistic, neurotic, immature. He loves nursery rhymes, messing about in the kitchen and flirting with policemen. His opposite number is a 'masculine' young woman in tweeds: gruff, anti-social and troubled.

These persistent and unbudgeable stereotypes, in whom 'effeminacy' and 'butchness' are inaccurately but inextricably linked with same-sex attraction and feelings, are derived from the music hall era, although they are to be found in most forms of popular entertainment down the centuries.

Blond-wigged and velvet-coated, Sid Field primped and pouted grotesquely in his classic 'Portrait Study' sketch ('Oh – I am *so* happy!'), while Max Miller, removing his ankle-length coat to reveal an exotic floral suit, would challenge his audience with an unabashed 'What if I am?'[1]

Sid Field and Max Miller were two of the greatest influences on the comedians who learnt their craft during the late 1940s and early 1950s. These included Frankie Howerd, Stanley Baxter, Kenneth Williams, Benny Hill, John Inman, Larry Grayson and the late Dick Emery. While the others incorporated effeminate inflexions, to a greater or lesser degree, in their stage personas, Dick Emery used them, undiluted, for only one of his many impersonations, namely Clarence, an over-dressed, flirtatious theatrical dresser whose come-on to (heterosexual) men was 'Hello, Honky Tonk!'

Such humour was, Dick Emery admitted, essential both for survival, and as a means of releasing what may be a peculiarly British tension:

> most comedians recognize that by becoming a little precious they can raise an instant laugh – a useful ploy in cabaret, for instance, when you're faced with an unresponsive audience staring blankly at you across their plates of steak and chips. Why the suggestion of homosexuality should be funny is an imponderable – perhaps our laughter is a defence, a reaction against hidden fears about our innermost tendencies.[2]

This collective vision of homosexual men as effeminate, ineffectual, pretentious, asexual buffoons was polished (or scuffed) during the 1950s by comedians whose popularity, enormously amplified by radio, television and films, has in many instances held firm into the 1980s. Their ranks have been increased by Freddie Starr, Ronnie Barker, Ronnie Corbett, Cannon and Ball; and by countless others, professional and amateur, across the country. The brittle voice, girlish giggle, hand on hip, limp wrist, mincing walk with protruding bottom can be seen and heard in cabaret, seaside shows, working men's clubs, pubs, offices and on factory floors. Often the formularised mannerisms are coupled with jokes about not turning your back or being careful when they measure your inside leg. Occasionally the gags embrace other minorities. Have you heard the one about the Irish queer? He went out with a woman.

Some people used this 'camp' comedy tradition to question assumptions about British life: its precise rules of conduct and the roles it demands we adopt. Spike Milligan was one, cleverly circumnavigating the BBC's censorship of any mention or depiction of effeminacy (just one of many taboos). In the early days of *The Goon Show* there was just a stock pansy, Flower Dew ('I could be *sick*!'); later, Milligan employed more subtlety in the relationship between the seedily suave Grytpype-Thynne and the taciturn, dishevelled Moriarty. They lived together.

> Grytpype-Thynne: You'll pardon the mess; we can't help it really; we're bachelors.
> Neddy Seagoon: Why don't you get married?
> Grytpype-Thynne: *I* would, but Moriarty doesn't love me.[3]

Outside these occasional signals received through Milligan's comic iconoclasm, the general public (heterosexuals and homosexuals alike) only 'knew' about sexual deviants from the mysterious language they were rumoured to speak, and by their appearance: suede shoes, long hair and perfume for the men; collar and tie, short hair and Brylcreem for the women. If anyone within the media had met anyone who didn't correspond with either image they weren't letting on; not that they would have been allowed to anyway. We were the phantoms of the night, denizens of the dark and the pages of the *News of the World*: vicars, guardsmen, scoutmasters, artists, spies.

It took the *Sunday Mirror*, in response to the Vassall spy case, to put the public wise in a double-page spread, 'How to spot a possible homo'. Now that long hair and bright colours were beginning to become fashionable for men, and women were wearing trousers and boots, the time had come to revise the criteria for our identificaton. 'Dropped eyes', 'shifty glances', 'a fondness for the theatre': all dead giveaways according to the *Sunday Mirror* (26 April 1963). Not surprisingly this kind of journalism helped maintain a climate of fear and loathing which Julian Meldrum chillingly recreates in Chapter 4 on violence against gay people. Yet some kind of thaw in the permafrost had already begun.

Post-Wolfenden: a new image

With the publication of the Wolfenden report in September 1957, the public and the media were asked to change their perspectives on homosexuality. From being a quagmire of unspeakable and unshowable villainies, it was now a pit of loneliness, sickness and blackmail. Television was quick to respond with a number of studio discussions in which 'experts' (psychiatrists, policemen, bishops and doctors) discussed our 'condition'. Also present at each sitting would be one or two men with their backs to the camera or in silhouette. They would haltingly vouch for the irrevocability of their condition, the blackmail to which it exposed them, and their utter wretchedness. A bleak picture, but at least it brought the subject into wide public debate. Previously, its only detailed consideration had been mainly within the pages of criminology and abnormal psychology journals, and rarified novels.

Then, in 1961, came *Victim*. Using a thriller plot and Britain's most popular leading man, Dirk Bogarde, the film delineated a wide range of male homosexuals: young, middle-aged, elderly; professional, labourer, artist; used car salesman, politician, hairdresser; 'butch', 'effeminate', 'normal'. Behind every line of dialogue lay out-and-out propaganda for a change in what its makers, like the Wolfenden committee, regarded as a cruel and unjust law. Backed by the Rank Organisation, *Victim* was an effective tool in helping to modify so-called informed public opinion. It remains a fascinating record of attitudes of the period, many of which are, regrettably, still with us.

Victim was one of a number of impeccably liberal films of the early 1960s, both here and in America, in which homosexual women and men paid their dues to society through unrequited love and subsequent (heterosexual) rebuff, loneliness, suicide, murder, or a broken marriage. In return, they received sympathy and understanding.[4]

There were exceptions, notably the stage plays (later filmed in the more accommodating 1970s) of Joe Orton. The pagan and sharply discordant black comedies *Loot* and *Entertaining Mr Sloane* continue to jolt audiences by their blithe amorality, and their prescient paranoia about the British police. The plays could only have been written by a happily gay man in response to an irrational and emotionally repressed society. They have survived better than most 'gay plays' of the period (1964–7), with the possible exception of Charles Dyer's *Staircase* (about two bickering hairdressers) and the then pro-homosexual John Osborne's *A Patriot For Me* (an uncompromising portrait of a homosexual officer blackmailed into espionage).

Orton's influence may have been abroad in BBC radio when Light Programme listeners suddenly found themselves assailed, at 2.30 p.m. on Sundays, by a mysterious language – *the* mysterious language of homosexuals. Words like 'varda', 'eek', 'fantabulosa' and 'bona' began to exercise a wide pull and fascination which their originators (gypsies and travelling players) wouldn't have been able to credit. Very quickly after the first broadcast in 1965 phrases such as 'Get you, duckie' and 'Oo, in 'e bold!' echoed across the airwaves into a large part of the nation's consciousness.

Posturing and squealing, Julian and his 'friend' Sandy were unquestionably caricatures, if not stereotypes. They straddled the old and the new concepts of homosexuals: the camp repartee, full of sexual innuendo crossed with an assertiveness and strong self-identity. Like the rest of *Round The Horne*, Jules and Sand brought into question, as the Goons had done, the British obedience to codes of dress, behaviour, patriotism, manliness and femininity. They became the popular idea of the male gay couple.

In the same year, gay women also became typecast, thanks to a play by Frank Marcus called *The Killing Of Sister George*. The central character, a radio soap opera star on the skids, fitted neatly into the brusque, tweedy mould represented by 'Miss Casewell' in *The Mousetrap*. Yet 'George' had vitality, vulnerability and honesty: she was recognisably human. Her girlfriend, by contrast, was manipulative and fey. Childie by name, childlike by nature, she was probably just a pretty girl looking for the right man to take care of her. In the meantime, she was happy to accept the devotion and attention of a surrogate mother/father.

Together, the mature, 'mannish' protectress and the pliable, 'feminine' child/woman stepped out of the play to become the template of a lesbian relationship until the present day. The image was consolidated by a sensationalised Hollywood film version. This odd couple could be seen over the years that followed in films like *Les Biches* or on television in episodes of *Within These Walls* and *The Gentle Touch* and *Smiley's People*.

Just before *Sister George* opened, *This Week* presented the first ever documentary about lesbians. This so incensed the *Daily Express* that it published a leader on the day of transmission (5 January 1965) telling its readership that 'you still have time to keep this filth out of your living rooms!' In the event, the programme was well received. Unlike *This Week*'s 1964 investigation into homosexual men, the women nearly all appeared full-face. However, perhaps because of the more pressing legal problems for the men, lesbians had to wait six years for their next television outlet (progressively entitled *The Important Thing Is Love*). Then nothing, at least nothing nationally networked, until Channel 4's *Veronica 4 Rose* in January 1983.

If gay women were virtually ignored (outside of exploitation films such as *The Fox, Emmanuelle*, and a conveyer belt of soft and hard-core productions with their obligatory 'lesbian scene'), gay men were seemingly everywhere, singly or in couples, in television plays and films. They were usually employed to add colour and kinky sexuality, as villains or jesters.[5] Fleet Street was much slower to respond to the mood of enquiry and curiosity released in the wake of Wolfenden. The occasional articles that appeared were dangerously open-ended, accommodating condemnation or condonation depending upon the reader's attitude or depth of experience. Furthermore, they were hedged around with qualifications and substantive clauses, lest anyone should suspect the writer of 'inside' knowledge or special pleading.

The silence of the popular press was broken in 1964 when Marjorie Proops, the *Daily Mirror*'s highly respected and widely read columnist opened up her problem page to male homosexuals. Other problem page writers eventually followed her lead, and, in the absence of gay switchboards and gay-run counselling agencies, these letters and their replies provided an important, if variable, outlet for some of us and our families. These letters still act as a reminder to the world that we exist, though as problems.

After the passing of the 1967 Act, homosexuality was increasingly alluded to in television plays, comedy shows, documentaries, pop songs, and, from the early 1970s, radio phone-ins. The link with effeminacy was reforged with the resurgence of female imperson-ation ('drag'), led by Danny La Rue, but enjoyed *en famille* in pubs and clubs all over Britain, some 'frequented' by us. The British felt comfortable with drag, and so did the media. Extravagantly attired drag artists could be contrastedly photo-graphed hunched over a car engine or baling hay: nothing 'queer' about them. Entertainments devoted to sexual liberation were drawing huge crowds, thanks to the removal of theatre censorship in 1969. *Hair, Oh! Calcutta* and, more restrained but still titillating, *The Boys In The Band*, an American piece of group therapy in which affluent, witty, self-loathing homosexual men talk about sex and play the 'truth game'.

In 1971, after a trial run (*Women In Love*), the mass cinema-going public was deemed ready for male bisexuality. Murray Head kissed and went to bed with Peter Finch and, separately, Glenda Jackson in *Sunday, Bloody Sunday*, then left them both. Mick Jagger, the moving force behind the pop culture's unisexual polymorphous perversity, played erotic fantasy games with James Fox in *Performance*. Even the Hollywood musical made a contribution with its bisexual menage in *Cabaret*.

Like the 'sympathetic' treatments of homosexuality, the above films (and others that accompanied them during this short-lived craze) followed a familiar pattern: tragedy (ending in tears, death or rejection) or just a bit of fun (hedonistic, affluent, a passing phase). No wonder the importation of a new movement from the United States caught the public — and the media — so completely offguard.

Gay Liberation: another new image

With its trappings of camp, cross-dressing and carnival, 'gay lib' *should* have been fun — and a nine-days wonder. The trouble was that its adherents appeared to take being homosexual terribly seriously, and the verbal and physical abuse of their own kind even more so. Besides, they answered back, were not ashamed, and they had misappropriated that lovely old word 'gay'.

At first, television lapped up all the colour (predominantly pink, as a reminder of the pink triangle worn by gays in Hitler's concentration camps) and movement (marches, sit-ins and zaps on publishers of reference books like *Everything You Always Wanted To Know About Sex*, wherein lesbians appeared under a section on prostitutes). Then when the gay liberation movement settled down and broadened out, television and the other media were puzzled, then irritated. Much of their irritation centred on the use of the word 'gay'. Once it was realized that gay activists at least were no longer prepared to have terms like 'queer', 'lezzie', 'poof' and 'nancy-boy' misappropriated to them, the media indicated their non-acceptance of such uppity behaviour by ignoring this usage of 'gay', or putting single or double quotation marks around the word (which was, however, nice and short for headlines). From 1973 onwards, a steady stream of articles and comments about this entymological outrage (including a campaign by the *Daily Mail* TV critic Herbert Kretzmer in 1979, to reclaim 'gay' for its innocent former use) met a larger number using the word unselfconsciously. The existence of the newspaper *Gay News* and its 1977 blasphemy prosecution helped publicise and familiarise the usage. It now has wide, if sometimes grudging, acceptance by the media, except in the time of national scandal (such as the Trestrail affair) when the clinical and cumbersome 'homosexual' is reverted to in order to indicate the gravity of the 'offence'.

What the gay movement also did fairly rapidly was to flush out prejudice and unreason from those whose liberal tolerance was shaky (including John Osborne, Jean Rook, and *Private Eye*'s Richard Ingrams who, none the less, published gay classified ads, unlike editors of other national publications).

The movement, in its various manifestations (Gay Liberation Front, CHE, *Gay News*, Sappho), also confronted the *Sunday Express* editor, John Junor, head-on by reporting some of his more pernicious remarks (appearing regularly in his 'JJ' column) about sick perverts and their organisations. However, the Press Council then failed to uphold our complaints against the now ennobled Junor, who continues his diatribes with unquenched self-righteousness.[6]

The greater confidence and self-awareness which gradually evolved as a result of gay liberation, has inevitably led to a change of image, despite the more clamorous voices of bigotry in the media. More openly gay people began surfacing on television discussion programmes; gay writers like Howard Schuman (*Rock Follies*) and Len Richmond (*Agony*), and film-makers (*Nighthawks*'s Ron Peck and Paul Hallam) tried to chip away at the stereotype, now raised to the level of a national institution. The media, as always, were slow and reluctant to respond to and accept the change. Well into the 1970s, gay male characters in films and television plays were still quite likely to be decked out by the wardrobe department in flowery see-through shirts, chiffon scarves and clattering bangles.

No longer did television companies receive enraged calls and letters from viewers about their 'endorsement' of homosexuality in a play or documentary. But what did continue to draw forth affronted hysteria was physical closeness and affection between men, except those tender embraces on football pitches and in changing rooms. Hence the shocked response to the television showing (in 1978) of *Sunday, Bloody Sunday*, and to the embrace between Michael Caine ('Alfie') and Christopher Reeve ('Superman') in the 1982 thriller *Deathtrap*. *Woman* magazine sent Mary Fletcher to interview Caine (31 July 1982) about 'the kiss that rocked the world'. She was able to report:

> Any lingering doubts that Mr Caine's screen role might indicate a change in his personal lifestyle are quickly dispelled. He is as macho as ever.

The actors' only worry, according to the article, was 'suppose we LIKED it?'

A similar furore arose over the (non-osculatory) relationship between Charles and Sebastian in the 1981 adaptation of *Brideshead Revisited*. This time it was the *Daily Mail*'s Herbert Kretzmer who put the readers' worst fears at rest in a piece headed 'Charles and Sebastian — an affair of innocence' (4 November 1981). It began:

> Perhaps nothing has perplexed, even antagonised viewers of the lush, continuing *Brideshead* as much as its central depiction

of what appeared to be, on the surface at least, an unarguable homosexual relationship.

Luckily, John Mortimer, the book's adaptor, when called by Kretzmer to give evidence, refuted the unspeakable possibility: it is a 'romantic friendship'. People who watched the series — and concentrated on the performances, writing, direction and camera-work: all sensuous rather than romantic — could, of course, draw their own very different conclusions.

Another panic reaction occurs whenever a heterosexual has been threatened by the stigma of homosexuality, a stigma which the media themselves have helped perpetuate. They will also come to the aid of those who, though 'self-confessed' (an enduring term for someone openly gay), are willing to endorse the things the media hold dear, like marriage and babies. Thus was Billie Jean King (sued for 'palimony' by a woman lover in 1981) able to survive the nastier press and television intrusions, although her forthright approach generally lost her a number of lucrative advertising contracts. The Labour MP Maureen Colquhoun, on the other hand, met outright hostility and a deal of sustained persecution at the hands of the gossip columnists and members of her constituency after it was revealed that she had left her husband for a woman.[7]

Openly gay men have met a variety of reactions. David Hockney, rich and successful but also fully confident in his sexuality for many years, is a fully accredited media celebrity: but he's an artist, has a flamboyant physical appearance (though a quiet, dry conversational style) and is a national asset. Tom Robinson, the musician and singer, completely and rigorously honest from the start, has also received fair treatment (though mainly from the more liberal music press). Elton John, his superstar peak just past, came out to a slightly sniggering media reception: but it was preferable to the insulting songs lobbed his way by supporters of teams opposing his football team, Watford, at nearly every game. Other openly gay men of reasonable celebrity complain that interviews, when published, omit the details of their private lives they freely and willingly gave. If they were heterosexual, every mention of marriage, divorce, separation, girlfriends and babies would be communicated to the public.

What the media find most appealing is the new (sensational/outrageous) and the familiar. This is why the most quoted and admired gay man in Britain of the past decade is a formerly reviled and despised Soho eccentric, Quentin Crisp. The adaptation of his autobiography, *The Naked Civil Servant*, caused a sensation when it was shown in December 1975. A new hero was born overnight: totally, unrepentantly homosexual. His triumphs, whether over violence on the streets of London or over psychiatric interrogation, were witnessed and applauded by millions of viewers here, and millions more all over the world in the year that followed. Suddenly the image of all that was best in homosexuals (and, according to the media, there wasn't much) became that of a man in his early seventies with tinted blue hair. The film remains a fine piece of work: witty, stylish and moving. It acutely charts Crisp's encounters with authority and all areas of anti-gay feeling (some of it from fellow gays). Apart from his enormous courage and much-needed gift for ironical self-preservation, Quentin Crisp (both through John Hurt's remarkable performance and through his own carefully constructed persona) gave the public and the media what they wanted: a victim who survived, a romantic who would never find his 'great dark man', an effeminate homosexual who wanted to be a woman, and a scratching post for the world's waifs and strays. Quentin Crisp was in accord with the mass idea of what gay people are all about. When he left Britain for New York in 1981, he was given a press send-off of articles and interviews bemoaning his departure from our shores.

Equally cherished, but in different ways, were John Inman (playfully outgoing as Mr Humphries in *Are You Being Served?*), Larry Grayson (a passive, hypochrondriacal Aunty figure on family quiz shows); and Melvyn Hayes (petulantly cowardly in *It Ain't Half Hot Mum*). They were family favourites, impotent figures of fun for people to 'mother' or feel superior towards.

'Real' life

Life as most gay people know it is only vaguely approximated by any of the media. The problem is that the media have never really made contact with us as people. They retain a very narrow definition of human behaviour and ideals which extends to physical appearance and desirability, financial success, thought processes and sexual preference. Some gays were becoming increasingly angry over the media's cramped image of us as half-men or sexual predators. A meeting was called at the beginning of 1978 with a group of television executives. Two turned up: John Birt of London Weekend Television and Jeremy Isaacs, then of Thames and now of Channel 4. Out of this fairly heated exchange came a discussion, *Gays: Speaking Out* (1978), and two series of *Gay Life* (1980 and 1981).

This second initiative (by LWT) began with a number of serious handicaps. It was shown in the London region only, and at 11.30 p.m. on Sundays. It was also fatally undecided whether it was *about* or *for* us, a point further underscored by the absence of an openly gay presenter. Important issues were aired (gays as parents, sexuality, police discrimination) but the reaction was primarily one of dissatisfaction with *Gay Life*'s lack of bite, humour and bloody-mindedness. Moreover, many gay women felt they were being both under- and misrepresented. Finally, a confrontation took place between a group of gays and the production team. As a result, the Them and Us bias was slightly adjusted, as was the relative invisibility of gay women. The follow-up series was much sharper, with two openly gay presenters, one man, one woman. But the spark — real commitment on the part of the TV company — was never really there.

Other attempts to get grievances through to the media have been successful; for example, a gay women's 'sit-in' at the *Guardian* newspaper to protest at irresponsible reporting of a Gay Pride rally in 1979 forced the paper to print a rebuttal. Going through conventional channels has generally been disappointing. The Press Council failed to uphold five complaints against the *London Evening News*'s methods of obtaining and reporting its January 1978 'exposé' of a doctor ('Doctor Strange Love') who was providing artificial insemination by donor (AID) to lesbian women. Nor did the Press Council allow that Maureen Colquhoun and her lover, Babs Todd, had been unnecessarily harassed by the *Daily Mail*'s gossip columnist, Nigel Dempster, and his staff the same year.[8]

The book *The Joy Of Gay Sex* was impounded by British customs (and remains banned six years later); the Thames TV series *Sex In Our Time*, which included a strong and much-needed programme on gay sexuality, was scrapped in 1976 after a veto from the Independent Broadcasting Authority (IBA); a BBC Radio 4 discussion with and about lesbians was yanked by the then (1976) Controller just days before broadcast because it was not 'up to standard'. Both BBC radio and television banned Tom Robinson's bitterly ironic 1977 record ('Sing if you're) glad to be gay'. A section on gay women in the armed services was removed from a 1979 BBC television documentary, even though this is the one area where gay women daily risk prosecution and dismissal.

What might have been affirmative sounds and images have been drowned out by the barrage of destructive ones. These could include a daily dose of anti-gay jokes; the archbishop's declaration that we are disabled (February 1981); or the vituperation meted out the following year to the Queen's bodyguard ('nasty little secret', 'sordid secret', 'amazing double life', 'forbidden love', 'seedy', 'disgraced'). In local communities, the penalties imposed upon gay men found guilty of so-called 'gross indecency' have been regularly compounded by the publication of the full names and addresses of those involved. A man committed suicide in Norwich in 1980 after reading such a report of his own case.[9] Others have harmed themselves in other ways, or left their neighbourhoods as a result of this public flogging.

Conclusion

With the promised explosion in communications in the next few years, it would seem reasonable to assume that we will be able to put our views across more regularly via local radio and television, cable and satellite, and videocassette. But although the choice of material and of outlets will be dizzyingly wide, the potential audience will be much smaller and more fragmented than the national one of millions we have at present. This will mean that a cable television station or local radio company may give us facilities to make the kind of programmes we would like to see − and like our families, friends and colleagues to see; but they will be unlikely to reach anything like the same number currently available through our four-channel system, or even the present local radio coverage.

There is also a danger, as seems to be happening after the advent of Channel 4, that those networks catering to the mass public will leave 'minority issues' to 'minority outlets'. In common with a number of other minorities in Britain, we have been on the receiving end of a great deal of misrepresentation and invalidation from the media: as emotional inadequates, as corrupting influences, as threats to children and family life, as people not to be trusted. Among the people who take in these false messages, at every stage of their lives, are judges, police officers, and other potential 'queer-bashers'. We ourselves take them in, by osmosis, as do our families. This situation must not be allowed to continue. The least we should expect from our mediums of information and entertainment is that they try to avoid dangerous oversimplifications and demeaning terminology; that they appreciate the need some of us have for confidentiality where our jobs, families and possibly our lives may be at stake; that they offer a degree of consultation in the planning of an article or programme which concerns us as a group; that they try to include us, wherever possible, in a wide spectrum of subjects (particularly those covering 'men and women' or 'the human race'); that they provide opportunities to openly gay people to work and express themselves *as* gay people within the media.

Even if one agreed with it as a principle, a watchdog body to protect our interests would probably either be ignored or, worse, encourage the media to further exclude gay issues for fear of giving offence. Better that we use the existing channels for praise and complaint: the BBC, the IBA, the Advertising Standards Authority, the National Union of Journalists, the Society of West End Theatres, the Campaign for Press and Broadcasting Freedom, even the hitherto toothless Press Council, and many others. To do this we must be better organised, less prickly and more determined than we have been in the recent past.

Sometimes the edifice cannot be scaled or breached from outside. For example, most national newspapers (including the liberal *Guardian*) refuse to take advertisements from us, even for accredited gay counselling organisations. However, all structures in the media are made up of individuals, some of whom will reach positions of influence within them. So one day, perhaps, things will change.

The National Union of Journalists' code of conduct states:

> A journalist shall not originate material which encourages
> discrimination on grounds of race, colour, creed, gender or
> sexual orientation.

Quite clearly this code is not being observed on our behalf. In November 1979 I interviewed the journalist Jilly Cooper for *Gay News* and taxed her on the subject of her book, *Class*, just published. In it, she declared that all gays (male) were pretentious snobs. Why, I asked her, if she had to single out groups for special attention, could she not also have looked at the class consciousness of, say, Jewish and black people.[10] Her response was flusteredly defensive. She felt I was over-reacting: it was a fun chapter in a light-hearted book. And, anyway, from her experience, gays *were* frightful snobs. I then showed Jilly Cooper a nasty, but quite typical, *Daily Express* gossip column piece about a 'nancy-boy writer' and his presumed tastes. I told her that, as a journalist and a writer, she did have a responsibility not to further isolate a group who were still vulnerable; or, having isolated them, at least not to make unsubstantiated generalisations about them. At this point, she left the room and the interview in tears.

Often the problem lies not so much in what is being said, but in the context. Therefore an insightful article by a young gay woman (in *Honey*, October 1982) about growing up in an oppressively heterosexual world is placed next to an advert for shampoo ('I wanted to look my best for him'): proving a point or, more likely, insensitive editing? A 'problem' letter from a mother asking what she should 'do about' her lesbian daughter was answered, well, by Philip Hodson in the *Daily Star* (24 August 1982). However, on the cover was a banner headline of 'Heartbreak mum's jail terror'. This story revealed how the woman was 'accosted' by a lesbian who 'wanted to start an affair'. Which will have had the largest impact? Advice to a mother to accept and love her daughter for who she is rather than what she is; or lurid cover stories associating defenceless heterosexual women with lesbians seemingly hell-bent on sexual harassment?

When we read stories such as that one, or others with headings such as 'The twilight world of unhappy gays' (*News of the World*, 25 July 1982) or 'Gays "corrupt" Third World' (*Observer*, 6 June 1980) or 'Jet-set wife's lesbian charge' (*Daily Mail*, 16 September 1982) all the old anxieties come flooding back. Our ability to ward them off depends upon our individual self-esteem, the degree of isolation we face, the deception we may be forced to maintain, and the support we receive from those around us. What we can't rely on is even a small supply of positive stories and images, in the mass media at least, as an antidote to this poison.

We also despair when jokes made at our expense are never challenged; or when the BBC's supposedly responsible science series *Horizon* produces a programme (*The Fight To Be Male*, May 1979) about gender which, uncritically, includes the work of an East German doctor who, for the past twenty years, has been experimenting on rats to find ways of preventing (male) homo-sexual babies from being born. If this theory (and others equally contentious, to say the least) had involved any other minority (with the exception of people with disabilities, who are themselves fighting back on this issue) there would have been a national outcry and questions asked in Parliament, had the programme ever reached the screen in that form in the first place. As it involved us, there were a few letters and a repeat was cancelled at the last moment. Apart from that, no apology, no right of reply.[11]

That is why we need talented people in the mass media, who feel good about themselves and confident of their skills, to come out of hiding and challenge the lies and half-truths that are daily written and spoken about us. It is often said that, with so many gays already working within television, radio, the cinema and the press, we should have little to complain about. Unfortunately, many of these people are beavering away — as I was — consciously or unconsciously creating the very climate that oppresses us — and them. Worse, if they are out of the closet, they may have ingested so many of the negative attitudes that surround them (which is what much of this book is about) that they are more anti-gay than people who base their 'truth' on instincts rather than experience.

What is certain is the value to those of us who are gay, of the example and the work of that very small, but growing, number of openly gay people within the media who are able to communicate how they live their lives — gay lives — to the outside world, whether through books, films, television plays and documentaries, articles, photographs, paintings and sculpture or theatre. It is through them, and people like them, that we can see ourselves as we are (though sometimes we may not like what we see) and begin to use the media, rather than let them use us.

Notes

1   John Fisher, *Funny Way To Be A Hero*, London, Frederick Muller, 1973, Chs 7 and 12.
2   Dick Emery, *In Character*, Robson Books, 1973, pp. 82–4.
3   Roger Wilmut and Jimmy Grafton, *The Goon Show Companion*, Robson Books, 1976 (script extract by Spike Milligan, p. 101).
4   Vito Russo, *The Celluloid Closet: Homosexuality in the Movies*, London, Harper & Row, 1981, pp. 112–79.
5   Ibid.
6   Andrew Lumsden, 'Sir John Junor of the *Sunday Express*', *Gay News* no. 247 (1982), p. 13.
7   Maureen Colquhoun, *A Woman In The House*, Scan Books, 1980, pp. 97–111.
8   Ibid.
9   *Gay News* no. 201 (1980), p. 3.
10 Interview with Jilly Cooper, *Gay News* no. 180 (1979), p. 51.
11 Alison Hennegan and Keith Howes, 'Man enough', *Gay News* no. 169, (1979), p. 29.

11 THE FIGHT FOR EQUALITY

Roy Burns

On to the streets

Legislators usually have precise intentions in mind when drafting new laws. However, the consequences of the passage of the 1967 Sexual Offences Act, which made male homosexuality partially lawful (see Chapter 5), were not only unexpected but were to be condemned by the proponents of this modest act.

Within five years a social revolution which had been simmering behind closed doors had exploded on to the streets. There were openly gay bars, gay clubs, gay social organisations, gay newspapers and even gay demonstrations. Homosexual men and women in Britain were publicly identifying themselves as gay, and were demanding to be recognised on their own, gay, terms. This had not been the intention of Parliament.

Why then did Parliament so misjudge things? As Nigel Warner has discussed (pp. 83–7), the Wolfenden report and the subsequent 1967 Sexual Offences Act represented the establishment's response to a number of politically sensitive homosexual cases. The intention of the 1967 act was not to make homosexual behaviour lawful (it didn't) but merely to reduce the susceptibility of male homosexuals to potential blackmail.

However this modest act was introduced at a time of major social change in both this country and the United States. The rapid development of television during the 1950s had exposed the marked differences in social life-styles between the haves and have-nots, and the introduction of commercial television in 1955

exaggerated this conflict by advertising the same goods to everybody, irrespective of their social class, aspirations, or geographic distribution. In the early 1960s, a new generation took over the rag trade (Carnaby Street, King's Road) and the music business (Beatles, Rolling Stones, etc), and *That Was The Week That Was* satirised the foibles of the Establishment. Overnight the young have-nots were rewriting social conventions. Hair grew longer and heterosexual sex (aided by the pill) became freer. Individuality, free from the reproachful gaze of one's elders, was the fashion. It was a social revolution which was to lead in the early 1970s to the birth of the gay movement.

However, in order to fully appreciate why gay people exploded on to the streets we must look at the parallel developments in the United States. Many of the same social changes were occurring across the Atlantic where the youth culture had won America's highest accolade: the presidency. The election of John F. Kennedy in 1960 swept aside the old guard and showed that youthful vigour could substitute for experience. Simultaneously, television was highlighting the geographical social differences, notably in the treatment of blacks, and this led directly to the civil rights movement. Public spectacles such as George Wallace barring the school door against blacks not only offended half the nation, it also made demonstrations a part of the national ethos. These two strands, the vitality of youth and the political effectiveness of nationally televised demonstrations, were to merge as America became more and more ensnared in Vietnam. By 1969 demonstrations were attracting hundreds of thousands of young protestors, angered by the prospect of being drafted for a war they didn't believe in. The streets had become the platform for political argument and for the expression of anger.

It was therefore natural that America's homosexuals should be affected by the blacks' demands for civil rights and by the youth-directed social revolution of 'doing your own thing'. The increasing importance of demonstrations raised the prospect that the homosexual response would be on the streets. Historically, it came in 1969 at the Stonewall Inn in New York when camp queens harassed by the police fought back. The resulting riot was a landmark from which there was no turning back, either in the States or here in Britain.

The incident at Stonewall was to focus the attention of

America's gays to the fact that the civil rights debate was not the exclusive concern of the black community. There were gay rights as well. Perhaps more important was the realisation that the fight for gay rights could equally well take place on the streets, provided that people would come out, and could be just as emotional as the black community's fight for their civil rights.

This vision of a fight for gay rights at an emotional level and on the streets was witnessed in 1970 in New York by two visitors from London, Bob Mellor and Aubrey Walter. They returned to London as prophets of a new age; Gay Liberation Front (GLF) had arrived.

GLF was to build on the preceding decade's overthrow of convention. Indeed, the theme 'proud to be gay' was revolutionary. It transferred the stigma from the individual homosexual to the bigoted opposition. This was a brilliant strategy. Homosexuals were now not sick or perverted: what was sick was the prejudice existing within society against homosexuals and homosexuality. If one was not sick or perverted then one could be proud to be gay, in which case one could come out and tell one's parents, friends, employers, everyone. If one was not ashamed, then being gay could be fun. No longer did one need to worry about how other people viewed you. Shock the opposition with radical drag. Zap the bigots at their meetings. Accept no compromises. Be yourself and enjoy it. The 'liberation' in GLF meant what it said.

GLF was an emotional solution at an individual level: it was not dependent upon the law or other people's attitudes. It depended solely upon the individual. Furthermore it was a response which knew no barriers; it applied equally to lesbians and gay men (unlike the law), to young and old, and across all social and economic classes. It was the ultimate challenge to a blackmailer, requiring only that people should have the courage to come out.

Gay Lib arrived on the streets of Britain just three years after Parliament had decided that homosexuals shouldn't be blackmailed. GLF's solution was far more radical than any of those of the liberal social reformers, since it turned the tables to say 'gay is good' and that the rest of society needs to readjust to this fact.

The emergence of the gay movement

The flowering of GLF was only to last a couple of years, but its effects were to dominate the decade. The importance to the individual of coming out is now central to the entire gay movement, and terms such as 'coming out' and 'out of the closet' have passed from being the jargon of a subculture to being a part of the general vernacular.

The crucial legacy of GLF was the concept of telling other people that you were gay. It is very difficult if someone you know and like comes out to you to retain homophobic attitudes. Coming out was to have an immense effect on public opinion, far more than any media coverage of gay issues, demonstrations such as Gay Pride Week, or pronouncements by public figures. GLF was also to impose lasting institutions on the gay movement, such as *Gay News* and the Gay Switchboards. At the same time, gay social groups were being formed, mainly by CHE and the Scottish Minorities (now Scottish Homosexual Rights) Group, throughout the country so that homosexuals could meet each other socially. These organisations had a combined brief of helping people to come out, to meet socially, and to campaign against the discrimination affecting gay people. As a result, more and more people came out. Discos, initiated primarily by CHE and GLF, became big business, and entrepreneurs (both gay and non-gay) began to cash in on the blossoming market. By the early 1980s, there were a wide range of leisure-oriented gay businesses, and most of the pre-1967 private, and rather closeted, clubs had closed: the last vestiges of the earlier secretive social scene for homosexuals were being swept away.

Despite the extent of this social revolution, some attitudes have remained unchanged. The preceding chapters have amply illustrated the continuing existence of homophobic attitudes and practices. Lest there be any doubt consider the following extracts from a letter to the *Guardian* published in December 1982:

Sir, — In the recent strike at the *Daily Telegraph* I yielded to the temptation to purchase as an alternative — albeit a poor one — your paper which I disregarded some years ago. . . .

There is, still, a massive conceit which pervades the whole paper and which in the sixties, helped to usher out manners, grace and style, and usher in churlishness, the great unwashed, jeans — preferably unwashed too — and other tatty clothing: in other words, the Permissive Society.

With it came the Age of Mediocrity and the intellectual trendies fell over themselves to condone gay rights; marriage for homosexuals; abortion on demand (for schoolgirls too of course); sex education (especially praiseworthy if deviant) for children; adoption of children by lesbians; and a special warm feeling for criminals and drug addicts. They, the trendies, were quick to worship pictures of inflated soup cans, electronic music, vomit pop caterwaulers, and yahoo accents.

What a society you have helped to create and sustain!

Institutional prejudice

Prejudice, as illustrated by this letter, is the underlying cause of the anti-gay discrimination described throughout this book. Many examples have been given, particularly in the early chapters, of the immense suffering, both psychological and, in some instances, physical, experienced by lesbians and gay men because of the illiberal actions of others. Prejudice is experienced by gay people at two distinct, interacting, levels, firstly through the actions and attitudes of individuals and secondly through institutionalised discrimination. For example, the sacking of a lesbian or a gay man is usually initiated by a single individual yet the formal reasons and subsequent 'justification' reflects institutional attitudes. Institutional prejudice not only backs up the individual's prejudice, but is also used by the individual as justification for their bigoted views. Clearly, then, the abolition of anti-homosexual prejudice must entail changing the attitudes of both individual members of society and institutions.

One might expect that these two would go hand in hand: that changing public opinion would automatically be reflected in changing institutional attitudes. This has not been the case. Institutional prejudice has hardened while public opinion moved between 1977 and 1979, according to Home Office statistics, towards favouring homosexual equality.

While the GLF ethos of coming out was effective in changing public opinion it had little effect on institutional prejudice. One reason is that institutional attitudes, particularly when the courts are involved, is governed largely by precedent and so is often insensitive to social changes. In particular, Lord Reid's view during the *IT* case (see page 87) that 'there is a material difference between merely exempting certain conduct from criminal penalties [i.e. the 1967 act] and making it [homosexuality] lawful in the full sense' established a legal basis for institutional prejudice. A further prop has been the ill-founded belief that children are corrupted by association with homosexuals. This argument has regularly been presented at industrial tribunals following the dismissal of lesbians and gay men whose jobs brought them, however transitorily, into contact with young people (see Chapter 3), and is used as a 'moral justification' for discrimination.

No independent evidence has ever been presented to support the corruption theory and we as homosexuals strongly deny that our sexual orientation has been determined by some childhood association with homosexuals. Significantly, a Gallop poll commissioned by the Home Office in 1977 showed that 12 per cent of men questioned claimed to have been approached by a homosexual during childhood. The Kinsey report found 4 per cent of adult males were exclusively homosexual and a further 10 per cent predominantly so, implying that association, if the corruption theory is correct, during childhood is phenomenally effective. The validity of the theory falls still further when the 1979 Home Office Gallop poll is taken into account, as it showed a *fall* in the number of people recalling a juvenile approach, suggesting that people's recollections may be coloured by prevailing social attitudes.

The institutional view that homosexuality may corrupt public morals, particularly regarding chidren, and its faith in precedent has permeated much of official thinking. For example, Lord Reid's view influenced the Charity Commissioners' decision to deny charitable status to Gay Sweatshop. It was then used in turn by the Registrar of Friendly Societies to deny registration to the Birmingham Gay Centre as an Industrial and Provident Society. Similar 'logic' has prevented the Criminal Law Revision Committee and the majority of the Police Advisory Committee on Sexual Offences from accepting the moral right of homosexuals to equality, industrial tribunals from protecting the jobs of homosexuals, and so forth.

While homosexuals are accused of conspiring to corrupt public morals, we might with equal validity say that there is a corrupt conspiracy involving Parliament, the courts, the police and the professions which is determined to maintain homosexuals as second-class citizens.

It is however more realistic to view these institutions as being inherently conservative, and made up of individuals who are wary of appearing too liberal. These decision-makers are often of a generation whose social attitudes were established before, or were unaffected by, the social revolution of the 1960s. Significantly, the average age of MPs voting in favour of homosexual reform is lower than that of those voting against, and the new generation of senior police officers appears to be more tolerant. We can only hope that the same pattern will become evident amongst senior judges in the years to come. It is patently wrong that the courts should view homosexuals as second-class citizens and that such a learned opinion should 'justify' physical and verbal attacks on lesbians and gay men.

Many chapters of this book have concluded with specific proposals for combating institutional anti-gay discrimination, which taken together would radically reduce the apparent support offered by the Establishment to individuals holding bigoted views.

The society we want

There is one school of thought which maintains that combating such institutional prejudice is a panacea for all ills. However, experience of the Equal Opportunities, the Sex Discrimination, and the Race Relations Acts clearly demonstrates that changing the law does not *ipso facto* change public attitudes. Yet at the end of the day, it *is* the attitudes of the individual person on the top of the Clapham omnibus which must concern us. GLF recognised this and by making coming out paramount it pitched its campaigning at individuals rather than at institutions − with phenomenal effect.

As we look ahead we must therefore have a clear perception of the type of society we wish to achieve and to ask whether this can be brought about by pressure on institutional attitudes alone. Discrimination will continue, overtly or covertly, until society accepts it without question.

To this end, CHE in 1982 published a Charter for Gay Rights. The important feature about this charter is that although it has been written specifically with lesbians and gay men in mind it is a charter which attempts to define a society which recognises the importance of the individual:

CHE's Charter for Gay Rights

Homosexual Equality demands the acknowledgement that homosexuality is a valid form of sexual expression, that lesbians and gay men have the right to lifestyles free from social and legal discrimination and that gay people make a contribution to society equal to that of heterosexuals.

This requires:

A. The elimination of sexism in all its forms;

B. The positive representation in education and the media of homosexuality and the lives of gay people;

C. The promotion of gay pride and of mutual support within the gay movement.

We demand:

1. The right to basic human freedoms: of opinion
   of expression
   of assembly
   of movement
   of residence;

2. General equality in criminal law for gay people and heterosexuals, and equal application of the law;

3. That consensual sexual acts should not be the concern of criminal law;

4. The right to have, raise and care for children;

5. The securing of freedoms for lesbians and gay men from all forms of violence and intimidation: at work
   at home
   on the streets;

6. The freedom from interference in our private lives;

7. The end of discriminatory harassment, questioning, arrest, detention or deportation of gay people;

8. The equal right of employment and the protection of that employment;

9. The equal access to all Public Services;

10. That gay people should receive equal treatment with heterosexuals in all aspects of the civil law.

The ideas embodied within this charter are radical. They represent as major a step forward as those of the 1960s. By making the interests of the individual paramount, the charter proposes, for example, the abolition of the 'age of consent' concept from criminal law (3), indicates that radical reform of immigration policy is necessary (1), and raises the question about the confidentiality of computer-held information (6).

Our *Guardian* letter-writer (pp. 217–18) wrote of the Age of Mediocrity. We write of a New Age which will encompass all of that writer's fears and more. We seek an age in which a person's individuality is the basis of society, and not (as at present) a society which imposes its views upon the individual.

Clearly, this social revolution will require major changes in the way that people view themselves and others, complemented by institutional reform − a combination of both the emotional approach of GLF and co-ordinated lobbying.

In the 1970s, we followed in the wake of changes initiated by others. This time, gay people need to be in the vanguard, to be the wedge which pushes open the door, working with the women's movement, civil libertarians, and other pressure groups.

The way ahead

In planning the way ahead, we need to keep these objectives clearly in sight, namely that we must campaign both at an individual and at an institutional level, and that progress will be the result of co-operation with a broad cross section of society. Part of our planning must therefore involve building a new alliance across all strands of society committed to radical change in favour of the individual. There is evidence that such an alliance is developing already: witness the attempts of both the Liberal Party and those parts of the Labour Party supporting Tony Benn and Ken Livingstone to develop a political base encompassing the rights of minorities. Gay activists have been involved in both, and we must continue to promote this political realignment.

It would however be a grave mistake to discard our current campaigning strategy of lobbying those bodies which determine public policy simply because we now demand more radical changes than minimal law reform. Continued pressure against institutional prejudice will remain a priority, although, as I shall expand upon later, we must also fight at the individual, emotional level. The lobbying of the last ten years has had a major effect, in particular it has challenged various parts of the Establishment to consider gay rights. For instance, there have been major debates within each of the churches, some trade unions are beginning to take gay rights seriously, and the media has moved from universal condemnation to ambivalence or even full support.

This pressure has had some effect upon institutional attitudes, even if there has been little progress at the legislative level. NALGO now demands the inclusion of a non-discrimination clause in employment contracts, and many local authorities have begun to take positive action in favour of lesbians and gay men. One effect of these welcome initiatives has been to place gay rights on the political agenda: a process which is essential if we are to change public policy.

However, despite this increasing acceptance of gay rights, there has been no new legislation yet to protect the civil rights of lesbians and gay men. The two parliamentary achievements, namely the extension of the 1967 Act to Scotland and Northern Ireland, were merely tidying up measures, and in the latter case it required the full impact of a decision of the European Court of Human Rights before a vacillating government would take action. Both measures were concerned with removing geographic inconsistencies rather than tackling the fundamental issues of gay rights.

Such legislative tidying up is unlikely to result in lowering the gay male age of consent to parity with the heterosexual age of consent (let alone the abolition of 'age of consent' from the criminal law) or extension of the Equal Opportunities Act to specifically protect the jobs of lesbians and gay men. These issues require an *understanding* of gay rights, yet they are contaminated by the prejudicial view that homosexuality is corrupting. Similarly, the overthrow of Lord Reid's interpretation that we are legal but not lawful is unlikely, by either parliamentary or judicial action, unlikely unless we are able to mobilise popular support.

This means that we must educate public opinion that homosexuality is not corrupting, yet this is the one issue that we have tended to shy away from, for fear that any public discussion of paedophilia would benefit the conservative lobby. If we are to build a new society we cannot avoid such difficult, even emotional, issues. To say that there is a distinction between gay rights and the rights of women, of children, of transsexuals, of transvestites, is to deny the very principles of our struggle.

Similarly, if we wish to build a new alliance we must be concerned with the rights of women, and of ethnic and other stigmatised groups. Our concern should not be on the basis of a *quid pro quo*: we'll support you if you'll support us, but because we have a clear vision of a non-discriminatory society which respects the rights of all individuals.

This demand for everybody to be treated as individuals means that we, as gay people, must continue to insist on our right to be equal members of society. Often this has generated hostile opposition, for example when gay groups have sought to hire public buildings or to lay a wreath on Remembrance Day. This intolerance must be exposed and countered. Similarly, we must continue to actively participate in public discussion on issues which are not exclusively gay. For example, CHE submitted detailed proposals to the Williams committee on obscenity and film censorship on the grounds that gay people have a particular expertise and experience on the public's definition of obscenity. Significantly, CHE's proposals featured highly in the committee's report.

Finally, we must continue with helping people to come out and supporting people in times of adversity. We have a remarkable track record: the self-help of the gay community has been a unique achievement. There are few other minorities which have shown such a degree of communal care.

Politics and people

This programme, and many of the proposals for action in the earlier chapters, might at first sight appear to require action by organisations rather than by individuals. If this were true, we would be proposing a programme which employed an approach at variance with our goals.

Organisations do have a role. They are a means of communication, they can bring people together, raise money, formulate policy. However, people rather than organisations sit at the switchboards offering advice. It is individuals not organisations who initiate new ideas and who do the work. For example, it was someone in the short lived 'Gays in Media' group who in 1979 proposed setting up a meeting with television executives, a meeting which resulted in London Weekend Television's *Gay Life* series, and which undoubtedly influenced Jeremy Isaacs who, two years later, was to launch Channel 4 with its policy of representing the views of minorities.

Similarly, the idea that CHE should document the extent of anti-gay discrimination was due to one person, and the subsequent work describing violence against gay people, discrimination in prisons and in employment, and the attitudes of the police and medical profession was done by individuals, not by an organisation. Likewise, it has been individuals who have marshalled the evidence submitted to government bodies, who have been responsible for raising gay rights within the unions and political parties, and for all the other campaigning. The message is clear: while organisations have their role it is *individuals* who initiate ideas and do the work.

We therefore need to create a climate which encourages people to fight for their rights. The expansion of the commercial scene has perhaps made the *status quo* too comfortable, particularly for many gay men. Why challenge the system, why rock the boat, when life is fine as it is? The 1970s saw a steady divergence between gay activists and the male commercial scene, as illustrated by the pitifully small turnout on the annual Gay Pride march (the largest was only 10,000, in 1979). If gay activists depict their lives as dull, being spent in smoke-filled rooms, it is hardly surprising that others do not share their dreams. We must not lose sight of the aims of our liberation: that being gay should be fun and enjoyable. We need to rekindle our humour: campaigning can be fun.

In this respect, I fondly recall the response to the Archbishop of Canterbury's comment that gay people are 'handicapped'. A circular, purporting to come from the Department of Employment, was sent to various personnel managers enquiring whether their companies complied with the provisions of the Disabled Persons Act in terms of their employment of homosexuals. Here, by using humour and imagination, the ineptness of the archbishop's comments were exposed, the employment of gay people was raised with both employers and the civil service, and, through press coverage, with the general public. A formal letter of protest could never have had the same impact.

What spark will fire both gay people and others committed to the rights of the individual to rise up and fight? In many respects this is a rhetorical question, since it is only with hindsight that we can identify the triggers of earlier social revolutions. Would one, for example, have predicted that television would stimulate social changes during the 1960s? Will rising unemployment, or cable TV, or microchips be viewed in retrospect as the trigger for a new social revolution in favour of the individual? It would be regrettable if repression were the only effective stimulus, although the prosecution of *Gay News* in 1976 by Mary Whitehouse did much to stimulate the flagging spirit of GLF.

Prejudice and gay pride

There have been two recurring themes throughout this chapter. The first is that gay people will not become fully accepted by society until we have changed society to respect the views of all individuals. The second is that much of the progress made in gay rights during the past decade has resulted from the GLF ethos of coming out. If we are to change society, then it will be through a similar emotional response.

The role of the gay community, together with the women's movement, must be to lead the way. Our ten years of experience will be invaluable in the fight ahead.

However, to take such a leading role in reshaping society will require us to put our own house in order. We must become beacons. We must show that we are proud to be individuals, proud to be gay.

Most gay people would probably claim to have come out. But do we share a common definition of what this means? Does it mean having the courage to go to a gay bar, to tell one's closest friends, to tell one's family, or what? Coming out is rather like peeling an onion: however far we come out there is still more to be done.

Too often, people seem to only come out to their close friends and relations as though self-honesty has some natural limit. This criticism applies particularly to people in the public eye, who shy away behind excuses that 'it would damage my career if it were to be known' or 'being gay doesn't affect the way I do my job, therefore people needn't know'. Yet such people are often public figures because of their self-advertising, and with that self-promotion must go a commitment to self-honesty. There is probably a disproportionate number of gay people in the Houses of Parliament, yet not one has has the courage to say from the floor of the House 'I am gay. This doesn't by itself make me better or worse than you — but it does give me a particular view on life.' The effect of such a statement would be devastating on the media, and would not (from Maureen Colquhoun's experience of being labelled by the popular press 'the self-confessed lesbian MP') be counterproductive.

Keith Howes has mentioned (p. 211) how few out gays there are in the media, yet if rumour is correct television is full of closet gays. Their failure to publicly come out has contributed directly to the poor media coverage of gay rights. Similarly, very few bankers, judges, policemen, managing directors and other establishment figures have publicly come out, yet maybe 5 per cent of them are gay. This argument of course goes across the social spectrum, yet people in the public eye should have a particular responsibility to be open with the people they purport to lead. Closet shattering, as in the case of various tennis and pop stars, is not enough. Individuals must find the courage themselves.

Coming out should also mean more than just telling people about being gay, it should also involve coming to terms with our own prejudices. After all, we know what it is like to face discrimination (otherwise it would be easy to tell people about being gay) but do we learn the lessons of that prejudice? Coming out must surely entail changing our life-styles and attitudes so that others don't suffer prejudice at our hands.

That means we must avoid drawing stereotypes and then ascribing these characteristics to a particular person, since to do this is to ignore that person's individuality. Stereotypes are a simple short cut: all women are . . ., all blacks are . . ., all young people like . . ., etc. Only if we banish such stereotypes will we break down the prejudice existing in modern society. Coming out should mean learning to ask whether this is what an individual thinks, feels, wants, . . ., and then responding accordingly.

As individuals, gay people have still a long way to go to banish their prejudices. We can only learn whether we discriminate by asking our 'victims', and then listening carefully to what they have to say. Certainly, many lesbians consider gay men to be as sexist as other men. Is sexism all one way? Is the growth of women-only events only because women feel inhibited to express their individuality when there are men around and because of the financial burdens of lower incomes, or is there a sexist element as well? Many young people find older gays ageist in their attitudes — it is often difficult for many gay activists to realise that they are no longer young, even at heart! One has only to read the views of the Black Gay Group to realise that they feel alienated by the racist attitudes of much of the gay movement — remember, being racist is not just a matter of disliking a particular racial group: fancying, say, an oriental guy just because he is oriental is also racist. Many of us have yet to come to terms with camp queens, with transvestites, with transsexuals, that is, we are still unable to see them as individuals rather than as stereotypes. Bisexuals find themselves sneered at by both heterosexuals and homosexuals. Sometimes bisexuality has been a convenient (and dishonest) half-way house towards coming out as gay, but for other people, bisexuality accurately reflects their individuality and we must learn to respect it.

This was the message of GLF, but it is a message that has been sadly diluted through the years. 'I am an individual; accept me as you find me. I am not a stereotype. I am me.' How can we expect to change society whilst we fail to treat others as individuals?

Yet the change we are seeking requires everybody, not just gay people, to come out, to come to terms with themselves as individuals. We shall not dislodge homophobic attitudes until this occurs, since prejudice is seated in a fear, through ignorance, of homosexuals. The Kinsey report claims that half the adult male population has experienced sexual attraction towards other men, yet few would be prepared to openly admit this. It is not just gay people who need to come out!

The challenge before us all is immense. All of us, whatever our sexual orientation, need to campaign for the rights of the individual using flair and imagination, using argument and logic. This is not just a concern of lesbians and gay men: it is the concern of all of society. We all need to come out of our closets. We each need to ask ourselves whether we are honestly living a life of our own choosing or whether we are being forced by others to conform. Only by asking such questions can we recognise the walls of our closets. Together, we shall shatter the walls of our ghettos. Together, we shall build a society which recognises the rights of the individual and which is at peace with itself.

FURTHER INFORMATION

CHE is an organisation of women and men who have come together to fight for the rights of all gay people. Founded in 1969, it has grown up with the gay movement and sees itself as a radical civil libertarian campaign not tied to any political party or ideology.

Through its Law Reform Committee and Gay Lobby, CHE influences MPs and government departments, and pressures for changes in Britain's unequal laws. The different groups within CHE Discrimination Commission monitor discrimination in employment, in the armed forces, in the medical profession, in prison and in police operations. *Prejudice and Pride* is very largely the work of these bodies. Discrimination booklets on 'queer-bashing' (*Attacks on Gay People*, 85p) and employment (*What About the Gay Workers?*, £1) are available from National Office. The Campaign is managed democratically, with an executive committee accountable to quarterly national councils and to an annual conference.

CHE's local campaign groups carry the gay rights struggle into the towns and shires of England and Wales. They are supported in this by a special newsletter and group, *Grass Roots*, set up to help local members.

The campaign could do very much more for gay people if it had more members and more money. CHE has two kinds of membership. Campaigning membership is for campaigns only, and costs at present (1983) £4 a year. Supporting membership is for people who wish to help the campaign with money, at least £1 a month by banker's order. Most supporting members do not campaign.

Could *you* help CHE either with money or by participating in the campaign? Would you like further information about the organisation and its activities? If so, get in touch. We'll be glad to hear from you.

National Office
274 Upper Street
Islington
LONDON
N1 2UA
01-359-3973

Other gay organisations
This list is accurate at the time of writing, namely March 1983. The addresses of many gay organisations do change quite frequently, so we have not included any. Any enquiries sent to us at CHE National Office will be forwarded. As an additional check on the current position of any group, ring London Gay Switchboard: 01-837-7324.

Campaigning groups
NCCL Gay Rights Committee
Liberal Gay Action Group
Labour Campaign for Gay Rights
Gay Social Democrats
Conservative Group for Homosexual Equality
Northern Ireland Gay Rights Association
Scottish Homosexual Rights Group

Youth groups
Gay Youth Movement
Joint Council for Gay Teenagers
NUS Gay Rights Campaign

Union Groups
Gay Rights at Work Committee
AUT Gay Group
CPSA Gay Group
Gay Doctors in England

Gay PO/Telecoms Workers Group
Gay Teachers Group
NALGAY (NALGO gay group)
NATFHE Gay Group
GMWU Gay Network
London Transport Workers Gay Group

Religious groups
Gay Christian Movement
Quest
Catholic Lesbian Sisterhood
Jewish Gay Group
Unitarian Gay Rights Group
Friends Homosexual Fellowship
Gay Humanist Group

Other groups
Gays and Housing Group
Gay Medical Information Society
Gay Rural Aid and Information Network
Rural Alliance
Action for Lesbian Parents

Counselling groups
FRIEND
National Association of Gay Switchboards
Lesbian Line
Sequel (elderly and isolated lesbians)
Gemma (disabled)

National information services
London Gay Switchboard: 01-837-7324
London Lesbian Line: 01-837-8602
Hall-Carpenter Archives, BM Archives, London WC1

While Gay Switchboard and Lesbian Line are national organisations, local details throughout Britain and Ireland can be
obtained from the London telephone numbers.

RECOMMENDED READING

The list below is a selection of books and pamphlets, most of which draw on the experience of lesbians and gay men in Britain. If you can't obtain them through ordinary booksellers, there are several specialist bookshops throughout the British Isles, of which Gay's the Word and Sisterwrite publish the most informative and wide-ranging catalogues. (Check the London phone directory in your local library for their current addresses and telephone numbers.)

Babuscio, J. (1976), *We Speak For Ourselves: Experiences in Homosexual Counselling*, London, SPCK.

Beer, C., Jeffery, R. and Munyard, T. (1981), *Gay Workers: Trade Unions and the Law*, London, National Council for Civil Liberties.

Bell, A. P. and Weinberg, M. S. (1978), *Homosexualities: A Study of Diversity Among Men and Women*, London, Mitchell Beazley (an American study).

Burbidge, M. (ed.) (1980), *I Know What I Am*, London, Joint Council for Gay Teenagers.

Burbidge, M. and Walters, J. (eds) (1981), *Breaking the Silence*, London, Joint Council for Gay Teenagers.

CHE (1981), *What About The Gay Workers? – A Report of the Commission on Discrimination*, London, Campaign for Homosexual Equality.

Cohen, S. and Jackson, B. (1979), *Queers Need Not Apply – A Report of the Commission on Discrimination*, London, Campaign for Homosexual Equality.

Crane, P. (1982), *Gays and the Law*, London, Pluto Press.

Dyer, R. (ed.) (1977), *Gays and Film*, London, British Film Institute.

Ettorre, E. M. (1980), *Lesbians, Women and Society*, London, Routledge & Kegan Paul.

Galloway, B. (ed.) (1982), *Grass Roots: A Campaign Manual for Gay People*, London, Grass Roots Group/Campaign for Homosexual Equality.

Gay Left Collective (1980), *Homosexuality: Power and Politics*, London, Allison & Busby.

Gay Liberation Front (1971, revised 1979), *Gay Liberation Front Manifesto*, London, GLF Information Service.

Gay Rights At Work Committee (1980), *Gays at Work*, London, GRAW.

Hanscombe, G. E. and Forster, J. (1981), *Rocking the Cradle: Lesbian Mothers: A Challenge in Family Living*, London, Sheba Feminist Publishers (paperback), and Peter Owen (hardback).

Hart, J. and Richardson, D. (1981), *The Theory and Practice of Homosexuality*, London, Routledge & Kegan Paul.

Hodges, A. P. and Hutter, D. (1974), *With Downcast Gays: Aspects of Homosexual Self-Oppression*, London, Pomegranate Press, and Toronto, Pink Triangle Press.

Meldrum, J. T. (1980), *Attacks on Gay People* (second edition), London, Campaign for Homosexual Equality.

Moody, R. (1980), *Indecent Assault*, London, Peace News/Word is Out.

Plummer, K. (ed.) (1981), *The Making of the Modern Homosexual*, London, Hutchinson.

Rich, A. (1981), *Compulsory Heterosexuality and Lesbian Existence*, London, Onlywomen Press (an American study).

Silverstein, C. and White, E. (1977), *The Joy of Gay Sex: An intimate guide for gay men to the pleasures of a gay lifestyle*, New York, Simon & Schuster (an American study).

Sisley, E. and Harris, B. (1977), *The Joy of Lesbian Sex: A tender and liberated guide to the pleasures and problems of a lesbian life style*, New York, Simon & Schuster (an American study).

Stewart-Park, A. and Cassidy, J. (1977), *We're Here: Conversations with Lesbian Women*, London, Quartet.

Walter, A. (ed.) (1980), *Come Together − the years of gay liberation 1970–73*, London, Gay Men's Press.

Warburton, J. (1978), *Open and Positive*, London, Gay Teachers Group.

Weeks, J. (1977), *Coming Out: Homosexual Politics in Britain, from the Nineteenth Century to the Present*, London, Quartet.

Weeks, J. (1981), *Sex, Politics and Society: The regulation of sexuality since 1800*, London, Longman.

Weinberg, G. (1972), *Society and the Healthy Homosexual*, New York, Anchor Books (paperback), and Garrards Cross, Colin Smythe (hardback) (an American study).

INDEX